Collected Poems

COLLECTED POEMS
John Gibbens

TOUCHED PRESS

First published in 2000
by Touched Press
4 Varley House
County Street
London SE1 6AL

© John Gibbens 2000

British Library Cataloguing-in-Publication Data
A catalogue record for this book is
available from the British Library

ISBN 0-9539153-0-1

Set in Palatino 9/11 by Touched Type
Printed and bound in England by
Redwood Books, Trowbridge, Wiltshire

For Armorel, Esmé and John

ACKNOWLEDGEMENTS

Some of these poems have previously appeared in the following journals: *Agenda, Ambit, As Well As, Bad Poetry Quarterly, Bête Noire, Community of Poets, Fire, Krax, London Review of Books, Moonstone, Navis, Ostinato, Outposts, Oxford Poetry, Poetry Review, Presence, Stand, Various Artists*; and in *The Gregory Awards Anthology 1981 & 1982* (Carcanet, 1982), *Poems for Peace* (Pluto Press, 1986), *Elected Friends* (Enitharmon, 1991), *Jewels & Binoculars* (Stride/ Westwords, 1993), *Return to Sender* (Headlock, 1994), *Things We Said Today* (Stride, 1995). 'Nostalgia' was a Mandeville Press poem card.

Contents

EYE CITY

THE SMELL OF THYME

BAY

ORPHEUS ASCENDING 137

INTIMATIONS 187

MAN'S LAUGHTER

THE IMPROVISED VERSION

PRAISES

PART I

PART IV

CHARACTERS

Star 355

I. YOU & I

RIVERBUS

I. FALLING DOWN

II. BALLADS

ENNEAGON
[*Poems of Don Plummer*]

A WILD INHABITATION

… a wondrous place, and in it grows much green
But it's a wild inhabitation for my true love to be in

AWAKE FOR EVER

I AM as the trees diagram.
I am as the rain illustrates on the window.

Cold wind drives me
from hills to the sea
along the scattering mist.
Fells outgrow their walls,
empty row of houses,
the thistled pasture.
The outside holds no promises.
The outside blows and rains
against the house.

So we wake together with the rain
floating against the window.
So we wander from bed
and watch the trees mobile,
sky tense with cloud.
There is only the day and then the night
and the uncertain weather.
So we waver, looking at the day.
So I say,

You are what the trees diagram.
You are what the rain illustrates on the window.

ODE

WHAT is this darting
by us,
its breast aflame in the crepuscule?
Luscinia megarynchos,
Sub-family *Turdinae*,
Order *Passeriformes*. The nightingale.

A Bird, his heart no bigger than a berry
pressed to the thorn.

What is this
stitched symbol
darting in the lines of nettle and branch?
An old dead bird, ribcage unpicked,
beak and bristles stiff.

The change –
Bouncing from the clutch
of hunger on the lawn,
the themeless, hardy robin,
his breast a spark
in the thaw of a winter's afternoon.

THE ESTUARY

THE first one, I remember,
must have been what we saw
in the late evening
(full of insects, oppressive air
on the greasy harbour
and the glint of the sea
turning on the rocks)
when we stepped out for a while
and held hands in the sand:
a lump in the water.

We had kissed first perhaps a week before.

In the morning the river was full of them –
peasants, from the remnants of their clothes,
the men with loose pants folded tight
over their legs as they drifted,
bunched up at the groin, pushed on
by the fast, full river.

Some of the wounds were terrible,
trousers pulled down
and dragging the knees down
into the water,
blouses torn and dragged
in the current over the women's faces.
And the flesh there,
where those wounds had run,
flapping gently like weed.
And sometimes only a leg or a hand.

Somebody said we should row out
and hook them in and bury them,
but then, if we did that, we might as well
string out the nets.

A baby caught in the bank and I
prodded it on again.

In the end we did that, kept them moving on,
out to sea, through two days,
waking up and rolling those caught in the piers
back in the current.

They must have been chucking them in,
back up in the hills where the rain had hung heavy
for weeks, in their hundreds.

And on the third day there were no more.
And on the fourth day, neither smiling nor kissing,
not saying anything, she came and woke me up
early, and said that the men were going out again
in boats. And the river wallowed round
an uprooted sapling in midstream,
and the wind wrapped her skirts,
rattling, round her thighs,
watching where the boats went out to sea,
where they had gone.

We went out into a hollow of the dunes
and made love for the first time
under the wind and the grey sky,
stared at the ragged grass
along the sand-ridge top,
hardly spoke.

RACONTEUSE

WE were so special and proud,
having a car,
but Uncle was fearful of falling
asleep at the wheel
and told us children to sing
to keep him awake.
With my brothers and nephews and nieces,
us in the back seat,
we sang
(that must have been
nineteen twenty-seven)
through Les Landes
with the pine-cones bursting in the heat.

TOWARDS EUSTON

THE small sounds of summer purged,
seats and faces still shadows on the glass;
the cinematographic flicking
of pylons and trees in reflection
and beneath, the piled clouds,
the glossed lowlands,
ivy on a barn end wall in sunshine.

The Netherlands, northern France,
north Germany are the same,
arable, moving in the muttering hide of history.
Bees return and return to the gorse,
cars gleam on the trunk roads.

Then it was different –
then it was ice
and our hairy hearts hurting
for the cooling fatal savannah.
Then it was the long straight roads
and sheep for pig iron.
The cumulus banks higher in the afternoon,
the vicious size of summer
silent beyond the air-conditioned compartment,
the cuttings secret, splashed with cow parsley.

Moving through the red brick, rust,
moribund industry,
through the remnants of the great north plain –
the climate is changing,
it cannot be leapt,
apocalypse more than summer rain.
The climate is changing.
Under the heat and the softly, slowly
boiling clouds
we are laying down our bones.

NOSTALGIA

NOSTALGIA curls up by the telly
and suffuses its peculiar orange glow
through curtains all along the street.

Kids shouting in the hot night
past the front window.

Nothing in the city comes quietly
except perhaps the cats
stalking and staking the gardens.
Nostalgia stretches and yawns.

Kids chuck cans at him,
the other cats call him Algie.
I catch him from the corner of my eye
pressing his prickled coat along the pane,
an empty mewl in his pink mouth.

THE LAYING ON OF WORDS

WHO would know,
hearing these quiet voices in a darkened room,
listening at the cracked door,
what subdues them so?

Sounds with no distinction,
sound with no mouth other than the door,
sound without sympathy,
loose gadgets in the wind.

Your mouth swinging and clamping
like an unhinged door
in the empty town you inhabit.

In the dark inside it is only the presence
and caress of words we can carry
from ruinous house to ruinous house
and the general repairing of worry.

The wind at the door ajar,
the spying ear at the door an inch open
would find nothing in our
gentle expedient dishonesty.

What transpires
lies beyond meaning,
a laying on of words.

KAKUA'S SONG

WHEN I have gone out,
regarded the earth, inspected the ocean,
traversed space in oracular, orbital arcs,
risen and descended through the dark,
pierced the sun through like a necklace shell
and peered
under the empty carapace of a crab;

When I have gathered up
the tickle of an electron
dancing in my pocket,
the centrestone of the world,
dust on my shoes;

When I have come, cowled, here,
to this same room and you
smiling knowingly,
knowing I have returned
to this same room and you:

Then, on your enquiry,
of my pursuit, the fruit
shall be Kakua's bamboo flute,
a one-note song.

*Sent by the emperor of Japan to investigate Buddhism
in China, Kakua's report, on his return, consisted of a
single musical note, which was the seed of Zen.*

MAKING LOVE

LYING up together
with our limbs curled
like something sunlit in the sunless
bed, like water in a bay,
like bark and golden leaves, or
water where golden grey and green lichen
diagram the sun,
clouds of green
and grey stone in their conjugations.

Each lichen expands, colouring a circle,
until cleft together.

Like an acorn in its cup,
like a string in its yo-yo
I cruise between your fine buttocks
after your bath, so your pink powdered lips
break gently a sweet sweat
smelling stale and lively like lichen.
You nudge the hollow of my groin,
the walls of my pelvis like a shadowed hand.

The broken sepals of an orange,
the last distilling of a smile,
the fullest, the little green star
in a creased expanse of glossy orange.

Like a rod on a piston,
we're well oiled.
Like pink flowering
wetly involved with the
latest attempts of the twigs and the wet.
Pink brave blossoming.
Good rain on the window,
the flowering well.

MONDAY

IF we parted now we'd be lost.
    If we split up, at least we couldn't say we'd lost
        the best years of our lives together.
    I hope these years aren't those,
        the best years we look forward to.
    These years are not for poetry for sure.
        These years happened on a day like this:

Went home, worn out, why are you crying?
    late supper, bed too tired to make love,
        late, late up, late for work.

If we split up, we'd have lost nothing
    but a lot of heartache and habits like
        holding each other in the dark
    and falling asleep.

If we split up, if the halves parted
    like a fruit, the husk of habits would
        fall off, and we'd fall off
    apart in the darkness.

Fruit withering. Blossoming tree of being in love,
    we hold it and watch it blossom,
        white, you wild hawthorn!

Your face floats on the darkness like a flower.
    I'm used to it. It's like a wooden handle
        well-worn with my hands, which are also,
    when I hold them up, like wood.

Why do I notice a split in the wardrobe?
    What was I looking for?
        Working clothes.

I only want winter clothes for autumn.
I only want to garden and garden and write
with you, somewhere, away from it all.
Leaves, flowers, leaves,
the wood springing up,
wet and wild and springing up,
and wet leaves and wild flowers.

ALL SAINTS', ALL SOULS'
AND HALLOWE'EN

DON'T suffer.
Remember there are good times after the bad
and bad times again beyond those.
That's where memory helps,
embracing good and bad together.

My work is now yours,
being all that I was,
for art is unforgetting.
Unforgetting and helping others
not to forget.

I love you, then I feel my pen failing
to produce anything here worthy of its source.
I love you but my pen is failing
to produce anything here but words.

Words are a common love;
they bind us as much as love.
Words and love both insist
that we continue when we would be finished
and remember, which we do not.

I hope everything works out well for you.
I can't draw you all into one picture

for a while yet, at least;
but I will. I hope
that works out well for me.

≈

PLENTY of fish in the ocean
Silverfish behind the sink
Her tears were quick as silverfish
Now they're dry as this ink

Bad times for lovers are cold little hells
Her grief's a white green sea
My heart was shrunk dry like an old orange
My love put me back on the tree

≈

O MY simple loves,
I praise myself for these:
Five white doves
That give my cold heart ease.

You are five
That my heart drowned in thought
Have kept alive
With answer and good report.

My five senses,
Five stars that have wooed
The bare recompense
Of my black crooked boughs;

13

Black as thought and black
And wicked and crooked as the river
That carries the stars on its back,
That is night and cold for ever.

You are five
That came in the snow
And kept me alive
And would not go.

ONE FOR SORROW

I WOULD talk, if I knew the world, about you.
A garden in the town I've seen
turned golden, black and once more green.
A pair of magpies, elegant as spears, flew
down through the golden leaves.

But there are yellow-coated trees in armies
on the hills, and a wide blue sea,
and deep forests across the sea,
and between stones and trunks in deep valleys
small birds change their voices.

I've seen winter coming into the city
gust between tall buildings,
I've heard news of killings.
On the tops the wind howls without pity,
blowing down broken walls.

I would tell the world if I knew the world,
and thought in their loss someone hears,
something of what a lover fears,
of the one death that means losing the world
in the millions of deaths.

14

GIRL'S TALK

ASLEEP, she is having another of her
little conversations with the night,
who will not stop talking while she is awake.
Brill selly woll
ard duwurren.

We listen and are half-afraid.
Does the beast's head rear now
in the dank arena?
The minotaur grows taller and taller,
his horns, scowl and metal-bound eyes
like the front of a locomotive.
His thick, flat, tilted brow
approaches you.
Sitting on the roof of the arena
like a dolls' house whose walls you straddle,
you look down to find
instead of the bright red flags and yellow dust,
a shaft, into whose green funnelling light
from the holds of sweet water in black
water-bellied darkness
the giant's frown is rising like a lift.

SLEEPLESS

SLEEPLESS in his globe, the goldfish blinks
a doleful mouth, incessant, startled,
orange paint rubbing off his tinfoil sides.
Look out of the window – rain starts up,
riddling the headlights, the streets seem submerged
and the houses broken moles where enlarged
eyes are drawn to stare through the glass, subject
to that cloud-wracked yellow moon.

But on finer nights you can breathe freely.
The streetlights of the city infiltrate
the sky like a dust, raddling its lilac,
and the back-garden trees are stilled under
a lick of warm light framed by the window.
He circulates clear water, nosing weed,
swivelling, flushing his gills.

THE FARRIER

A BANTAM cockerel strutted on a wall,
his rust and black mineral feathers stirred
by a little wind. The farrier yanked the nails
from each foot and cut off four dirty crescents.
While the firebricks glowed in his portable forge
and the steel blued, he talked, finding a way
for his eagerness round the blocking stone
of his cleft mouth, determinedly, yielding;
told about his job and tools, the forge
in his smithy that would weld white-hot steel.
He bedded the shoes, bending his head down
into the sulphurous yellow hoof-smoke,
and finally shod with bright clipped nails
the hoof rasped pink and flush. That bird of slag,
displaying, unbridled sun, raking the ground
with his claws, cried aloud.

RHYS
In the kingdom of the blind

IN the crisp flesh, on the underside
lain in the grass,
a woodlouse has scoured a crater.
I dislike turning over this windfall

to see it, scaly and grey,
wiggle in the light
to which it has exposed the rich seed.

If you eat to the core
it's spoked with translucent cases,
thin green eyelids that tear like fingernails.
A tadpole or a teardrop, the glossy pip
tastes like sweet wood.

Rhys, when we first met you
I wondered like everyone does
what was under your black patch
and later where they had cored your cancered eye
was a dangerous place to look in.
I kept my attention turned
on the single blue living one.

You said you admired my
dealings with the world.
Once you looked at me with
level despite. I said,
"If you can be a reasoning wild animal
why can't I be
a sentimentalist with a heart of ice?"

Memory's a long exposure
in which the quick becomes solid.
Shrugs, grins, shy duck of the head
and a resumed stare
gain fuller and fuller flesh.
Your whole headstrong body
is a curtain of milk.

You remind me of some red or yellow dog, Rhys,
with a black-lipped grin, sat

so your legs are laid open
like the honey-furred segments of a fruit
split to the glossy dark pip
on the maned fibre up your underbelly,
panting, pink-tongued, joyful.

You gimlet your little finger in your skull
to relieve its itching socket.
A philosopher's memento, the spoils
of generation, bitter milk-white apple:
the hole where knowledge gets in.

NAN
From Broadstairs to Sheol

WILL you come down, brother,
to the sandy beach, where the wide brown rollers
roll in, down the jetty in the blowing rain?

The sea pumps over the sea-wall,
falling along the car park in buckets,
sliding up the windscreen
of a white car,
running back quietly.

Your thin hair clutching at gusts,
droplets in the black wool of your donkey-jacket.

Shall we run to the rail and look down,
brother, at the sliding sea, wild,
tearing up sand and chalk,
for the risk of being
belted by a wave?

Why should we smile so frankly
at our windblown smiling faces
when this air's blue with autumnal storm's
depravities, when all this weather
tastes like tears?

Over on the leeside, the mud-brown beach
receives the swell. A flotilla ducks close
in the shelter, all empty, like the streets.

Our grandmother lies curled
on her side, and we don't know,
don't know if she knows.
"It's a shame to be so weary":
to just lie there with blue-clouded eyes
looking at the light, small, unknown,
incontinent, unknowing, dying.

"Look at that dreadful weather."
Small trees dandled on the wind,
in here the gusts and rain quietened.
She subsides, a small sound,
a near moan on the turning of each breath.
"No, not in pain, dear, no.
Just this terrible ebbing feeling."

"When I'm up you come down again,
come down for a real weekend
and we'll go mad, won't we?
I'm not much fun like this.
I'm so tired of myself
just lying here and wasting the day."

And afterwards we saw the seafront
where we were as children,
deserted and autumnal.

We're real friends, brother.
We share and we're close to each other's hearts.
All our problems end like this,
look, that blue storm breaking
over a brown, muddled sea.

STICK CURVED TWO WAYS

A SALT rind or the limb
of a small animal;
stick curved two ways;

thick flint needle, lighter
than any wood; yellowed
bone; dry driftwood.

I hold it like a key
and hear water clocking,
shaking wet stones,

tone of a beach-ridden
history. The slightest
part of a tree

split by a tail of sand,
it points to destruction.
A pointed tool,

I lick it and turn it
in my fingers to feel
eternal salt

and see thin, arched grain left
in a sea-used, spent stick
stitching the waves.

I learn how needlework
could not undo a turn
it had outlived,

stripped it to a lesson;
how green, deep, air-trailed waves
cleared high water

by lacing its chance shape
for luck through the joints of
my locked fingers.

WINDSOR TREES

THE jets' flight path, overgrown with silence
and birdsong, is excavated and metalled
by their ravenous din. Quiet reweaves
blue, white, green, still river and clouds, in shoots
of level sunlight, until orange leaves
the far black trees suffused violet, enamelled
green water, and the near trees' eloquence
in a blue bloom, as though their drinking roots
in night-bearing earth fed fountains damping day.

January night grows cold. Writhed, leafless
wood spreads out like the maps of black rivers.
If these are gestures then they do not speak
but by example. Their twisting is not
suffering, nor adventitious. This bleak
rigging holds up fistfuls of green slivers
to the sun in season, which should redress
their injury, each leaf a broken clot
where light flows, buds ravelled from the knotted tree.

21

No necessity enables me to see.
Because the branches bear contracted hands
to heaven, although I am a witness
to the deal, they do not reach down to me.
The branched canals of their extended ears
feel in the air for summer's flowering key
turning locked earth to dance. Hardy fitness
of turned words dies or lives, and river sands
aren't fed one silt-grain. Long hollow years
in books won't raise the sap in fleshless time.

Why accumulate insubstantial rhyme?
There was a gardener who knew his place,
had hands wide as shovels, whose patina
and polished grain shed starlight of cells when
plunged in black earth, and nails gathered its crumbs.
He shared his body among saplings then
under the crown of turrets. An inner
gold stood where the red sun, hiding its face,
fell among the offspring of his bald thumbs.

Some misunderstand this in another way.
Drunkards' sick turns gold-dust in distillers'
vats. Their green bottle breaks and they strangle
order. Their knuckles bud through fingers split
like sausage-skin between the cold and fire.
Unfit, they've found the common tongue to spit
and gozz out snot and curses. Hooked, they wrangle
off the iron fence, falling on a killer's
waste-ground. Half-buried, almost entire,

> they turn up two cuddling bodies,
> arm in rotten arm. Nobodies:
> the forms of need and desire.

A WILD INHABITATION

I. *Creatures*

WE tested our new heads, grey in the early
immanent light we saw come back slowly
like memory gathering. The clouds tore
over the thorns, spilling and thickening
a tally of glassy droplets. Before,
still in the blue dark, birdsong notes, quickening,
had splashed on the glass. All night long, in fawn
electricity, we'd smoked and jived, shucked
our husks and laughed. The birds floated up, borne
to the nets, the tree-top twigs. The wind chucked
rain that scuttered like gravel for a dawn
call. We plunged our heads in cold water's scorn.
The ten thousand things had clear outlines, drawn
in water. We were empty vessels, daft.

II. *Gosforth Cross*

They grounded their beast- and bird-headed craft
on Braystones' milling pebbles, at Silecroft
overlooked by dunes, on a beach of suave
slick mud up an inlet at Ravenglass.

A summer day. Standing on a green grave
watching a breeze slowly heave and then pass,
stifled among yews, looking at their cross –
carved rust-red sandstone honed on hot blue sky.

23

The fells mount up, Atlantic pitch and toss
and swell of rock. Their mark is the long I,
five yards tall and ten centuries across.

They made land in ships of dust. When the heart
describes itself, its pride is raised in art
and stands by lies though all of time's denial.

III. *A.*

You always seemed to move free, in floral
wide smocks. I saw a lifting, dancing style
learned from the light. That house was made of glass,
the light of water and the grass of flowers
where I'd watch you bend, blue-jeaned curve of your
      arse.
A stripped pine clock opened its hands. The hours
chimed in the blond grain and brass. The current
you sailed in full sail, like a clipper-ship
on a polished leaden sea, was rampant
delight in your design. Each rounding hip
bred it and bore it on, loved, content
in your trades of husbandry and childbirth.
You wove grass and printed flowers on earth.
In my arms Lady Lion lies hot and dark.

IV. *Offcomers*

My Mum tucked her nightdress across her dark
red, riddled and swollen breast, painful, stark
bag of curds that suckled me.
               In the warm
fog, as I walked the road towards her, I saw
the lights of Windscale – glowing, ordered, calm,

like a city-sized battleship come to moor
alongside the fields. Then I stopped to watch
an intermittent blueish fire flutter
and chirr on a pylon's power lines. Such
a soft, fatal sign I thought the mutter
of moth-wings frying.
                The red, fat-fisted clutch
of an appalling, fist-faced baby, cancer
is an affection I cannot answer.
Smile at me, hold my hand, hide it from sight.

V. 7/7/77

That highest summer I'd listen till midnight
to the airwaves' flutter, hot as summer's height.
I hitched around the roads under a pall
of dust and dark leaves, a green boy at play,
fair-weather visitor. One date was all
sevens. Knowing Thomas had saved the day
to give me California Sunshine on.

The world in the woods was unscaled. We shed
our clothes, a pale stripling and a limber one.
Lean foxgloves clung like flies' tongues in the red
clay banks. Dun calves grazed the greenleaf in the sun
and looked on. Testicles like pink sea-urchins
in the cold beck. Straight gold light was searching
along buffed railway lines, among reaped hay.

VI. Snakes

In the Snake House, over scummed concrete, they
raise their heads and stare point-blank past those
       who pay.

Some lie thick as tyres, asleep. Inertia
doesn't exist behind their glass. They dream
no dreams. If we tried to live there, pressure
would smear us thin as our reflections seem,
margarine-yellow and with hollow blue bruises
for eyes. Their wills police their whole bodies
and their heads are hard. One green one cruises
lithely from a pool, its eyes regardless
as split-shot. They move so slowly, time loses
heart. We fidget in coats, thinking we've spent
our money well, only later to relent.
"They shouldn't live there, and die, and not kill."

VII. *Bird*

Somewhere among wires and chimneys the skill
of a songbird starts. His practice is to fill
his gizzard with flies and sing all he knows.
His song is a game played with stones, the play
of water over water-polished stones.
Now is the twilight of a working day.
Brick is dry, rich and absorbent like bread.

I sing a few small drops of rain burning,
big river-stones gleaming black through wet, dead
grass in the walls, in the flood of night-wind turning.
As I walked out on New Year's night, my head
was a bone-pale prow like a seabird's lifted
on the clumsy swell, my heart was a gifted
needle flickering in a gulfing sea.

THREE TRAINS
i.m. Grace Elizabeth Gibbens, 3/6/25–6/6/81

I. *InterCity 125*

THE low land lies submerged.
Great open-hearted trees
in leaf feed on the surge.
Its surf is white clouds
rolled along dark skies.
The underwater quiet holds.

Running North, into rain,
scratches of scattered drops
line the windows of the train,
so people can complain together
between stations, where it stops
and they lose one another.

While our land floods back
and out of sight to the pylons'
time like an elaborate music,
our brightly-lit compartments
brighten in the darkening silence
of storm we rush against.

I hold my tongue
and listen to the weather-sense
of the passengers I sit among.
In the sick thunder-light like morning
their holidays and gardens
are bright as straws to the drowning.

II. *Whitehaven Train*

That I'm bound back where I lived,
down Cumbria's harrowed coast,
whose harvest of rust and slag and thrift
is blighted by salt, must indicate,
with close, soaking rain and my lost
feeling, a pre-terminal state.

The most part of my belief
is only that the clear and beaded,
tearful curtains fall from grief.
Squalls draw my perfect fallacy
from blanked windows and unweeded
plots to the level waves of the sea.

In the dim quiet of the ward
a nurse gets up from her lit station
to steer an old man back towards
the bed he's left, barefooted.
"Where are you going, Mr Mason?"
she asks him, drifting in the dark, befuddled.

And I know nothing.
I value these live details.
My brother's touched a button
to illuminate his watch display.
Number after number, each entails
the next one flickering into place.

I wish there was a light to cast
those fluid, inky shadows,
shining now as in the past,
letting tears drift down also.
You're going where nothing follows
any blank instant now.

III. *Bound For Glory*

Once upon a time I dreamed along
to the dreamtime in my brother's room
where my heart learned its rocking song.
I watched the ships with tattooed sails
from a beach 'neath a silvery moon
on the sand where empire falls.

Once upon a time a tall castle stood
on a high mountain, surrounded by cliffs.
In its cellars, and in caves and woods,
young underlings of the cruel king
hoarded their leather armour and their gifts
to bear to a birth where angels will sing.

You were my fair queen and in a rage
my pale skin turned to shining armour.
I lay still in the night's cage
and called when I heard red wheels
that rolled over the world like thunder.
I became invisible with secrets I concealed.

When I came to say goodbye last night
you were leaving the flesh I'd left before.
You were drawn on a line into the light,
hand over hand, by the soul-fisher.
"Be happy" was the magic mirror
you left me of your wisdom's treasure.

ONE OF A KIND

ONE morning moment, when your hair's
red-gilded by the sun above
those blocks of flats, all unawares,
maybe I'll stumble on a dawning love.

Then, when you stumble from my side,
running your fingers through your mane,
switch off the clock and throw one curtain wide
to lean your brow against the pane,

you'll be dancing all mysteries.
Though flat, sour days may earn our daily bread,
such ordinary life histories
are leavened by the full, blood-red

potential of that morning sun arisen
from our dreams and from the concrete,
stained, tiled and balconied prison
of the dwellings across the street.

IN MEMORY OF BOB MARLEY

ACROSS the lake at Crystal Palace
you were dancing, tiny in the afternoon
from among the crowd where we'd sat restless,
spaced out, wilting, waiting, sheltering from
        showers:
tiny in your black, ites, gold and green,
cultivating the fruit of the sower

and giving thanks continually.
On your right hand there, one of two beautiful
willow trees planted by the bank broke slowly
under its load of spectators –
reckless, keen, foolhardy souls –
and let them fall one by one in the water.

*   *   *   *

There is a bird that sleeps over the sea
and cannot land, unless it drowns,
yet day and night, and week after week
it braves the Atlantic: sooty tern.
The angry wave flies up to snatch it down
but like the wind it laughs the depths to scorn.

In London on its feet of clay,
beneath the golden heads that dome St Paul's,
you are not remembered in your day.
The crown of the pride of the towers of the city of
      Babylon
gather round about their mirrored walls
the intensifying thunderclouds of mid-autumn.

Sending the mind's-eye's bird away
across the rock of the quartz-like waves,
over the world's sea-pendulum sway,
to painted water and a painted isle,
I follow in the sunken wake of the slaves
to see Jamaica smile.

As we walked in the sun to the demonstration,
from one radio after another
the voice of the Rastaman gave salutation,
upful commandments and meditations,
so we knew you weren't dead, my brother,
as we walked in the sun to the demonstration.

In the final stages of his melanosis
they shed his locks and he cried.
But did they tell you "blackness" was your Greek
      disease?
He cried, "Fear not, for mighty dread
shall be there, by your side,"
and shook black lightning from the crown of his head.

KAL 007

High in the cold and rushing, before-morning
Dark, mercy was not shown. Sleeping, yawning
Into the unknown opening of the
Immediate future, lit so softly,
Two hundred and sixty-nine lives waited
To get off the plane, anticipated
Or doubted, in dreams or out, elated
Or troubled. Who knew they were fated?

    They cross the alert, ever-dreaming screens
    And the star-fighters drop their magazines,
    Stub cigarettes and run for their machines.
    With combat gear they put on pride and fear.

Now we know more. They flew too near hidden
Suns and burst in flames from the forbidden
Air. The air itself continued to chase
Smoothly away from the forbidden place,
But the water broke and received burning
Wreckage, bodies, bits, engines still turning,
Which it gently embraced and took to heart.
They suffered and died and have played their part.

    Scattered, floating or sunk, unseen, untold,
    The non-arrivals do not know their cold
    Flesh turns solid political gold
    Nor hear great mouths mourning them with
        warnings.

We hear that we are angry. The paper
That lusts after Justice wants to rape her.
Our most glorious comrade rises from bed
Today with the world falling on his head,

Which may yet crush him flat. He picks a hat
And heads for the office. A dying cat,
Once, squawling under the wheels of a truck...
Another of God's creatures out of luck.

> One idle thought, remembering that call,
> Can bring cold and rushing dark to us all,
> A high wind to break you and make you fall
> In the end, if your head will not bend.

So spare your judgement, heads of state, until
We've seen your tears. For if they wouldn't fill
One silver salt-spoon – and they do not yet –
What do you propose to bring and set
In the scale-pan? Let the father's wife,
Brother's sister, mother's son and daughter
Bring tears drawn from the well of each life.
Fire and air weigh nothing against water.

> If you don't know pride and fear are the cause,
> If you don't know what's ours and theirs is yours,
> Then no sleep will creep past your locked doors
> One night, and you'll lie, startled with remorse,
> Going down, feeling the great unfeeling.

STORIES FROM THE HEART

I

I MET a travelling party on the road.
Among their number, none was more beautiful than
                another.
But while one kissed my cheek and laughed
and laughed and ran ahead of me,
one alone took me by the arm and walked with me.

II

I met no-one on the road.
Sometimes I walked in a fog of ghosts.
Sometimes I turned
and there was an angel alongside me.
Sometimes we'd talk – stories about heaven,
the contents of their scrolls –
and sometimes they'd play on their trumpets
and the sun would jump up from its sleep
and day break.

III

The road stopped.
Its place was taken by the room,
followed by the street,
the city,
the country,
followed by the broken sea.

IV

Down by the shore
        her face only
moving in and out of the lovelight.
Down by the sea
the hot-blooded needles of her hurt
        moving
burned in the darkness.
She turned her back on the land,
letting go of my hand and crying for home.
There was no holding back.

V

When you phoned me last night from some deep
            dreaming
your voice nearly took me off my feet
right then and there, standing
barefoot on the floorboards in the empty light.

Though you were miles across the midnight sea
I dreamed and I believed and saw
two people kissing tenderly
somewhere dark and electronic,
between the buzzing cables under ocean.

NO COMPANION

THE moon's no companion
though I'll smile to see her,
though I have looked in her face like a lover.

I have seen her exalted on a clear night
and a fragment,
the statue of a breast in daylight,
and footprints in the dust of her veil.

Heavenly mother of images and madnesses,
long dead,
the scarred face of a blank clock
white beyond any comparison,
you are the form of all wasted messages
to whom I fall
solemnly prey.

LITTLE BOY THINKS AGAIN

I'M taking back the fire, smoothing back
faces, recondensing eyeballs
and returning the leaves to the tree.
Bone, bricks and timber reassembled
and flame and ashes sifted together
to remake paper – the breath of the sun
indrawn – I can suck back the first fragments
of steel to clamp down and stifle.
Now to divide the critical mass.

Holding the two pieces firmly apart
I ascend gently on my parachute
which collapses in a moment like a flower
folding and recramming itself into the seed
before I hop back in the belly
and snuggle between my fastenings. There.

Now you can take me home.

Little Boy was to Hiroshima as Fat Man to Nagasaki.

THE ETERNAL

LEGS crooked, back pressed on the wall,
he looked sidelong at one among
that drinking company. This one opined
that they were all securely damned
in God's forbidding, downcast, regal eye
brooding over the sphere of his dominion,
unless they turned old age to shaky prayer,
and thus double-damned for premeditation.

Got up off the floor, dusted down his doublet,
brushed the sawdust off his thighs and,
grinning a foolish grin, departed.

Only to lose his way in a bare pasture.
Only to lay his head down on a plump tussock
under wheeling stars, to spew up red wine
thinly in the grass roots and, looking up,
begin to praise the eternal
in iambics that almost came out right.

WORDSWORTH AND BLAKE

THE Williams, like two fells abutting
At the valley's end. While we mount the one,
Though gravity and stepless, boggy spots
Resist the aspiring tread, the other's
Head is locked in snagging mist or, clearing,
Is plotted with fleeing sunshine and shade,
Particoloured and sombre, the sky's speed
Registered on that brave massiveness.

The streams are so cold and so clear
They're dark on the bedrock. The mountain sheep
Run from the path, mountain birds fly up
From the long grass, and the sun rains lark song.
Above, blunt-winged ravens call, circling the crag.
Below, the force mutters in the oak wood.

Climbing a mountain, as night approaches,
To find at the top a place of bare stone
That the wind rushes over, and the rain
And gloom fall upon.
Cloud is a torrent from the sudden peaks.
The rock is lifted as a breast with breath.

NIGHT BOY

THE hairy-chested hunter and the long-leg fisher too,
    he bid them both adieu,
the breather in the darkness and the angler with his
                                 light,
    and set off in the direction of the night.

In a meadow that the milk moon flooded
    the paleskin child was blooded
and a sea of grasses rustled to receive those drops
    where they hid him from the cops.

When morning light rebounded on the ice
    he popped his lice
and watched his breath and woodsmoke intertwine,
    wrapped in furs beyond the treeline.

At noon he skinned a rabbit among prairie flowers
    while the guards in wooden towers
leaned and smoked and noted no particulars,
    then moved on under their infra-red binoculars.

Near dawn he stepped out from the station
    to the city of the nations.
Near dawn he crossed the rust-red tracks
    with a crown of knives and a bundled axe,
an armful of junk, a new box of tacks,
    a bottle in a bag and a stolen sax,
to go knocking on doors among the tarpaper shacks.

LIVING WRECK

THERE'S a half-built sun comes up
and a ruined sun goes down
on the living wreck of London town
and the long red reaches of the river

where slumbering commerce stirs
between dead jetties and weed-grown wharves.

Through the wind from door to door
the workforce comes in hordes,
silent, with eyes full of words,
putting their coats on hangers
and warming up their machines,
with a spoonful of coffee for their dreams.

When the morning's half worn off,
styrofoam blooms in the park
where pigeons flirt and strut enlarged
and sparrows stuff themselves with crumbs,
and the overcoats tied up with string
go up to the oxter from bin to bin.

While the afternoon DJs warble,
the clocks play all their old tricks
till starlings fly off in slicks,
filling the evening air
where an anticyclone broods
on the meaning of office moods.

The weatherman drawn in dots
consolingly points to the chart
but there'll be no change in the heart
that jumps in the dreams of the night
like failing vertical hold
on the last television in the world.

Down the black lanes of their flight paths
clumps of lights wink slowly past
and the show goes on with a smaller cast,
none of whom are famous names,
who knew this morning when it came
over the roofs in a ball of flame.

GRASS

NOW the grass is coming into flower.

Poets call forward in time,
Whitman and Wordsworth and William Blake
asking at the entrance,
or they find us work
hammering swords
while the grass is coming into flower.

I planted nothing but left the bowl
with a dead plant in it, on the windowledge
and now it's a windsown colony
shaken by the wind
and spikes unrolled for the feathered head to nod.

Where you may lodge and hold
the wind will take your seed
I trust.

Sprouting from rooftops
gutters and chimneypots
thrive with me also, ever.

FORWARD

FORWARD from here, drawn
        from one to another
as the fullness lapses into waste,
        the waste heaps to new growth,
until the final sheer waste,
        death that is utter and complete,
and a long drink from the shadow waters
        muttering
like dead souls over the shadowy stones.

Forward from darkness entanglements,
    the hollow ground where we woke,
to reach the threshold of the open field
    and lie among our clothes beneath the oak.

Upward sprung from the thin green blade
    to the white grass flower,
sun-burned and lordly among the first grape-crop,
    squinting up the hill-slope at her.
And she a twist of hardy fire
    still, like a rowan tree in sunlight.

Onward carrying a baggage of small verses,
    of destiny and bright-painted wooden objects,
downhill along a solemn colonnade of books
    – cool the stone
of the calm, broken faces –
    to the harbour antiquity built,
to cross the great stream in a wooden boat.

To be at the last an old man on a bollard
    among salt-stiffened fisher-tackle tangled along
                     the cobbles
on the quay, on the qui-vive, mending the nets,
    but doubly happy in the glare or shade,
whom I would listen to now
    making light of my youthful obscurity.

BY GLASTONBURY TOR

SPIRITS rise from out the soul
of this green flesh, old England.
    A green hill and a tower
and in the tower nothing but the wind
and shelter from the ocean wind

41

that the kestrel rides
where the small birds sing.

Small birds sing out
where the kestrel looks out from his
towering on the wind.
Where the heart of earth goes out to space
from built-up England–O,
where Michael's fell on the hill that Mary's rose
and, all but one strong arch,
was razed below,

those feet did tread, bled
when the gallows tree was sadly set
in the name of God.

Two cross-shaped scars
where the ram was polled that crops the tor.
The apple trees kneel in the orchards,
reaching out low
like the Magdalene to touch her Jesus.

BRIGHT EARLY MORNING

SUNDAY, bright early morning,
and St John Street's deserted,
a gulf of darkness
chilly at street-level,
but in the top-floor windows on that side
from one to the next
the sun blooms and flashes
and the sky behind is pure blue.

It's a foreign country
and I wander down the road like a newcomer,

Sunday, bright early morning,
reading every date and foundation stone,
tatty plastic or polished business nameplates
by unpromising stairways,
the ghost names over boarded windows...

And I find that Bartholomew Fair
was deemed a public nuisance and prevented
in the 1850s,
conveniently perhaps.
Now the Smooth Field that was Smithfield is
⅛ acre perhaps,
a fountain and a ring of benches,

and the rest
with the bulk of the City's square inches
from here to the river
hidden from the sun by the price of land,
stone-cold
even on Sunday,
bright early morning.

THE LAUGHING STICK

THE laughing stick, odd man out and stumbler,
even my own right eye
shies at the sights the world has to show me
and fills with motes.
The only voices I hear I fear, fill me with trembling
like burning scriptures conspiring to put me wrong
so my last state's worse than my first, and that's
only the start of sorrow.
The skin of my countenance grieves and weeps to
face the world
and sores break out on me like barks from a dog.

My bones are being turned back to front in the
        middle of my spine
and spiteful thoughts are my only consolation,
for which my breath is barred, and my heart fattened
        with lusts pinched hard from time to time.
Every wise creature flies me. Perhaps those with
        appetites disgusting like mine seek me.
Would you cure my sore-ridden self then
set me in the world of rosy whole again?
Then take hold of me, hold of me under your
        downpour
love round all your flames deep thunder rose.

EYE CITY

EYE CITY: ONCE

ONCE I was living at ease with time on my hands.
Now before the blow lands, would I spend half the
        time on my knees?
And what would I do with the other half?
Laugh? Laugh or cry? Cry to whom?

The room is quite warm and quite secure
Though a breeze makes the blind-string shake.
The flowers of tulip and flag are still
Though a broad tulip leaf that has sagged and
        folded
Wags when the grass on the windowsill
Surrenders its rags to the wind's tugging.

Ill on Ash Wednesday I've lazed abed
In mid-February snow's lenten melt.
But bray the mortal artist in his bedsheets,
Still you'll not part conceit from him.

                *   *   *   *

Home's withstood the stone-cold year's first weeks,
Ceding a breeze by the backyard door,
Snuffing the pilot-light but freezing no pipes.
We've kept the music of gas-fires up our sleeves,
        under our belts
Recited the poetry of the soup-pan and the sturdy
        waterproof shoe,
Through the tireless bread-knife's toil learned the
        psalms of the rounds of brown bread
Conveyed from board to table by palm of hand.
But how such few bare facts might uphold our
        temporary dwelling

In the new moon of the biggest bills, under the
      blows of the telephone
And onslaught of electricity, countercharging gas,
      offensive rent,
I don't know.

*   *   *   *

In Sainsbury's sleepwalkers sail, trundle, dally
Trolleys along the aisles, while household goods and
      ills
Snatch at multi-family-size-pack fingers
That empty their pockets like sockets
To the sleeptalker's tune of the scanning tills
Eyelessly telling us, one by one, ingredients of dreams
They have of their Next Customer Please.

I mingle from meat to biscuits,
Seeking my Mis-shapes and Part Rashers, my Rich
      Teas,
Singing under my breath and my eyebrows,
Are you here O my Self-Raising Flour?

*   *   *   *

I met a man by the meat market
On a snapping spring morning
Not going anywhere special.
He was hardly, walking on clockwork legs,
Going anywhere special when I saw him
Stumble, knock a boot
On a jutting flag and fall dumb and hard like a
      fencepost,
With his legs kicking forgottenly, still working.
He was stiff and flat like a frozen cut of beef
When I set him on his feet

48

And cold as a frozen cut of beef.
In a bony face raw and hacked-looking
Blue eyes and a blank mouth working
Couldn't name me or recognise me or thank me,
But the two coldest hands in my life
Clung like some long-lost somebody to me,
While for the couple of seconds I could stand
The look and the speech that weren't there
Remained not there. I told him to take care
And ducked, feeling panicky, down the narrow
    alleyway
To the left, into the old church boneyard there.

*   *   *   *

The elderly types in the library
Are not looking for information,
But to be in the warm – that's their wisdom.
They might pursue unlikely topics
Or rustle the dailies for a while,
But soon they are brought to the doors of great
    learning,
Of sleep, whence their breath mists these windows
Like the panes in an aquarium.
Our coughs, snorts and snivels echo
Below the high ceiling like jungle birds.

As for me, my eyes are shot –
Can't help but be – black sun-spot shot
And dancing, with the grime of a million words
I looked up, like "spring" – "unburdened" –
    "overground"
Where the blackbird drills his song through the
    stony air.

*   *   *   *

Spliff booze & powders
Spliff booze & powders
Can't you play any
Louder?
Play some blues.

Clit tits & nates
Clit tits & nates
Come out to play in
The 80s,
In the sand-pit.

Many faces made familiar with love's
Shortage, cocktails raised
In places made similar through spiritual wastage,
Dimness and indirection of the light,
Cash flow and fun with elastic
Inhibition...

Would you be wise in bars and beware
That strange girl's beauty you're watching
Whisper in your brother's ear, tenderness
You'd spy out under her adornment?
Cause every he in here's seen her,
Mummy-lovers, sugar-daddies, hard boys,
That she's a shape-shaker, hunger-tonguer.

*   *   *   *

When one who weeps will walk the streets,
When the superior man asks that his tower fall on
        him
And the wise woman her mirror and her thread to
        hide her,
Pity the fool, petty, proud and poor,
Who believes in this world and says,

Bless the harlot and the violent that they would be
      healers;
It's behave or be saved if the next wave's the last;
Though everyone's saying it's a small world,
Really there's just a big God.

*   *   *   *

Comfort to one afflicted is the transformation of the
      earth
And Messiah a loving act.
A fit object for devotion is the son of man made
      hideous
By the torments of a sinful generation,
Not for the contemplation of fault
But that the glory of God be made manifest in the
      healing.

*   *   *   *

Suddenly a black vaporous tide rushes upon the full
      moon
And engulfs it. The perfect lesser light completely
      vanishes
As it had never been, but soon shines again un-
      vanquished, at which
The clouds, brows beaten by her gentle light, bulk
      under a new head
And mount broad-winged against it, till the simple
      disc reveals in time
The assailant unsubstantial, beaming from fissures
      and chasms
Her splendour. This play it seems they'll play all
      night, while our desolate
Sister rises high, obsolete and small as a silver
      threepence.

*   *   *   *

51

(Even in this dictionary,
Though "Messet", from the Irish
For a lap-dog comes between,
"Messenger" is before "Messiah"
As "Fairy-tale" before "Fait accompli".)

*　　*　　*　　*

The feet's writing read
Three toes forward and one toe back
Here's the snow and there it isn't

&

Melting patches still
Describe round Mum's eyes when she smiled
A footnote I forget what to

*　　*　　*　　*

Logical snow, repentant water;
Mariner gulls row likewise,
Counter-clockwise.

Ruffled songster sits like a comma
In a measured wall-top line
And looks both ways.

Promising they'll be pineapples, blind
Hyacinths with open arms
Receive pure crowns,

Speechless, proclaiming shame and glory,
And an unlettered starling
Recites over-

head of one coming endlessly soon.

*　　*　　*　　*

Never one to stint on options,
The Enemy, His Short-lived
Serpentine Majesty, Old Bendy,
Has thrown two wayward coils
Of false religion round the world.
One is clad in iron, gleaming white;
He holds out his left hand and his right hand
And in them and his garments are graved wrongful
      names –
King of Kings and Judge of the Earth, Sword-Arm of
      the Lord.
He is known in the spirit as false Emmanuel and
      false Prophet,
Whose true character is death,
Warlike inhumanity of self-righteousness.
Another, whose garb is softly glittering
With embroidery of signs, ever-moving
And seductive, dealing pleasant-tasted words –
Prince of Pieces, Star-Haired, Coming One –
Is the false Orient, leading into slavery.
Never one to stint on options,
The Father of Falsehood puts forth
His left hand and his right hand,
Both Satan and Lucifer.

*   *   *   *

    I can't see you though my eyes are closed
    Nor keep silence before you but by singing
    Your word the poem is made on,
    Alone-good.

EYE CITY: YET

I

YET Adam's mode of locomotion
Remains from grief to grief (after you,
Lover), an ungainly gait he makes
His way by, through the door marked Progress.

His heart ailing and his left foot clubbed
In a box-like boot, his shamble like
A bear's in forest darkness under
The interminable entrance arch,

He stumbles out on the desert glare
Where clouds bearing the likeness of cups
Evaporate southwards before noon
And sand sinks and fills the portal in.

Alone on the face of things, footloose,
He starts his round of the city walls.

II

Another starveling camel straining
At the needle's eye (to be taken
Unliterally, though without God
It's still impossible) must shed his
Bales of various colourful stuff,
Finding out how not to keep back light
Laid on us in perishing places
But to let more in.
                    Do it, driver,
And then head for market, where children

54

Pipe and drum in disinterested
Earshot of camels that kneel relieved;
Stones underfoot are more worth than cash
And would cry blood before shedding blood;
The manifold fruit is of one tree.

III

Ah, that deep-throated American taste
For surfeit, waste and self-destruction,
For the sun like a pizza setting
Behind the industrial thicket
And night-purée roiling on the sea.

The pioneer's heart burst into flames,
Whose ash in lines the backward breeze makes
Waver on the page of a novel
And soles crunch on the lakeside cinder path;
Whose heat goes nowhere, whose light goes home.

No sky-blue-pink berry tops the rise.
The bush is clogged with man-size tissue.
If Huck Finn had lived he'd have taught us
The worth of an elder's crown, downcast.

IV

Madness is setting in so much more
Quickly than we expected, doctor,
And not only in the mind. But still
The small, orange, early-waking bee's
Coming to make her honey from the blue
Hyacinth and from the pink; house-flies
Consider all the angles; the bug
Half-trod holds one remaining feeler

Out and shuffles painfully backwards
In circles, till pulped with a jug's foot.

Rosa Schulmann, killed between the blossoms
Of your Christian name, and the infants'
School of your last, teach in those mansions
Without prisons, prayer for the slayer.

V

Half-dark stirs with presences
That get me jumping upstairs,
Spooked in the tinted urban midnight.
There are no stars near the ground
And the sky's the limited
Colour of television,
Constantly simulating morning,
And the same square, rounded shape.

The Lady in the Chair shows,
Cassiopeia, the capital
Double-you of Why?, who was
Queen of Ethiopia;
The Plough, too, and the Hunter,
Though not the Scorpion that hounds him.

VI

Even twilight we prefer
To mask our revelations.

Not fleeting daytime's meeting with night:
Cautious lukewarm restaurant
Light contents, conceals our stained
Indifference in a void embrace.

Feel free to touch each other
Here, since in broad sight you won't
And in true disillumination
Won't know which each is other.

These stretched moments of decline
Incline us to acceptance
Of all their shady machinations
And speech of less than wholesome wisdom.

VII

Cut-lemon sun in potato sky:
Must be Sunday. (That whole bright star's rind,
Life-oil-glistened, later shines.)
Through white midday's placid, lakeish light

I plough my macaronic furrow.
Wind bloweth where it listeth
And I've leagues to wake before I sleep,
But stop now and then, considering

My condition of this soul,
Gift you have got to learn to give back.
The nothing I'd have if I lost her 's
As utter as losing you.

Goose-girl, your scandalled heart is the king's
To be, not to be denied his love.

VIII

The half-moon shines on the man himself.
A three-way thing, it seems his emblem,
Compound of earth's shadow and sun's light

Met on a small world speeding debris
Pocked, or the frenzy of vanished fires:

An upright bowl, or slightly tilted,
Pouring whiteness out though not away
Nor into the absent half induced
By the light. "A bright right's growing,"
He thought. "The dark that's left is going,
And now she begins to cast shadow."

Before this saw had sunk in truly
It slipped his mind like a ship that steers
By taste for shores of milk and honey.

IX

Yes turn but turn where? It's salt aside,
Aback, affront. Unless some high land
Catch the waters falling to their own
Where thirst can drown, thirst must die self-killed.

House-sparrow beaking raindrops piled on honey-
          suckle leaves.

Air's been lately full of signs like this
Police helicopter harrowing
Over the wine-bar's backyard's chatters'
Heads, where moony disco bubbles up.

Limehating navelwort blooms once and fades, a spire
          of tiny trumpets planted wrongly on the cob-
          webbed bricks.

Who perfects friendship enters the gate
But who perfects a love perfects earth.
There a tree in a summer shimmer
Darts off light in a Whitsuntide wind.

X

I thought because it was doubtful
the world turned
but I think because it's certain
the world turns.

You hardly stop talking like some children.
Like some child you're hardly there at all
or rather we're not,
busy on the outside
in our world of make-believe-we're-busy.

I couldn't see you smiling
so close,
only the star in your eye
shining out of the blackness,
shining out of the blue.

THE GROUND

I REACHED to speak familiarly of God.
By self-elevation there is no way to him.
Come soul and I will walk along the ground, not
        tiptoe.

The cherry tree buds against the cold,
    green sparks along the branch.
The sparrow gang heads up,
    heads down,
grazes the paving for crumbs.
And a woman with black and white down
    round her one-toothed mouth
folds her bent hands, waiting.

YARD SPRING

IT starts with a bump; bright, unmistakable tints.
Mint slants through the grit like fuses, balm
    discloses
A leaf wrinkled like foil, vigorous and spreading.
The scarlet creeper's points set foot on unmapped
    brick
And some buds on the branch, thumbs-up and
    multiple,
Plump for ghost-white blossom. She's never so
    human,
Nature, as in her childhood's gradual, careless time.

THE WHITE HYACINTH

LEGGY from the darkness where it grew,
The white hyacinth has settled horizontally
Across the stem of its pink companion.

Underground they leant for a basement's seepage
Of sunshine, and lived till British Summer Time
    began.
Then the column of opaque stiff stars,

Ivory-carved, sank on itself
Like a sea-creature, shrinking and turning trans-
     parent.
March southerlies, varying from boisterous

To huge, blew the first death-day blue-brilliant.
Our loss was made clear by this flower becoming
     glass,
Wrinkling like water by the hour

And doubly beautiful. Now it seems sad as skin
And forsaken as only something human can.

RAGWORT

I HAVE forgotten the earth
and when I walk away
dwindling in your perspective
I dwindle also within myself
almost to nothing
as though turning to dust
and when I come back I will not get large again.
You will not see me then returning
or say, he forgot something.
Inwardly I will have dwindled away
and you will not see me.

Only grant me to say,
almost to nothing, almost forgotten
and I shall be blessed dust, not cursed
dwindling to humility.
Only grant me like the earth
to nourish in my smallest parts, inwardly,
like the earth putting out its weeds
under the sun and the smoke of humanity;

putting the ragwort forth,
the rosebay willowherb from gravel;
from slabs the bitter-milked dandelion
and in grime the pineapple-scented mayweed;
the nettle, the elder and bramble on dumps
and the medallion-leaved mallow in unlikely places.

Like the earth, thinking nothing of itself,
grant the vagrant seed may go unregarded
and the crooked tenacious weed
to stand up on its pale feet
and swell its unappealing
or appealing flower, an emblem of the sun,
as common as these prayers are to life.

TO THE BICYCLE

HUMANE chariot, most valuable,
most laughable of machines,
complete companion of the human form
and to the human bottom bosom friend,
we are more intimate than most friends.

Cousin to the umbrella
and elder brother of the sewing machine,
an example to all your family,
you testify of an heavenly engineering
which angels do not need.

Once you went unrecognised,
bore eccentrics asymmetrically about,
stopped to pose for engravings.
What you gained in simplicity and equity
you gained also in beauty and usefulness.

You are our invention's
hymn to balance;
with the horse and the steam-train
you write the perfect poem of distance
overland – its sonnet.

Poised between your wheels,
between your pedals,
I feel I know your future
is secure. You cannot be replaced
any more than I can.

AN ABC

A IS for Apple, an innocent fruit,
Put here first for the aliveness it shows.
The core of its globe, far from evil's root,
Reveals to teeth the fiveness of the rose.

B is for Birds, which are nowhere confined,
But make on the air, in water, on earth,
Pictures of freedom they seed in our mind,
Of flight beyond bounds of death and birth.

C is for Cat, most luxurious creature,
Accustomed to walking while others ran,
Thing exquisite of habit and feature,
The only one to domesticate man.

D is for Dog, model of loyalty,
A born companion though we've proved unkind,
Stunted his sturdy frame, made a frailty
Of his faculties, his sharp eyes near-blind.

E is for Ear, the labyrinth of sound,
Whose winding ways lead direct to our hearts.
Musical instruments look to compound
In their forms the forms of this organ's parts.

F is for Forest, whose dark fills with fear
Some, gives their sole belonging to others.
Whatever the dangers lingering near,
The deadliest is elsewhere – their brothers.

G is for God, who's called Lover of Souls,
Father of Jesus, and not him alone,
Thanks to him, whose love is least own of goals,
Who draws us near his universal throne.

H is for Hunger, the breaker of hearts,
Third of four horsemen to ride in the End.
Upon a black horse from heaven he starts...
Now remember starving Lazarus, friend.

I is for Islands, which we cannot be,
And also for Is, a wave of the sea;
Also for It, which is other than me;
Also for I, who am other than thee.

J is for Joinery, Jesus's trade,
By which the last table he shared was made,
The cross the next day he hung on and prayed,
And the boats wherein his friends were afraid.

K is for Kisses, O my fair sister!
Moon-faced, modest, silent one, unpainted.
It takes a fool's courage to resist her
And brave folly to be better acquainted.

L is for Love, humbler and stronger than
Everything – the everlasting law,
Our passions, death itself. The longer man
Is in longing, the more love he longs for.

M is for the Moon, planet of feeling,
Whose courtly dance leads on variation,
Whose light-washed face, concealing, revealing,
Is Sorrow's and Beauty's illustration.

N is for North, the home of the winter,
Whence cold wind goes forth and the days of dark,
That leave summer's fruitful pride disinte-
grated; whose power and glory are stark.

O is for Orange, the fruit of the south,
Where they drop like harvest moons from the tree
And stand in the hand, and taste to the mouth
Like rising suns on a deep leaf-green sea.

P is for Poetry, fruit of the tongue,
Rooted in the heart and branching in thought,
Language-leaved and music-flowered, whose dung
Is grief. Spirits are birds the fruits support.

Q is for Quest, best gift of the giver,
By the hard way through terrors and torment
Of doubt, rock chasms, flames, a deep river
To cross to the groves and dwellings foremeant.

R is for Rocket, technology's pride,
Lucifer launching himself at heaven,
Or a flame from man's heart sent shooting wide.
Back to fallen earth fall NASA's seven.

S is for simple Souls, Spirit and Sin,
Sex and Snakes and Superstition; for Skin
And Skeleton, Secret and Seeming, Spin
And Stillness; for Saint, Soldier, Searcher within.

T is for Trees, the pillars of the sky
And guardians of breath, which give hearts strength
To feel the force their limbs are twisted by
Established in a harmony at length.

U is for the Universe, the "one-turned",
Whose spinning fragments, clouds of glowing gas
And starry consorts came to be, we've learned,
When God the pin pulled from the primal mass.

V is for Vulture, bird of ill-repute,
Counted a villain for an ugly look –
An undertaker in a shabby suit –
One of the shadier turns Nature took.

W's Water, without which nought lives,
Molecular image of trinity,
The lowliest, loveliest stuff earth gives,
Up from which emerged Christ's divinity.

X stands for the unknown, as in Xmas.
Most letters live in the sociable port
But X only leaves its home on the isthmus
At night, sax in hand, to coax and exhort.

Y is for You, and I wish you were here
For I think of you often and fondly.
Yours was the voice I was longing to hear,
Even when what you said was beyond me.

Z is for Zion, the hill of the King,
And Zebidee, whose sons Christ did befriend;
For things that don't end or begin, like Zen,
And Zeal, whereby repentances spring.

> That completes this criss-cross row.
> Reader, with your leave, I'll go.

SUNFLOWER SEEDS

STRIPED like stones, I pile sound ones
to the right hand of the fold,

scatter of husks and the brown
tongues, twisted closed, of flowers

emptied from their broken heads
on the left. Their sorting place

is a full-page ad for personal computers.

Words would be such seeds, newsprint-
coloured and ordinary,

our grimy smooth currency.
The sheen of slate is on them,

as rivers mouth to the stones
they carry, that carry them;

their shape has the chisel's deep, dignified bevel.

I stuff one envelope with
one year's harvest from our yard.

Flags raised, a patch of good earth,
though filled with the centuries'

rubble, has looked at the sun
now from every angle,

fruit of its travel these quarter-inches eager

to tell again the eight-foot-
tall story, of rough green hearts

and heavy heads, temple-form
of flowers inside opening,

mixed like bells in carillon,
arc on arc, to the centre.

The keen kernels, like loaves, slip their papery shells.

FIXTURES

THIS small blue book is *Fixtures Ready Made*,
Grandpa's one bequest to English letters,
Ensuring matches in your league are played
In a fair rotation of home and away.
I'm sprung through him from the class that betters
Itself – upper working? lower middle? –
From printer's pence to sub-editor's pay.
Courting culture, he practised his fiddle,
Versed, and took up oil painting in old age.
Once, in his dressing-gown and in his rage,
Short, stout and bald, he squared up for a fight

With a wayward grandson who'd larked all night
Doing *what* with these questionable "friends"?
But now he sleeps at peace, his lifelong page
Off stone and gone to bed; no more to light
And tamp with flameproof thumb his thickset pipe;
No further proofs – distributed his type,
Until our Author's final and complete
Revised edition his devils amends;
Whom now, as I close my eyes, I entreat
To see that Gabriel his name appends
To the great gold book when the story ends.

FIVE SONGS OF A STEPFATHER

I

SHE looks a girl, our neighbour,
In the way she holds herself,
The first grey above her brow.

"He asked her to marry him
The first night, so my mother
Never got back to the farm."

Once they mingled streams of talk…
"You never know, next year,
You may be a grandfather –

Rather young!" Opalescent
Nightfall brings wild song, caring
Nothing for his melody,

From a bird, that one warm day
After two of rain is spring,
Begetter of the seasons.

"I got married at twenty" –
Turning her mild, child-wise look
And ash-threads to the window.

" – Thirty years. They seem happy,
You know. They knife each other
And talk again the next day."

II

Ill-tempered because the job ahead was a botch,
Old wood, old screws were made to serve,
And the wall to which they were attached
Plasterboard and nothing,

I drove the screwdriver in my hand such a twist
A disc of skin driven from it
Left an eye or mouth palely weeping
In centre of the palm.

What it says to me or sees in me is not clear
Though often I've looked into it.
Now the boy's in the room the girl had
And she's to be married.

To be married, and I should compose to bless her,
In mauve, though first she'd thought of black,
In dark of the moon to a stranger,
New moons on each shoulder.

Is it my heart and my fortune cross there, tell me,
Or life and wealth? Under the wound,
Whichever, in the rough and tight spot,
The junction grows the same.

III

The tulips' grace is dilapidated,
Their beauty run wild.
Whereas their cups were held bated
Now they open shameless wide,

Blunt iron stars on their nonchalant stalks,
Fresh from the furnace,
Nearly flat, or twisted half back,
Half forward in tenderness.

A week since they were set out in the vase
From son to mother
Their entirely uttered voices
Declare they soon must wither.

IV

All his life,
Grandpa rusted tins of screws and hooks,
Once-used fittings,
Time-eaten tools,
Memorials of a bodger.

New York time
Was the morning of your wedding day.
I cycled past
In evening rain
A burned-out hearse by the roadside.

"Love is fire,
Strong as death," mouthed its wreck. Twice en route
To the menders
The chain derailed,
Fetching the fire that needed fixed.

71

V

One week since we had your word
That in five days you should be wed
She goes to pray for her daughter,
To the prayer-house with such an air
That if I should lech
She would stay and make love with me.

Be well wed, love,
Who are what no lover could be,
More dear to him than any,
As she is who goes on her knees
Just now to beseech your welfare.

THE PROSTITUTES' SONG

WE warm earth with our blood impartially
as we did you who kill us with our loving –
you or your brothers in need
of ease from their seed's insistence.

We recognise them in you;
you share first names
and your second names – fearful lust,
shame, tenderness unknown – are also the same.

Fathers of our fathers made the law to kill us
and the money to keep us alive.
I don't see you look in our eyes
at the moment of penetration.

With us strange women you turned aside.
In our arms, between these folding legs

you gladly forgot to be earning paradise.
You'd bought it for a moment second-hand and half-
       price.

Bullet smashes a breast you pressed,
tears the nipple you triggered.
Our sister's unwon heart is burst in mid-beat
but her cry doesn't show how God is pleased.

The beauties he'd given us,
when you had confinement and labour to offer,
we used to be an arm's length free of you.
At arm's length you rid earth of us.

Earth is awash with our life
as with righteousness in a just day.
Oh men, then where will you go from the earth
or into what heaven can you be received?

FULFILMENT

A GLORY we who are condemned can only faith
Is the glory of one-in-all that Paul confessed,
For the human is not whole apart. Even breath
We borrow and return, as song, with interest.

The blood shed of love's fools who felt it must be so,
Though it pollutes the earth, puts life into the heart
Of hearts, whose pulses hearts in all will one day
       know.
Those who held out for the low against the upstart

Tyrant, the self-made god, defended the juster
Against the unjust act, the more against the less

Equal share, even if the good they could muster
Fell short of the sum, trusted the sum of goodness

Has need of every little, and takes it in.
A glory we who have been pardoned cannot law
Is community of the pure in heart. Begin
To build with passing acts. The foundation is sure.

And a woman sings there who found no forgiver,
And the hair of those who were shaved, blood of
       those killed,
Sways together as a forest, pours a river,
And their rushing revoices her song of love fulfilled.

A QUESTION

WHERE'S an art so good it's impossible
To speak well of it, that will render
Inconsolably the inconsolable,
Though form's consoling prompts the heart's
      surrender;
    Off the white, right-angled page
    To head with difficulty
    For its lair in the ribcage?

Whose laborious pen can make guilty
The dancing eye and fluting mental voice
For concentrating their strong faculty
Here, not in the making of a life's choice?
    To undress the injury
    Without healing intention
    Is a worse-than-perjury.

"Harmony, that mends the soul's dissension,"
Replies my flatterer, "is the great sun

To which your wings bent draw our attention."
When what is done now in the world is done
    I'd not teach a soul assent.
    God the Son confessed himself
    An arsonist, impatient

To set alight the planet's selfish pelf.
How can the poem so stir the embers
You'd not even return it to the shelf
But yearn to act while the heart remembers,
    Leaving the pages unclosed
    In stillness of November's
    Light, like a true question posed?

DEVIL'S MASS

I CANNOT think you chose to be adored
With babies impaled on a sword,
Though like better-chosen presents
These also announced your infant presence.

Unbelievers know you didn't relish
Burnt, broken offerings, hellish
Rites for the choking heretics'
Conversion into meat by fanatics.

Who ventured, then, to make a blessed name cursed?
What deep returned the words reversed?
Finding the height unscalable,
Who'd poison to his praise each syllable?

The tortured alone are like one tortured,
No matter in what faith nurtured.
When the tormentor wears the cross,
All Hell rejoices in Jesus' loss.

FOR THE DOOR
OF A VANDALISED CHURCH

THE thousand breakings
of earth
and thousand leafings,
leaf-falls,
the sanctuary remained,
and three times
one hundred thousand times
darkness within
gathered and stars scattered
without looked,
were as one night one woman
kept her lamp
and watched for the bridegroom
to rejoice with the bride,
that he came a long journey
for her.

THE EDGE OF FAILURE

THE first night's shaving off the moon,
that edge of failure mortal things endure...

"You don't see things with black lines around,"
the art teacher teasingly chided,
but you do, and everything has
a stronghold in nothingness.

Not even a stone is chaotic;
within it is a cathedral
and a pile of stones contains the seeds of order,
which time that waters also eats.

This flower that builds it, the human hand,
believing the moon's not green cheese,
although flesh may be nervous grass,
sets the bark of light a-sailing
on the bight of dark.

BORE OF FROTH

THE city takes away dreams
        phallic rigidity
she must not bend
The dream that makes us well
that leads to the heart
        by its paths
Instead by the billboard
airshot, broadcast
is the networked fantasy
industrially uniform and seamlessly apparent
Well-being and strangeness banished
nothing issued from the difficult
        gate of horn
The core of this porn is not soft
but a nest of covet, stinging
and with a bite less good than death
Out from the ivory, elaborate gate
        pours a bore of froth
surmounted by an eunuch Eros
Scuds with ravishing technique
unloveliness displayed in the teeth of need
To call it an idiot menu
insults the idiot's fenny
        flat reflective mind
and it slights even cunning
to call it cunning, inseeping drivel

Timber turns paper with this dry rot within
Our last consumption
and most ruthless appropriation
        with improved ruthlessness
larger than life and bold as brass
broad daylight robbery of dream

LEVIATHAN

WHEN did you come to and when go
from our shores, these continents,
their immensities, condensations,
swathes and buckles no more than spits and bars
to your one ocean, mothering and continuous
        element?
Denizens of earth and air as you were once
we are woken of fire and its wakers as you never
        were.
However cumbersome, you felt the strider's pride,
the contentment to lie down here
where we walk between weather and geology.
Your universal now is only our companion and
        visitant,
water: while we grapple and couple them,
air touches you only lightly above,
earth holds you slowly below.
What can your mazy, leviathan, musical minds
understand of the erect, difficult livings we make?
What can you make of us, your quick, light,
splay-formed slaughterers? Between your eye
in a bulwark of oil and bone, and mine,
glancing electrically in a blooming networked box,
the beam of mutual intelligence persists
to be unblinded. Like the hunter once we could hear
in our own your mammalian hearts.

THE VIOLIN RECITAL

BY the streetlight the tree's hair squeals,
bark bowed on bark by February wind.
Out of the brutal cold, an air
of expectation circles slowly
in the light made of brass and graphite.
Her gown is electric blue,
her hips are broad as a river,
as the blue air over a Russian river.
Where does the little box come from
if not from the farm, the evening,
the feast day? She holds it under her chin,
which is bald and creased like my granddad's head,
this defector. Her debut night
in the day-blue gown, she makes the bees fly,
the cats and horses dance.
Where does it stem from, the honey-coloured box,
if not the forest? That cultivated scream
as high as civilisation speaks of
the national character. Her husband's left behind.
She grasps (as on the tree
the gleaming, leafless tress vibrates)
the violin by its top-knot.
We catch in our hands enough shadows
to fill a small wood, and let them go.
They clatter up as ripe, pink-breasted pigeons
and circle in an air of appreciation.
Outside, the luminous plastic wheel
of the night twists and creaks in the sky.
Fiddle the dial and the radio harps,
"The city's a jungle and I'm its beast."
But the women, Rapunzel-haired,
led by the arm, did they abound
like this, before her programme?
"This city is not quite a ruin,"
their taxis hum, "and I am its citizen."

79

THE SMELL OF THYME

OF THE GODS

THE gods run ghostlike through the present world,
Discredited, unpropitiated,
Their worst slight to be the self-created
Punch and Judy show of our inner life.

Where lives of a place gather to a mood
In glistering acres of cereal,
Or moor, or waste woodland, the gods are real.
These leaves give news of Pan, that he is dead.

Who is Diana, or bright Apollo?
The fine-boned woman who dreams a dancer
On unmolested ground has the answer.
Ask her tanned rival, the hot young talent.

By night, the tornado struck from the south.
A bus-shelter roof has been kung-fu-chopped
Where the long, smooth branch of a plane tree
        dropped.
A frantic god is shaking the storm-bared crown.

Who now would turn stag, be run and torn down
By one he glimpsed in her moon-specked river?
Respect of their precincts fades for ever
Into the map, the grid's sheer location.

Bleached phantoms walking the western horizon,
Whose polished limbs and robes were battle-dusted
And blooded, with hearts scalded and lusted
And faces like stars, older than the sky.

THE GALE

AUTUMN came without gentleness,
One wind ripping prospective gold
Off the branches, branches
From the trees and trees from earth.
Few, yet many green, the decimated leaves
Shine and play in the strong sun
And urban birds, that don't know resignation,
Have unseasonably naked homes.

A fade to glory I thought was lovers' fate;
That too, this weather fears me,
A single fury can pre-empt.
If a blow should empty my arms
And every torn leaf turn to rot
Perch in my heart still to sing our distress.

THE HUNTRESS

SHORT as ever of time,
two meet in hourless gardens.
The colour of her sleeve subjugates him,
the colour of her hem and the blackbird's beak
scissoring airs to strand them on the lawn.

"In art," she says, "there's plenty and enough
of mess, disguised as decoration,
an emptiness that blackbird's never known.
Don't trouble your fingers with the frets
unless each string can strike a dart into my breast,
for I am Queen also of the hunt."

Her cheetahs on silk leashes
give his ragging hands no room to fail.

CYGNET

SINGLE on the dusk canal
this yearling sails,
whistling for company.
I stop the bike
and whistle lowly too
for company.
She swims close up to look,
long-necked like you,
and gaps her noble beak
for a hedge-bird's three-note peep.
Afloat in her cygnet-fawn,
and as yet unaloof,
on the City Road Basin,
unfinished perfection.

BURNING VENUS

BURNING Venus takes her sentinel station,
Over the fencing blocks she mounts her watchtower.
Let the night begin
With adolescents' cries of mock-pain, ululation
Of sirens and blue light spinning through the final
        leaves.
Winter needn't lessen
Our pursuit, nor cold skimp the crimes of Eros.
If we go well wrapped, the point still enters,
His aim is no less naughty.
The real God can't deflect the tearing barbs
Nor hate us when we step defiantly
Towards them, shirts open.
Does it grieve him when the terrible queen rises
Indifferent to the distant, sedate and ordered stars?
It must, since of all things

He knows the end. She wavers and beams more
     brightly.
His love is quiet and still enough to consume all
Many times over.
It cannot be filled or emptied, ultimately,
It cannot be avoided, yet is in the best sense
Unprepossessing.

THE BEAUTIES

MANY beauties must've read of another's
And thought her themselves, though assured
On the poet's most solemn word
She was dead, before they formed in their mothers.
    In flatteries burnished near the shine of truth
The fair consider their features,
Old lines made a new love's teachers,
For dust surely wastes the heritage of youth.
    A lively praise deserves a livelier eye
Than she has now who inspired it,
Don't you think? He who admired it
Would prefer to her lip, yours who lips his lie.
    Yet may beauty and her poet pass unblamed
When each shall rise, new bodied and new named.

PARIAN

THE town museum has displays upstairs
Of rustic and of prehistoric life;
Downstairs some old and mediocre pictures,
A cabinet full of Parian ware.

Flour and milky fairings of an Eros
Still hanging on his mother's apron-strings

Once teased the civilised mantlepiece,
Limbs disporting what the talking skirted.

Here are Milton and Prince Albert, both blank-eyed,
And languid, dimpled nymphs on stumps and rocks
With bums no bigger, smoother than two thumbs,
An arm across the breasts, a modest twist.

Though the veiled bride marks the summit of
        technique,
By whose nostril the porcelain almost quivers,
The pastoral couple's dateless charms
Most absorb the gaze of a daydreamer.

Paul and Virginia on their grassy knoll
Loll on the threshold of an unlike world
Whose haytime breezes lead their locks astray,
Where no shell bursts the birdsong of those fields

They seem to survey. They smile, unminding
The lovers bound for frozen mud, laid low
On the burning childbed, whom they misled.
Mutely they cant to each other, Life is sweet.

FEAR OF LOVE

THE strings are vainly twisted
because I cannot sing the old songs any more
though the grease of them is still on the fingerboard.

The previous songsters charge me
that sloth ate up my thoughts of you,
the cut of you sank to an ulcer
and I made you out to be like others.

I opened an inward eye
and more instantly jetted in than I dared fear
but the strings will not reach where you are now.

Here is your mouth and a line under the underlip;
  its smile.
Here is your face from this side and from that.
The inward gloom of the eye and its moss-green
  surround
roll out from memory.

I would search in the seeing blank for reproach,
that indifference prevented my overturn,
or indifference, that it didn't,
and I am afraid of neither.
Of that I am afraid.

THE THORN

A LOT you'll learn of upset, the obsessed
Man's twinges, and little of loveliness
From forced, arch verse, barren and overdressed.
The fluctuation of air, her light dress
Against the dusk breeze and low voice sounded
Over the water and through loud chatter,
Still warm to recollect, are confounded
By absence, dissolved by teeming matter.
The part of beauty that's delight of sense
Culpable memory will shortly fail
And words unequal. The part more intense,
Harmony of sentiment, time can downscale.
  No wonder lovers keep a buried thorn
   When flowers themselves all else seems bent to
    scorn.

THE SMELL OF THYME

THE smell of thyme, fresh thyme,
earthy and subtle,
opens a landscape of white
dry limestone to the spirit,
a wide, high-lit plateau
from a narrow herb, winding and low.

Dark green above and dusty underneath,
the tiny spear-point leaves,
the reddish stalks, though slight,
breathe unstintingly
odours of courage and hope,
glinting in the mind's eye.

Unlike the enrapturing rose
whose scent whelms us back,
as when we begin to embrace,
to beginnings the heart almost knows
how to retrace, the smell of thyme,
fresh thyme, speaks of the future.

Each leaf-pair is a door
opened on a setting
where companion goes with companion freely,
not in the flowers' plangent fragrance
but new love, subtle and earthy,
in the smell of thyme, fresh thyme.

THE MOCK

MOCK me now you later times:
This strain's high-flung
From one so young,
Ill suits the lumpish echo of his rhymes.

But on this count mock the most:
Love unbidden
And kept hidden
Was the form these archaic lines enclosed.

The dense and subtle splendour
Of the domed brain
Reflects in vain:
In the heart's forge truth is hammered tender.

They say the holy city,
The angel host,
God, Christ and Ghost
Find room in that chamber's infinity.

Mock how heart the mind enjoins
In its great need,
Though she'll not read,
To build her place there, her columns and quoins.

And when you've soundly derided
Unlet passion
In the old fashion
Feel your heart too, set in your breast lopsided.

THE LEGACY

I. *The Gardener*

YOU fructify me. I set the hard fruit
That daily swells your praises. The moons swell,
Diminish and are swollen. The dull bell
Counts another day, cancels it to boot.
Another week: the sharp buds make to shoot,
And you can't come approvingly to tell
The total of my labour, whether well
I work to draw up sweetness from the root.
    The branch aggrieved its store is left to waste
    Sheds round its foot the good mouths failed to
        taste
    To feed the gentle and the gardener worm.
    Your dextrousness put pollen to this style;
    Don't let me yield decay what's due your guile,
    But pluck now, while your harvest's bloomed
        and firm.

II. *The Dowser*

A wanting is an unwise heart, it seems.
Where care might breed the tender act, neglect
Comes this way. Disbelieving, I suspect
Regards deeper than signs allow, as dreams,
Too inward to open among the schemes
And scandal of a day, still intersect
Its speech, like leaves over water, sun-flecked…
Pathetic fallacy, which wit redeems.
    Not that I think you want me. Even love,
    Though blind, could not that wilfully miss sense.

But your intent's unkindness I'd disprove
At once. Unhope persuades that me you move
You are unmoved towards; this diffidence,
Hope answers, is the careful heart's defence.

III. *The Eclipse*

Fire doesn't draw me aside more simply,
Nor reflecting tidepools call to explore
Their otherworldliness, nor do the four
Panes of my window give more openly
Than do the eyes, the lips, the ten shapely
Fingertips. As restless as the uproar
Of surf on foreshore, patient as downpour
Of beck from stone, is how you pull me.
  Perhaps like paired stars we may neither meet
  Nor ever part, or like the sun and moon
  Keep on divergent tracks till crack of doom.
  But I have seen on the summit of noon
  The queen of waters hold the king of heat,
  The stone rolled away from the blazing tomb.

IV. *The Frost*

This growth is forward since the frost so far
Through winter has forborne its tight embrace.
Is the season forsworn? Our devious race
Might teach the cold to subtilise its war,
Matching strength with cunning, thus to mar
The delicate trustful spring, and abase
That rival summer whose unaging face
Ice's shrivelling touch is jealous to scar.
  Likewise time, withholding the end of hope,
  May leave an opening love some seeming scope

Just to blight at one blow both its present
And its future. This my green heart believes:
You are the sun that mounts to spur my leaves
And the ice to shear them when you're absent.

V. *The Ward*

Split-minded and prey to the intruding
Of prompting voices thought to emanate
From others, deranged wrong-doers: my state,
In all, is barely better than such brooding
And self-consumed spirits as these, colluding
With themselves to populate their dim, strait
Hospital midnight, bound to contemplate
Terror-embroidered shadows, denuding
    Their reason. As nature by dividing
    Gets increase and proliferates in species,
    So shall I (I argue disjunctly),
    Drawing out my rhymes. But time's deriding
Jaws pursue them, and not her pregnant peace.
She parts to add. Apart from you, I die.

VI. *The Palace*

Add moans to aches as mortar is to bricks
And build yourself a mansion of despairs,
Then daub it, as the Medicis did theirs,
But not with pastoral-Olympian mix.
Show sly coquettes who lead on puffed-up hicks
By their over-eager noses. Paint fairs
Where geldings fetch a better price than mares
And fools outbid to get some filly's kicks.
    Hang a sign there, charge a price to enter,
    Calling the place the Palace of Love Shows,

Though how untruly, mercy only knows.
Proclaim a Lavish, or Slavish Revue.
But you, keep out, and to the true be true.
Stay to this crooked house a stiff dissenter.

VII. *The Summons*

Be praised and leave me be. Why must you knock
And call, and startle again with the claim
Of interest words on the loan of your name?
I've already rifled the clouds and rock,
Flowers, fire, the lot – exhausted the stock
In comparison with you. Let my lame,
Remiss invention take no further blame.
Don't make me come down limping and unlock.
    Or if you'll force an entry, everything
    That comes to hand is forfeit: the brass ring
    Of rhymes, speckled mirror of my skill-
    less images, glass beads of verse I string.
    All which won't even pay the bailiff's bill,
    Let alone remit the name I keep still.

VIII. *The Dream*

As when you wake and keep, at the outset
Of day, the ebbing after-turbulence
Of a dream that morning's brash incidence
Frightened back to its reticent thicket,
You can neither recall nor forget it,
A voice of which I catch the resonance
But not the sense, of vanished provenance,
Urges me to heed and to abet it.
    What, though, should I not retain within me,
    Which is far too long withheld, enemy

Of my peace and ally of my action?
Now the blackbirds' matins are distraction:
I'd retrace that place of speaking sleeping,
Find what I should give, that's in my keeping.

IX. *The Archer*

Though I assign you all my love yet you are not,
There being others that I love as well,
Though none that remained in return, come hell
Or high water; so tended me, forgot
My faults so often. None that brought, like Lot
A better self from the busy pell-mell
Capital of lusts, before the fire fell,
And set me shaken in a desert spot.
    Eros, smiling, counts you his truest shot.
    The wound of his barb's at your heart's centre
    Which can hardly, for hardness, enter
    Mine. That tempts him, whose pride was always
        hot,
    To set those further arrows to his string
    From which you get the hurt, and I the sting.

X. *The Bandit*

Composing your praise is my nightly ease,
As to bewail its failure is my load;
Between which fire and water my sole road
Is steeled, resistant as an epée is,
Risky and edged with possibilities.
I thought from the height some green refuge
    showed:
Now through alien wilds the going's slowed
While I battle the robber Time, who'd seize

And spend my living, minute by minute;
Who digs his pits and traps the bends ahead
With deadfalls, from which I rise more wary;
Who moves marks to set my course contrary,
And always seeks, till he or I am dead,
My life's end, before I can begin it.

XI. *The Eagle*

I never loved so fervently before:
Before were prophecies and shadowings.
The greatest birds stretch out the most slow wings,
Unhastening to the long hours they soar.
Before were sparrow-flights, short and unsure,
Fast-beating, full of comings and goings
From hedge to hedge, flung out like winnowings.
Now love's eagle eyes vale and open moor.
 But the eagle's sudden and love is meek;
 High-born one, while the other is lowly
 And stakes no claim on clouds, from which to
  glide
 To strike down the lamb with imperial beak.
 No fault surpasses the false-named holy:
 Do not let me, love, mistake love for pride.

XII. *The Earth*

Earth should have shaken when we put her first
Beneath our feet; trembled in forewarning
Of her current throes; shrunk from the morning
Glare of our eyes; and when the first blade burst
From the flint, shuddered at the beast she'd nursed.
Soon the rich, folded robes of her spawning
Would be stripped from her back by these scorning
Offspring of hers, the latest and the worst.

How long she laboured to provide the store
We'd waste in twenty thousand years of youth
Our time-ungrasping minds dare not conceive.
Stunned, depleted, cracked, earth lies at our door,
Past hoping that within one voice will grieve
Above the coins' din, brassy and uncouth.

XIII. *The Fashion*

Should naked-born desire don old clothing
Or that which turns time take the latest trim,
Lacing a bold body up in the whim
Of fashion's current, gushing and frothing?
Beauty unashamed courts public loathing
Though in another morning age, less dim
With durance, to Venus' Parian quim
Nothing was so well suited as nothing.
    That day's gone. Go get your wildest show on
    And we'll step out tonight to show the town
    In garb how we delight ourselves undressed
    When in each other's arms we're host and guest.
    Love inspires a style bested by no one,
    Though like that emperor's, bare but for his
       crown.

XIV. *The Trash*

False medieval fripperies – swords and hawks
And undying loves – out with all these;
Also artificial similes
Drawn from Nature – roots and buds, soil and
       stalks,
That bric-a-brac at which the poet gawks
While the planet's overwhelmed with sleaze.

Now find among our trades' and industries'
Cantankerous clatter and hi-tech squawks
    Your emblems of a profitless pursuit.
    Strange how, in this light, chivalry is brute
    Warfare and rank oppression like today's,
    And Nature's womb has borne a matricide.
    But world's old ugliness is undenied;
    Just that it holds her beauty still dismays.

XV. *The Grass*

So much complaint and scarcely one word's praise:
Is that the due of the god who sent you,
His chaotic prodigy? I pursue
An apparition, finding thorny ways
To lose me, prick me, sadden and amaze.
So not by light, but downfall, eyes renew
The emanation, as the grass askew
And winter-weather-beaten, spring rains raise.
    As the year revives in cold and wetness,
    Your unfinished beauty rises in me,
    And I cannot add to its completeness,
    Nor take from it good substance for my lines.
    It is enough that it should seem and be
    Just as you are, and that like you it shines.

XVI. *The Down*

If I romanticise what loves I've known,
Little loves as brief and bright as spark-falls,
I'll remember, when on me the dark calls,
Your love as true to itself as a stone.
Cold to each other as we've often grown,
Each eyeing through the slits of steep, stark walls,

We'll remount the high air where the lark stalls
Over the down in the wind's pleasant moan.
    Harsh to each other as we may have been,
    Sharpening on our hearts knives of resentment,
    Heavy and piercing, serrated and keen,
    We'll lie again like two empty crosses
    In the deep meadow of our contentment,
    Concurring as the grass nods and tosses.

XVII. *The Fountain*

Companion in pain, I'd better in mind
Than you've ever received of me... But hush:
Promises will even more quickly crush
The heart, unfulfilled, than the lies that bind
The gross burden of one's unconfined
Unfaith to another without a blush.
Truth's breaking injures once, in the first rush:
A vow's torture's long-stretched-out, refined.
    So I'd promise nothing, to keep you consoled
    But nothings already and manifold
    Pour to you from my soul's overflowing.
    Then take my word: by all that's never told,
    So long as days keep coming and going,
    My love shall stay, truer than its showing.

XVIII. *The Fork*

Neither the fury nor the silent scale
Of elements, not mountains in tumult,
Nor seas, nor the bare night where stars exult
And sheep like dropped clouds drift along the dale,
Outweigh the passion and the joy of frail
Humanity, where nature finds result.

Before a footsole trod, earth moved occult
From itself, but with that tender, low and pale
    Foundation laid, hand and eye, tongue and mind
    Began to build, see, speak and plan in kind,
    Finding in themselves the root of those rings
    Hurtling things describe, joyed and terrified
    Likewise in the plummetless scope that brings
    Wild orchestras to tuning forks complied.

XIX. *The Stars*

I'll liken you to these for being far
Beyond earth's thin and troubled, spotted skies
As you from me, which to my living eyes
Live in former light, present as you are
Absent. They're fire that does not smoke or char
Or warm, unbrightened by the round-mouthed sighs
They draw; agents of fortune, in disguise,
Whether for beggar or maharajah.
    Across lacunae, learning has me trace
    The emptied images and ramping creatures
    Of our nocturnal selves. So scattered speech,
    Remembered, and so moments of your face,
    In constellate, horizon-spanning features,
    Illuminate the dreaming that you teach.

XX. *The Night*

Bless the night now that the human motion
That takes the name of life harangues the day
Incessantly and has all life at bay,
Busy as cancer in self-promotion.
Bless the morphine moon that tilts the ocean
And stills a bit the world under its sway.

Bless the needled night that civic lights fray,
That pointed three the way to wise devotion.
    Bless the night with all its bright retinue.
    Loose us from the power of revenue
    To find our ancient selves again within you.
    Remind us God makes earth and heaven new
    As you make that seem splendid man made
        cursed:
    The fresh day that you cede to at dawn-burst.

XXI. *The Heroes*

What makes a heavenly heart is simply this:
The hell-like deep it reaches to below
And lays it down in, where lost spirits blow,
The bottom of whose worlds, with a dead hiss,
Fell out so long ago they never miss
The floor. There with the basest of the low
They go on calling on the good they know
And keep in flame till all climb safe to bliss.
    Tireless as times accumulate zeroes,
    These are the deeds of the holy heroes,
    Who outweigh hate's pound with their loving
        ounce.
    While brains secrete thought and the belly bile
    And while each is needful and neither vile,
    The heart, the heart, the heart is what counts.

BAY

GREY SPRING

GREY spring, and the lovers in arms
Tickle and pinch in their lunch-break,
Birds sing at night like car alarms
    And flies half-wake
At noon, staggering in the rain
Among the rooftop's greening weeds.
    Motley pigeons pirouetting
    Make a prelude to begetting,
Take up their mumbling amorous strain
Insistently till she concedes.

Pushing the jonquils left and right,
March, the month of many weathers,
Menaces their miniature height.
    On stiff feathers
The city kestrel mewing
Hangs overheard, then stoops away.
    May no lovers' fondest petting
    Be overture to regretting
And nobody's buttons' undoing
Be theirs, dear lord of love, we pray.

LOSTNESS

THAT sense of lostness that you thought you'd lost,
Of the world a place too tall and chill, broad
And without light, is a bus-ride away,
To an unfamiliar borough by night.

More than menacing floodlit blocks or barren
By-passes and industrial compounds,

105

BAY

Tidy terrace houses with people in,
Lit curtains drawn, bring home to you how far
And wide's the country where you're not at home.

Though maybe where a yellow seam is seeping
Out from a bedsit above a closed laundrette
The world for one and one becomes complete,
Comprised between four ugly-papered walls.

HER LAST LANDSCAPES

THREE pictures on the wall:
of summer, the rosebay willowherb waving
on a railway's abandoned embankment,
a vanishing fence and various sky.

Of spring, the shrunken stream
under a triple-arched bridge;
under bare trees, of one tone with the stone,
some bulb patch, bright green, fledging.

In the centre, the year's sap consumed
from bracken, rush and grass,
the brown fells blent in the air's royal blue
to an umber more burning than burnt,
where the first dust of snow lies,
signify that winter where the artist shortly went.

ELGIN MARBLES

STRANGE that classic grace should end as totems
of our own fragmentary aesthetic.
Once free-standing figures are embedded
in the air, as though stripped by their falling.

A goddess flutters in headless grandeur,
other amputees lounge like the damned.
Man and man-horse combatants, their sword hands
broken off, never press home to the kill.

Hell for these heavenly lumps is the snap-
shots constant flicking at their muscled stumps.
Poor immortals, reft of the dignity
their artful servants long since claimed, of graves.

ABOVE BROTHERSWATER

I

DRYSTONE walling vertebral,
Bright grey in the headlights' beam –

But the rhythmed dark on dark
Beyond I have not words for.

The radio-cassette glows
In the car's heavy cradle.

Our heartbeats drop to the tune
"Cry for Home" in the slipstream

Taking our place between rocks.
Skull-faced sheep fleeced like doormats

Scutter skance-eyed from the road
Through bracken on dancers' feet.

II

Our climb seems through thought's levels.
Following the beck's course, books

And such, till the valley head
And scramble from combe to col

Where hands do service for feet.
Breathers at the halfway view

Stand to tackle aesthetics
A minute, then bring the lake

Round the hill with ten more steps.
In the saddle of the ridge

Fresh wind flexes the spirit
And five words of love suffice.

III

Under speeding mist we squat
Down to lunch behind a wall

At the top, in a ramblers'
Gaggle, having seen the lake's

Long gleams break steely beneath
The blowing cloud, vanishing

Last of the valley below.
While photogenic vapour

Pours like tide waves between peaks
The shutter's stuck in the cold

Wind hammering on the crag.
Wrestle to stand and listen

To a wrath zealous as fate
Wrenching the gates of the earth.

IV

The force tears its web of sound
And moss cradles drops. The may-

Tree perches in the beck's breast,
By the collarbone of rock.

Water falling from above
Me and below, before me

And after, speaking a word,
One endless omega.

DAUGHTER'S DEPARTURE

AN indented circle,
the mark on your cheek of her earring,
tells the force of your parting, tearful clasp
a quarter-hour after she's gone.

Unforeseen, the osprey young's first flight looks,
a slight leap into the wind
off the rough circle her wings'
beating has fanned for days.

Before northern weathers have wrecked that nest
she'll fish African waters,
with luck. Now limbs twist to control
her climb from sticks to eaglehood.

BAY

I

for Hank Williams

THE path's edge is busy with baby birds
where a thumb-size sparrow casts a hand's-length
      shadow
and though the starling young have not yet learned
the vandal manners of their speckled elders
they already shrill at each other fiercely.

Just as I think my making phrases,
even out of them, disturbs them not at all,
of a sudden they fly off into one tree.
I brought the frame of mind, as chance would have it,
that small things please.

Looking more closely what glistens in their beaks
I read their common pursuit.
It's July, the first fine spell in weeks,
a day for winged ants,
easy pickings, coming out to breed.

To forage or threaten and thieve
is all one to the birds
but then wasn't the Christian first
to get through paradise gates
also a thief after all, worth many of these?

II

O TO be intelligent to the very ears,
to the toes and tail as the black dog is

with her eyes on the stick,
or with one eye caught by the candle
deeply lit:

to walk without this volume of negligence,
distress of impulse,
and to talk less and less
haltingly;
to sow the seed of flame in each other's look.

III

COME back, dissatisfaction,
I haven't finished with you yet.

Ink my nib that's dry without your blackness,
blind without the shine of what I wait to come
from below the skyline.

Absence of complacency:
that lack is truly luck.

IV

I HAVE dallied too long,
the work is thin and sullied,
however troubled over,
unfulfilled, precocious.

The blocks I noted
I have neither means to possess
nor the skill to manage.
Wash off my pencil lines, begin again.

Like a grass tuft
out of shallow ground
my first growth sprang up easily
and is already sun-bleached yellow.

A new green crop is coming,
all the same, soon ending.
The quarryman's scornful look
he has given me rightly.

V

COMING death in kindly light
illuminates failure, defines a gift,
though I must be yet and am afraid
how fierce it yet shall be.

Bless them who call it unfriendly,
who say as I have heard
Jamaican voices threefold sing,
We live to live, we do not live to die.

Death circumscribes
the gift I have
and all the gifts I have
no need to envy others.

Lack of singleness
in loves, in purposes,
the fault that I proscribe –
though who was ever wise

enough to say?
As rock by circumstance
reveals its flaws, strength
expresses likeness to its weakness.

VI

CANYON and prairie, cactus and pine,
in infancy without wilderness,
entered the setting of fancy,
the plums I pulled from the pied screen.

I may not get to sign the neon poem
that says Welcome to the Home of the Lonely
and Hamburgers, one of the last few things
Leonardo didn't think of first.

Still I've the map of the Cumberland Gap
at heart, where the Cherokee nation thrived,
country music was tapped at source,
and Hank Williams' heart stopped short, passing
         through.

Settled for this outlying, outworn spot
of the old world, colonised by phantoms
of the new, I feel Jackson, Mississippi,
where Tommy Johnson moaned, come home to roost.

VII

THOUGH another shadow than the fell's
returning one falls over all such idylls,
the patient body, slow to anger,
implores the frustrate mind to dwell on them.

The cows are to their knees in the gracious water,
and the rushes to their waists.
The lake receives, this late each day,
the same exact reflection.

We could make, if anywhere,
this valley like a vowel our home,
let spill, like the grey hill in the mere,
last light between our elbows on the tablecloth.

VIII

WE finger in our affirmers a hollow centre –
they feared so much they had to make up such a lot –
and feel slip through at the heart of negation
a marble nub of substance.

Will I be or when will I be shed
of childhood's pink slim slippiness,
that unerring urge towards what shall be
growing up should rid you of, fulfill?

From fantasies provided to grow out of
lie no outlets, ways of growing into,
and we collapse like balloons
then set our lips to ourselves again.

Mother, father failed –
O find another friend
to play the playful parts between your struts.
O friend, if I offend

take my right hand,
peel off the pink thin glove,
for sentimental detachments leave no fingerprints,
however assiduously inked.

IX

SUNLIGHT through the leaf-chinks
though irregular
is circles interlocking on the wall,
over which other, fingery shadows swivel.

All will course as one like a river,
left, say, then flow back again,
and out of this watery mobility
the single pointed shade of a plane leaf focuses.

Let me resolve as these bright striated discs
that need not be unmoving
to be still, these calm recurrent patches.
Then the sun drops at once, and dimness moves on
          dimness.

X

HOW can we turn back
to nature now?
Disorderly summer's
bouts of sun and sudden showers

– are these disturbings ordinary
or does her illness begin its crisis?
Whether emanated
or reflected from her,

concentric harmony,
when we turned, once met our gaze on her,
and she could balm our madness
like John Clare's,

who called her spirit Mary
and could be himself around her,
though all his talk in company was skewed
and he had to be Byron, or a prize-fighter.

He was less crazed and knew it
than the captains of rationalisation,
whose one faithful nurse we've wounded and
      deranged
in rage at our own sickness.

And yet she rises,
despite the abrupt, heavy rains
of malady, with her green fervour unspent,
her succulent passion in millions of plants,

despite the insidious damage
in abrupt rains and the wholesale demolition,
because hers is the household of eternity
and from her graveyard garden the spire of the
      human breastbone rises.

WAITING FOR BUZZARDS

ON Helman Tor the roundness of the world
is plain, the small trees bent to its turning,
and coarse granite gives back warmth at the end
of day. Unseen buzzards mew as we go
downhill, wishing for a view, a blessing.
A fit of screams in the grass, a crippled rabbit
starts and flops, crawls along the ground.
We've interrupted a stoat at the kill
who dances back, away, back. We step back
and wait for the thing to be done. He comes

at last, a minute later, glides forward
and the helpless head judders when he bites.
We hear him lap, and move. He vanishes,
a clean hole made to the skull already.

EPIC

OF these particular finches
A solitary male is singing
In the last bit of undrained swamp
Of his need to copulate,

To reproduce his brilliance
Of colouring and unrivalled song,
Phrase upon phrase upon phrase
To the exhaustion of his stock:

A canto as never before
On the grey-green stump of a branch
Because there are no females,
Because he is the last of a kind.

FISHMONGER

Gemmy and glutinous, mineral pinks and whites,
The flesh-fat fish lie in tribes on their bed of ice,
Gifts of the alien, endlessly refreshing sea.
Choked and troubled, the city air reverberates
Out from the narrow distance. From lobsters to
        plaice
To purpled, milky squid we inch by patiently,
Calmed in the bustle by their chill potency.

Knobbly fruit of scallop, sprats like stainless bay
     leaves,
The wild salmon glittering, the flaccid whiting
Soft and grey as tin, coral slabs of skate wing,
Thigh-thick halibut, and flounders' flower-dotted
     turves.
Wounded knights, the magnificent armed crustaceans
Rise, then fold a jointed feeler in submission.
Below, the blood-pinked ice glistens and grieves.

    But those who weigh this split silver
Are brisk and full of savour as the sea itself.
Levantines, Chinese, Greeks and West Indians
    Queue for what we have in common,
    Salt of the multiplying ocean.

ANGELS BANDITS

DOWN in the belly of the Festival
it was the second night
the site was drying out
singing Angels Bandits
People were tramping back to camp
twenty deep along the causeway
and mud in lakes on either side of the causeway
singing Angels Bandits Casualties
A Transit van buried to its axles
and burned out like some skull
sunk to its chops in the muck
singing Angels Bandits Casualties Dead
Beside every thoroughfare
at every junction like prophets'
voices in the wilderness calling Black 'Ash

Black 'Ash Black 'Ash Black 'Ash
Acid Mushrooms Grass Black 'Ash
The Mutant Waste Disposal Company
had their Carhenge up on the hillside
and when night fell the crowd were up there beating
      on them
on their Batmobile vehicles and heaps of wrecks
We kept a fire and stayed up with it
going on all night on the last night
Sunday, drifting across at dawn
That was Ivan the Mutants' music master
the one who died in the Kings Cross fire
singing Angels Bandits Casualties

DAWN'S EARLY LIGHT

BLACK Kettle watched amazed
who had cried, Come under the flag,
under the flag we shall all be saved.
The bullets closing in from every quarter
stood on end and started
slowly to circle, bobbing,
the huddle of mothers and children,
the elderly, the trusting,
then broke from their ring-dance and one by one
with small mosquito voices
fell among the breasts and heads and bellies,
fell as sure of victory
as the Cheyenne had been of amnesty
under the white stars dipping and floating
on midnight blue and the scarlet
stripes bravely snapping on the morning air.

BEFORE THE EMPIRES

IN the time before the empires
when the people of three rivers stood up
they said, We are they who fight naked
and they are the armoured.
They have no families
but where our daughters serve them
and we have no metal. What will they not take?
This was before the nation,
nobody thought of tomorrow then,
and the mothers asked about the children
and the men said, We have no metal,
and they said, The children will have children.
They stood up and pointed to the west
and they looked to the east
before the nation broke them,
when this song was made
and their name was not forgotten.

BABEL

EARTH at the mountain's foot went down
on her knees, and on her side,
sad for him who had left her incomplete;
turned nightwards, cherishing
in the hollow of herself
groves, the river, memory.
We built the city for a gift that might console her.

On the skin of a white bull-calf
compasses of ebony marked out the scheme of
        terraces

120

and the walls were drawn with a copper foot-rule,
corresponding to the stars.
We sang at the laying of the corner-stone
to the north-east
a sacramental song.

While it was yet dark
donkeys labouring up the gorge road
brought pressed figs and woven belts,
honey in the comb,
the prized silverwork of villages.
Women on the rooftops
shook out colourful rugs in the early morning.

One sang, "O sun, I am made ungrateful
for the greatness of your light
though it be the fire of mine and every life.
You rise and speed at the bidding of God
and I alone in the world would turn you back
for I've another god, another sun, another life
and all night till your peeping he was with me."

The old tunes tangled with the new
in snatches and the colours flashed
where dust was flapped from the fabrics.
The windows were wide open in the chamber of the
        dying king
that his last breath should mingle with the hubbub
according to his wish. He had not died in the night
but already the king's sons were divided in two
        parties.

What was murmured in the counsellor's ear
meant terror on the terraces,
blood and iron unloosed.
Those who lent their voices to election

of the one king killed by order
of the other, by the armed men of his house.
A terrible song broke from their bearded mouths.

Weeds have seized the paving,
a sapling buckles
and tumbles a portion of the wall.
The same swift lizards bask
and dart on the white well rim
but the dovecotes are peopled with kites,
long-eared owls have roosted in the astrologers'
        tower.

The skull heaps of the tyrant,
bones without sepulchre,
the bones buried with honour,
all are stones to the silence of the earth.
The cisterns fail but the brooks run still.
Nomads' black tents in the forum,
grey smoke from their watch-fires.
The beasts shake their harness in the dawn.

DEATH AND THE HANGED MAN

I

In Tewkesbury Abbey

THE last Abbot – Wakeman, John – is shown in stone,
Long, worn and lowly, and he has no clothes,
And even flesh has left the bones alone.
There he moulders, effigy of those
Who glory in garments to no avail
As they must end. And over the corse

Humble frog and mouse, worm, snake and snail,
Five beasts with dust for meat, do slowly race
To fill their bellies, while the stone itself
In which these things have life, is scribbled
And scratched with years of hands in idle stealth.
It would make his father sad he dibbled,
But for the fact of the case laid bare:
The tomb is empty, and the man elsewhere.

(In Gloucester Cathedral, to be precise.
His bishopric there was the gracious price
Of giving the Abbey up to the state
Embodied in the gut of Henry Eight.
And there he shares the ground he once mastered
With the first-born son of Bill "the Bastard".)

II

In Gloucester Cathedral

Bright, thin, elfin in his red and gold,
Robert, son of William, Duke of Normandy,
Conqueror of England, still makes bold
In wood, with armour on and dancer's dandy
Legs crossed. But they've carved him all askew
And not at rest. The knee across is lifted
And his right hand's reaching for the sword it knew.
What of deathless daring left him gifted
Thus with art? History remembers
And the world forgets. Tourists pass an odd knight
Oddly twisted like low flames on embers.
But one who stoops may start to see the light
In the open eyes of one about to jump
Up smiling at the playing of the trump!

A PORTRAIT OF THE SUN

I

THE sun looks through the windows of the twigs'
rhomboid interstices, their architect,
who builds a building he cannot live in.
They fill with the faces of leaves, smooth and
solicitous, acquisitive courtiers
who bow and whisper, turning to him
their keen reflective profiles, all in his
silk livery of green. But no: they are
orphans who crowd each other and point
to see their benefactor riding by
in his carriage. The dapple with the star
on her grey forehead nods towards the west.
He settles back in the crimson plush
as the wind gusts chill, and looks suddenly old.

II

Have others among your trillion brothers
such praises? Have they such creatures to praise
        them,
to whom your friendly fire, as theirs to us,
is a heatless indifferent winking
and distracting wonder, clustered in night?
Your companionship, constant and kind, is
temperer, primer of our conceiving
our creator and yours, our elements
all once being in you, every atom,

first furnace of life. Of the I who looks
to you, each particle derives from you,
dead were you nearer or farther away.
Hydrogen, carbon and iron, the humming
systems hymn, as you do, factive brilliance.

III

I am the son of the Father of suns
and image in fire of the unseen fire,
your fellow creature. When the tongue-tip touched
the upper palate, at the "la" of "Let"
we held our breath, through "there", till the plosive
concussion of "be" that clove through nothing.
We leapt at the "la" of "light" with "Selah!
Alleluia!" Then the sons of morning,
not as yet distinct, momently going
our ways, sang in a body together.
I am the song of the Word who walked then
among us, who imparted the glory
he had before us, as in the furnace.
I sing it again to all below me.

EC1

A GLITTERING day of the favourite season,
the short sun unblinking in the hazy air
on the town as ever hectic
and disco-ordinate, making its motion
serene and equal-seeming, almost still.
The mother with her child on either side
walks in a wreath of breath under peaceful sky.

125

EXILE

FAR from a hero, far from saint,
Either in an action frozen
Or burning in the lamplit paint,
You were uncomfortably chosen
To stand dumbfounded in the fellside light,
To witness all the restless human night,
    And have what came as words in youth
Come in the dry September of your years,
                In truth,
                In tears
You would not let fall, being bent on rhyme;
Eternity's exile in love with time.

*   *   *   *

Monkey in a Chinese story
        Reaches
    For the moon in a stream;
Can't let go his branch, can't grasp her glory,
        Can't shun her gleam,
    Stuck between deed and dream.
Fall through the quicksilver light and go down
        Into darkness and drown,
            One sage teaches.

LIGHT

BEYOND the sphere of mist
and water, wind and weather
    that green things have exhaled
for us, huddled together,
we conceive of space, discounting the grist
of dust, as an emptiness unassailed.

Yet from countless sources,
all ways, at a single pace,
the unseen light courses
and crosses without a trace,
not straying nor slowing unless it flies
against some intervening object's face,
or in at the tombs of our eyes and dies,
becoming there the light we recognise.

MISS P.
for Stevie Smith

GENTLE and staid
They thought the old maid,
The spinster
Who lived hard by the minster
But she had iron in her soul
That when swung and struck
Like a bell would toll
And masses of pluck.
A lion in the way would find that Anglican old maid
Unafraid.

Sad and single
They dubbed Miss Pringle,
The old biddy.
He never came back from the war her boyfriend did
          he?
But her corsets like a brazier held a fire
That in matters of faith
Would kindle and aspire
So she was even as the Apostle saith
No tinkling cymbal
Miss Pringle.

CORVINE

IN the city of Cork the pigeons are crows,
Larger of muscle and thicker of nose
Than the paraclete's reprobate cousins
Coming in London to call by the dozens.

So first there's the full-scale carrion thug
Yanking at a bin-liner, walking off with a shrug,
Then the whole family – magpies, jackdaws, rooks.
They take off like somebody throwing a Bible.

There's one overhead with a cake-paper gripped
In one foot, eating the crumbs at his leisure
On a telephone wire. His eye fixes you
Defiantly, or with a glint of amusement.

FISH FOR BREAKFAST

IT'S been going slowly wrong now for a long time,
Spiked with sudden disasters.
Remember the flood? Remember the wind?
Remember the ship and the drunken master?

It's been twisting round somebody's little pinky
Till every word's bent out of sense.
Find me one with a decent point left
To hang a house together, let alone fix the rent.

The meadow's black and yellow like last year's
        paper.
Cluck, clack – the bell's been rung.
Everybody's talking about the weather
And the leaves all summer like unwell tongues.

If God was alive he'd be turning in his grave now
To hear the captains praise him.
The saints are sleeping quiet in the light.
We'll never blow our horns enough to raise them.

Mocked and saluted and run up a pole,
He's been hounded from pillar to post,
Hung out to dry and crammed back in the hole
        again –
No ghost, eating fish for breakfast on the shore.

BIRDHEAD

SEED-SHAPED mouth gleams like a flint,
dotted eyes pinned down in feathers.
The head prises open a little to let the sound out,
the split-note chirrup of scissors closing.
This air-tight case is one incisor
that pivots faster than you can write,
each move smaller than a lower-case a.
The two-edged wings spread out
around its black and white flower,
the feet come out below the neck.
Heavier than a fly,
lighter than a crust,
commoner than a sunny day,
mister the excellent lord sparrow to you.

THE GENERATIONS OF OMO

OMO begat Daz; Daz begat Flash; Flash
begat Oxo, Bisto and Andrex; and the sons
of Andrex, Gloy, and Bostik. And the sons of
Bisto, Anodol, and Bisodol, and Euthymol.

129

These were the sons of Bisto. And the sons of
Oxo, by Nivea, Paxo, and Nimble, and Vimto;
and the sons of Oxo by Camay his handmaid
were Izal and Dettol. Dettol begat Be-Ro; Be-Ro
begat Us; Us begat Milton and Nesquik;
Nesquik begat Harpic; Harpic begat Bovril;
Bovril begat Domestos, in the land of Uhu.
Domestos begat Timex and Copydex, by Savlon
his wife. Timex begat Jif; Jif begat Actifed;
Actifed begat Pyrex; Pyrex begat Paracetamol,
when Tampax was king. Paracetamol begat
Brillo; Brillo begat Horlicks, and Bemax, and
Gunk, in the reign of the first Coco-Pops. These
were the sons of Brillo which his wife Ryvita
bore him. And these are all the generations of
Omo, from the reign of Phostrogen, the son of
Radox, to the coming of Kodachrome.

THE HERON'S BRIDE

WEIGHED in the ballroom
dancing and found wanting,
a would-be coquette
wishing she'd a pocket-
handkerchief, preferably
of scarlet, polka-
dotted with white, such as
the gentlemen use
for resounding blows
and achoos of a noise
to rival the brazen
trumpet, not the scrappet
of lace tucked up her sleeve,

having no-one's leave
to ask, stepped out upon
the balcony. A heron
quite as elegant
as any gentleman
indoors in evening threads,
sleek and not ill-fed
on frogs who were not princes
washed down with minnows,
seeing her silhouetted
against the windows
alighted, unafraid
and addressed her thus:
"Madam, I am but
a humble wader
bred on a backwater
while you undoubtedly
are a duchess's daughter.
However, since it seems
your love is unrequited
I should be delighted
with the pleasure of a flight
into the falling night.
Do but climb astride
(if you'll forgive the phrase)
my back and let my wide
grey wings carry you away.
My house, though in a swamp,
I assure you is not damp
and why should we a moment
longer waste in talking
when we could be stalking
even now, knee-deep
through silent shining streams?"
She lifted up the hem

of her oyster-coloured gown
while courteously he crouched down
and without a backward glance
for them by whom
she had been scorned
accepted his advance
and climbed aboard. The horned
moon rose on the lagoon
and leaving her guardian
aunts, alas! behind
she felt his wings unfold
and lift her where the world
of dance-cards nevermore
would cross her mind.
He speeds and leads
her to his palace in the reeds.

THE BAPTIST

THE honeybees have built in the hollow
Of a locust tree. All the queen's daughters
Dance. I hear the voice of many waters.
He who follows me is him I follow
Into the wilderness. The veils drop one
By one, until blood brims the silver dish.
I dip and dip until at last the Fish
Comes up in my hands from the Jordan. "John"
My dumbstruck father wrote, and found his voice.
I breast the stream that Moses never crossed,
Greater than all before and less than all
Who come. I go out crying like one lost,
One last man, to afflict you with your choice.
I seize and plunge God's head, but mine shall fall.

TO A CIVILIAN CASUALTY

CONGRATULATIONS!
You have been kept to
an absolute minimum.

The ministers
raise their clean hands.
No more questions.

This madman Hussein's
beyond the pale,
him and his white horse.

Meanwhile Madam Russia
turns over in bed,
crushing her little ones.

Saddam can be relied on
to pour oil on
troubled waters.

The Mother of Battles
makes ready to suckle.
Blood trickles from the nipple.

The B52s roll out the red carpet.
She lies down in the grit,
she spreads out her arms

and licks the marine sergeant's ear,
whispering, After 28 days
of combat 98 per cent

of all frontline troops
are psychologically debilitated
and require evacuation.

That means forty-nine
out of fifty; that means
mad to you and me, soldier.

I'm telling you this
because I have an objective
and accurate view of the war

whereas yours has been partial
and distorted
ever since your house fell on you.

I see wet rust
falling out of a head.
I see a Bush speaking

between two bundles of firewood,
INGODWETRUST
in letters of gold on the wall.

WATER

CLEAR and impenetrable,
mother of awe, of sisters
who run to meet us, turning
with outstretched transparent arms
and the songs we name them by,
stream, force, wave, rain and fountain.

We divine ourselves in you,
little mother. Meek, stubborn,
mizzle or Mississippi,
you go your way submitting
to rocks, to a grain of sand,
to nothing, soothing the earth.

Flung back unhurt by yourself
with thunder and big words, bone-
cracking shoves, you bear your slow
and unturnable surges,
you make your exclamations
and whispers sharks and elvers.

Where the king of crabs pavanes
as a green star in the gloom,
thought makes the rounds of a drop,
and the high chants of geese join
the deep ones of whales under
responding swells, the dry moon.

VALLIER AND CEZANNE

I

The apples bruise themselves
blue, from the inside out.

They're bronze, going
oxide green, granite,
brass, pushing each other aside.

We feel them push the iron
in our blood sideways.

They're beside themselves
in a calm beyond terror
and loss, the fruit of knowledge.

The light goes over, behind them,
the double-edged sword.

II

The gardener becomes his garden,
this earthen face no longer seen
beneath the flowers – the glancing
watercolour that invites the pollinating eye.

His glance is downward, to the earth.
The sepals of his eye leave undisclosed
what fruit it holds.
The painter's eye, for its part, won't intrude.

Persistently set to this fruitless task,
his long frame shaped by unregarded work
in the motley shade settling on a chair.
Geranium red, forget-me-not blue –

the master applies himself to the servant.

ORPHEUS ASCENDING

Till, turning where the god
    who leads us up is shown
    by light I left alone
    as clear as flesh and bone,

flare of his guiding torch
    that fixed our eyes ahead,
    as step by step we fled
    the household of the dead,

just equalling the first
    grey inlet that the day's
    unequivocal blaze
    reaches into the maze,

I watch her stop mid-stride
    and fade. Her clay lips quake
    to keep the breath she'd take.
    At twilight, as they wake,

the white owls make the moan
    that goes from her, to die
    outside. Dry alders shy
    and shake by the brook, by

a backward glance bereaved
    of her in her young, green
    season. Dark falls between
    us and our budding queen.

I. HER FLOWERS

ONE

WHEN the evening singers had all but finished
A wren appeared on one concrete fencepost
And flew to the next, darted from platform
To thicket and, after a moment lost
To view, perched in a diamond of the mesh.
Over the post the bird had graced a calm
Round moon inched up from its branching niche.

Surveying the sleeping river of rails
While behind him in a faint electric hum
The train that had brought him slept, its lights still on,
Paul waited for the nine-thirteen to come,
Steel's complaining chirp forerunning its wheels.
Parallel, tilted, recurring reflections
Beguiled the short journey, and the petals

Fallen from short ostentatious cherries
Bleaching the neat verges of suburban
Ways he walked. Taking himself a plateful,
He sat down in the feast-littered kitchen.
A large-browed man was scorning the Tories;
Another, his dope-wide gaze sceptical
And glistering, mourned art's difficulties.

He glimpsed her for the first time by the door,
Hesitating, looking in; quizzical,
Timid and dark-complexioned as the wren
Out of the garden night. The light tussle
Of bracelets accompanied her quick four
Steps between the pairs of silenced men
Reluctantly resuming as before.

Paul studied her smooth profile as she leaned
Across to serve herself. She turned to bear
His inspection frankly for an instant
And, fumbling his fork, caught unaware,
He spilled rice over his chair. As he gleaned
The scattered grains, he thought a slight, distant
Smile was on him – amused but not unkind.

TWO

LATER her cinnamon fingers
    whispered on the goat-skin
and he sang a song he wrote
    to the handful of late guests.
She crossed her fishnetted calves
    round the drum's skewbald hourglass,
with someone perched on the sofa
    vamping them on mouth-harp.

In a pink blanket on the floor,
    a hand under his head,
his thoughts were taut, unresting,
    bolstered with hashish reverb.
They circled her being there,
    sleeping, elsewhere in the house,
upstairs? He sipped a stone-cold tea
    and fell asleep at dawn.

It was a chilly and drizzling
    mid-morning when he woke,
seemed the first stirring, stumbled
    into his jeans and jumper
and found her in the kitchen,
    staring into the garden.
He mumbled "Morning", lit the gas
    and put on the kettle.

"You're up early." "I couldn't sleep."
    He hunched against the cold,
holding his hands to the flame.
    "Couldn't stop myself thinking."
She turned to volunteer it,
    leaning back on the counter
and watching him closely.
    Her eyes showed signs of wear and tear.

Last night's luminous blossom was
    a pale plastered litter
on the Sunday-lifeless streets.
    The sun was virtually down,
hanging clear of level clouds,
    when they went to get their train,
numb to their stomachs and
    hollow-headed from exhaustion.

She sat down unexpectedly
    beside, not facing him.
He was waiting to ask her
    what she couldn't stop thinking,
but there was no opening.
    Instead, within two stations,
simply as might a child
    she lay her head on his shoulder.

He watched her curved lashes quiver
    and wondered if she slept.
She stayed close, she gave no sign.
    He wouldn't move to stir her,
though the arm around her was
    nerveless when they reached King's Cross.
She woke and raised her head
    to squint at the bleak terminus.

"Well, this is where you go your way
    and I go mine," she said,
turning to him on the steps.
    "And which way's that?" In answer
she asked for a pen and wrote
    in eccentric capitals
"BEA, FLAT 5 – " etcetera
    on her dog-eared ticket.

THREE

    THEY met again by chance
    In the upstairs room of a pub.
    They called it The Advance,
    A weekly shoe-string jazz club.

    An improvising trio,
    Clarinet, bass and percussion,
    Were blowing with a brio
    That precluded conversation.

    When in time a broken
    Elegiac theme connected,
    The greetings they'd spoken
    Mouth-to-ear in the impacted

    Furor of the intro
    Seemed enough. Instead the rhythm
    Coiling through the long slow
    Passage did their talking for them.

    The bass player, masterly
    And presciently empathic,
    Building from one shadowy
    Arco phrase to an ecstatic

Fierce cadenza – thrummed chords,
Skittering harmonics – was met
By a cry twisting upwards
To a scream from the clarinet.

Then gently on a thermal
Of malletted cymbal splashes
They circled to a formal
Close, holding the note one spacious

Exhaled moment. Her dry
Light hand was closed on his, assured
Through the music, but shy
Now they parted to applaud.

FOUR

THAT'S just the point, she is "already spoken for". ...
I remember what I said, but that was before – ...
I wouldn't let it, but it has. ... Don't ask me. Some
        man. ...
Well, obviously. ... And back in the frying pan
Again, I know. She isn't happy with him, Rex,
You can tell. She told me herself. ... A few. That sex
Was the big thing between them. Not in the porn
        sense,
Mechanical. An "animal experience"
Was her phrase. Something in the bone, in the gut,
        far– ...
It's not a matter of boudoir or abattoir –
Leave it out! ... Listen, will you. Basic romance,
        charm,
Is what's missing. Plus, whether he would do her
        harm
Or not – well, maybe. But she goes in fear of him,

I get the feeling. Not his temper, but his whim. …
Hunches, I don't know. Plain guesswork. This
    character
Ain't what you would call a gentleman. Sure, to her
He may be wonderful. … I'm not justifying.
She moved in on me. … Alright, there's no denying
That. … Of course I haven't. I've only met her
    twice. …
Nikki's got nothing to do with it. It's no dice
Now with me and her. … A trial separation,
Yes. But it's really a dead-end situation. …
Right. Once at Ronnie's party, and then at The
    Advance.
Talking of which, that bassist, the fella from France,
Played a blinding set, just staggering. I'm in love.
I want him for the band. … So? If push came to
    shove,
Mo would have to go. … Yes, but that's the way it
    is. …
OK. Leave it till rehearsal for talking biz. …
I know, the phone's no good. How about me
    standing
Dinner at the Diner? There's some mind-expanding
We could do here, too. … When's good for you? …
    Cool. Eight o'
Clock, let's say. … OK, Rex, great. Bye. See you later.

FIVE

WHAT your friends say about me,
    It preys on your mind.
You'd do better without me,
    My dear lucky find;
For you've no cause to doubt me
    The man-eating kind.

146

But the tigress grown vicious
    Confined in her cage,
Whose tail-tip as it swishes
    Confesses her rage,
Though her temper's capricious,
    Your touch would assuage.

I've no power to force you
    To undo the door
If the prospect appals you
    Of facing her jaw.
It's only pity calls you
    To the killing floor.

SIX

LONDON shows to the ebb of day
that blackens the spire-crowned skyline
her moment of tranquillity,
her regal mood. Iniquity
goes on yet, innocence is forced,
the five-year-old child undresses
for the video camera,
and worse takes just a moment's thought.
When Dame Town wears this evening gown,
you leave it out of the picture.

Clad in the eyes of your lover,
black and pale-rayed aquamarine,
she's mistress of forgetfulness,
a hypnotist. Her head weighs down
your shoulder, her spine's cool as night.
Her Soho starts to palpitate
to your spreading hand. You'd abuse

her kindness by comparison.
To her she's him, a darkling prince
under a wasting, penal curse.

The silent toiling river turns
to oil at your feet, where you bend
together at the parapet
and lean apart to strike a match
for her cigarette and your own,
then fumble the latch of her lips
to learn her mellifluous tongue.
The Thames like a contraband tape
of perpetual nothingness,
glittering, streams and flickers on.

Until we two secretly meet
again, remember me this way,
mouth open like a simpleton
to catch whatever time you say.
Or will it be "… madness!" "Wednesday,
Six o'clock, then?" "Look who's talking… "
Apart from headlights, streetlights, moon,
neon, pub lights, stars and your eyes,
everything's out. We're in the dark
of fairy-tales and betrayals.

SEVEN

AS he paces
the emptying of his can
to the length of another film in the Burt Reynolds
        season,
she clasps him to her
in the windy crook of a street.

Burt's good-natured moustache
ambles over his lines
as he clasps her to him,
her arms thrust under his coat,
her ear to his heart.

Blue and green, the big
spaces open up
around the all-white teeth.
A brew of wrath has settled on his stomach with the
        Special Brew.
He squashes the tin with a clack.

EIGHT

LOSING track of who I am
He's the romantic one
She's my little brown liar
I'm thinking of her body as guitar
Stroking thru her tangle with an idle thumb
And I'm the one plays trumpet

Cock-eyed embouchure on her womb
Her windings' ecstatic pressure
Till the pure cry and the tongue
Moving out in the lips sounding it
Again a different way again
A differing way away

Taking me back with her into her
Eyes a distant blue
Opening and she can be beyond
Out there and still come back for me
When I'm beyond already
Losing who I am

NINE

REX is in the kitchen
with a teaspoon in the teapot
he's been stirring as long as he can remember,
which he drops and reaches in after.
Finding the black aromatic interior
hot, he snatches two red fingers back
and the pot almost tips. Saves it neatly.
Passing the scalded digits through the air,
"Jesus," he reproaches himself
aloud, "I must be wrecked."
Inspiration comes from a table knife.
Running it under the tap
he smears the butter and toast crumbs thinner
then manages to fish the end of the handle
of the teaspoon free of the steaming brew,
seizing it between thumb and
forefinger of the left hand but,
since it's as hot as the tea,
not for long.
He manoeuvres it patiently into view again
and bending down, squinting
against the wisps of steam wafting through his lashes,
aims a cooling stream of breath
at the hoisted end of the spoon.
"Jesus," says Jasper,
having just remembered where Rex went,
coming in from next door,
"You must be wrecked."

TEN

I HAVE set my face against fate
that bars us pettily
so when I sit to write away
delays and obstacles

and bring you near me
your round face moves
like a compass in its gimbal
in a ring of silence,

all I have in the grey-stricken world to follow.
Foam flies in the wind's teeth, the speechless needle
points the north of love and grief
where green land lies out of the storm.

ELEVEN

"WHERE have you been?"
The false livid colours
splash his cold expression from the muted screen.

> "Hi Paul. Where you been?
> Roll a number. Look at this –
> bizarre! Weird shit, I'll tell ya."

She folds down on the floor
beside the armchair, puts her head on his knee.
"Just out, you know. Out and about."

> "See what I mean?"
> "What is this crap?"
> "*Tarantula.*" "Surreal."

151

By the ledge of your cheek
and perilous gully of your lip –
     "Oh no, not the giant rabbit!"

Where downy hair
beyond the eyebrows' hedge…
"What's that supposed to mean?"

There are two lakes
fed by meltwater.
"You're lying to me."

TWELVE

"BROKENHEARTEDNESS and manic anger,
But still it's upright, dignified.
They say it's a feeling
Yet it's more than a mood.
Angry, sad and wild and funny,
It's all round human. Not just standing there.
You know, God, if I could get that feeling… "
"Well," says Rex, "it's simple.
You sell your soul to the Devil."

THIRTEEN

THE flood tide sets the buoys clanging
In midstream, and gurgles and clacks
Like a tongue through branches hanging
New leaves in the deepest of blacks,
The black of the broad midnight Thames.

"Come along. Be rid of your shame,
Your foolish unremitting need.
Leave behind on the empty walk
The hope you'll no more watch recede,
The pointless work and fruitless talk.
Make these redundant as your name,"
Croons the bride, the wide, brimful Thames.

But let me live, the heart says, tempted and oppressed,
To take again on her quick, quiet breast
The first long shot of lasting rest.

FOURTEEN

OVER in that block of black
One orange light remaining.

What are we up to still
Together my friend?

Wondering over a woman
Wondering over a man?

They can take the guitars of the world
And bury them if they leave but one

And that one mine.
I'm a man of simple wants.

Am I the one she loves
Or the one she doesn't hate

Enough to leave behind?
Of simple wants –

And that one mine.
Then why are we up

Together with the dawn a distant blue
Behind you, behind you my friend?

FIFTEEN

THE stars that haven't fallen fade,
mist creeps off the river.
The distraught limbs assemble,
they stand up from the pile
and go back into the yards.
I'm a winnowing, a husk
blown from the sieve of occupations.
The slaughterer changes aprons;
the first calf, pale-headed, totters forward.
Soon the runnels and gutters
are healthy again with blood.
Where is her gate of bronze and lapis?
All the slaughterer's cash in my pockets
is yours if you'll lead me to it.

SIXTEEN

GOES musingly among the pied flowers
Beside him. After irascible gales,
Days that lately clear to candid sunset,
Now all that frets the sky are vapour trails
And summer gathers its stilling powers.
She follows the bright sliver of a jet
Westering between two council towers.

"Fucking vulture bastards! Why should I go
Down the police station? Just because I'm –
Yes, and what's it fucking got to do with –
What are you looking at anyway? Time!
What do any of you lot fucking know?"
The pitiless pressure with which we live
Pumping through the dentures of old mad Flo.

"Perhaps if us two ran – ?" "To some islands
The world hasn't reached." "Or sail on and on."
"There never will be peace." "Not even now?"
"To somewhere no-one's been." "That's right." "Be
        gone."
"So long. And vanish." "To live in silence."
"Naked." "Really?" "Absolutely. Somehow
Still to keep us." "You lot, keep your distance."

The same sad joke that lovers always tell.
Railing shadows stretching out like harp strings
And the flowerbeds leaving their colour
To motionless air where a blackbird sings,
Transmuting dusk's cold ashes through his spell
To pointed blues, grown fuller and fuller
Of the coming night: sings that all is well.

II. LADYWELL

The Source

THE new moon on the hill ahead
draws us on like an open door.
The road twists down to the bridge
then climbs once more towards our omen.

A shoulder to the swollen door
releases it, complainingly.
Smell of uninhabitation
where we'll live four days together.

He finds the pump and the fuse-box.
The first fire ticks out in the grate.
I relight it while he conjures
a meal in the empty kitchen.

*   *   *   *

While a Welsh wind exults outside,
drifting off in each other's arms,
we huddle in our lifeboat bed,
and my dreams are so much flotsam.

Between the recent scenes twisted
into a new recognition,
I'm met by a woman, a friend,
it seems, though her head is cowled.

Familiar faces and strange
at a casual, elegant feast,
insecure in their shiny clothes,
and her across the gathering

157

approaching me, a blue mantle
down to the ground. My spine feels her
force from a distance, and I wake
as it enters me, beside him.

*   *   *   *

The sky is calm and brilliant
in the small uncurtained window.
He sighs something inquiringly
in his sleep, starts, then turns over.

When I wake again it's the eye
of his prick nosing up between
my cheeks, his tongue at my ear that
stirs, finding the way gently home,

takes possession of all it sees.
I back against his kind flat loins
riding up against me, shudder,
and just as I come remember

what it was I'd been dreaming – this.
The thick cloud drags and tumbles by,
attaching itself to the glass
with trembling, splintered filaments.

*   *   *   *

He falls back again and dozes
till I kiss him to consciousness
to speak to me. "What should I say?"
"Say you love me." "I thought I did."

"Well, tell me again." And we do,
tongue to tongue, tell each other, both
hands gripping on stiffened buttocks,
and then both sleep till afternoon.

*   *   *   *

There's time for no more than a turn
around the garden before night
comes quickly. The four o'clock dusk
breaks open at the last minute

and a broad gleam like the sickle-
blade of Revelation's angel
is stretched out over the valley
from a rift between clouds and ridge.

The shaking, soaked, neglected shrubs
and stunted trees glitter wildly
for that minute of light worth more
than many whole previous days.

*   *   *   *

His head always down in a book…
Our semi-occupied house holds,
along with the damp and the dust,
half a library, still half boxed.

Why not this eagerness for me?
For instance, he says, the tamed well
fitted with winch and fairy-tale
gables and neat surrounding wall,

that stands on the paved patch out front
is the actual "Ladywell", once,
before that prettification,
devoted to the trinity,

the triple goddess. He shows me
the photos of stones where they're carved,
the hooded women, in granite,
threefold – and stops to see me stare.

I stumble out my dream to him,
blessing what goddess, so to speak,
or movings of whatever have
denied me disillusionment.

                    *   *   *   *

Only the moment before sleep
falls, my head on his arm, the thought
jars to, that tagging the symbol
runs counter to reality.

And sure enough, she doesn't come;
but beside a placid water
I find the mantle on the ground
and trace the track of her diving,

a wake of brightness lingering
in diamionds of reflected sun.
Her path was downward to her source,
invisible heart of clarity.

The Bird

DRIVING across the bare plateau
we round a bend and a buzzard
starts from the top of a hawthorn
suddenly in front of the car:

a dark-barred breast, the broad blunt wings.
The wild uncommon things we meet
touch us with the force of omens,
the engine idling a moment

as we taste our benediction.
The sheep's forlorn, prosaic cries.
He takes my hand and kisses it,
smiles it's going to be alright.

*   *   *   *

Where are we fitted in this world
like the farms into their hillsides,
I wonder as the lanes meander
down the Teme valley into Knighton.

Nowadays it isn't clergy
but shopkeepers bless marriages.
If to them you count a couple,
you are, you're two-for-one. People,

you forget, don't have to look a-
skance at us, like in the city.
The young girl tallies us brightly
The till bell is ringing our change.

*   *   *   *

We load the boot of our borrowed
elderly Saab and take our walk
by the river. Out of season
for ramblers, beyond the parkland,

we're left with the paths to ourselves,
outside the orbit of the town's
joggers and dogs. The single-track
rail- and footbridge, some rough pasture

to cross to the foot of the Dyke:
a thousand years old, he tells me,
and now almost landscape itself,
just a few feet proud of its ground.

It snakes above the other ridge,
coercing an outcrop of rock;
on this side it makes its own rule,
built straight up the slope to the col.

*   *   *   *

The leafless woods are dry, the hill
soaked in the late afternoon sun.
From the breathing, beating silence
that comes with effortful climbing,

we turn back to take in the breeze
and the view. He points out where a
buzzard is leisurely circling
stone-white fractured clouds over Wales.

With him I enter into scenes
and have the eyes of anything
I see – learn this geography
from that lone, regal point of view.

This is countryside thick with time,
with being seen and lived on, held.
The soil beneath our feet feels dense,
potent with graves. We climb a gate

out onto the height. Wind-shaken
grasses stretch out under the crow-
queried sky. The Iron Age rampart's
a low, discontinuous mound.

He stands on top with arms outspread
and turns about as if to say,
all this is ours for the keeping.
His hat blows off and rolls away.

*   *   *   *

The path between birches and larches
comes down to the back end of town,
council estates and the station,
cattle mart and farm supply stores.

In the steep and tightly angled
ancient backstreets we find the pub
for our pint and claim two barstools.
Wood and lino, plain as you please.

Here is all of community
we two as two may ever know,
that looks us over, barely nods,
smiles and reverts to the talk of

last night, and last week, and last year;
that needn't care and has no cause
to bar the odd pair of strangers.
We sip, relax into ourselves.

*   *   *   *

Only one raggeder, louder,
unsteadier than the others,
the others' foil, their fixture drunk,
lacking their reserve, circles us.

He eyes me brightly, says hello,
and seeing I'm not unattached,
extends his welcome to us both,
his staggering, spirited charm.

He has tall tales, as usual,
though it's hard to tell what they are
for thickness of his drink-blurred brogue.
He surveys us for unbelief.

Not a local, an Irishman,
who left County Clare at fifteen
to work the roads and building sites;
fruit-picker, potato-digger,

farm-labourer and forester;
even, for a while, a shepherd.
When we tell him where we're staying,
he thinks for a moment, recalls

his best friend laid in the churchyard
with a handful of hill-farmers.
Riding his Triumph into Wales;
just twenty. Never been back since.

The portentous theme and reeling
panoramic graphics flash up
in the corner. Paul turns to watch,
but it's only news of trouble.

The Fire

GEORGE'S hands are work- and weather-
bent, his only debility
from forty years of farming here,
a single man, in the same house.

Alone, he welcomes company,
we're told, though not with such hunger
as haunts the stranded urban old.
We take our place on the settle

whose high panelled back bars the draught
and makes this corner of the room,
though sparse, a warm nook round the range,
burnished with decades of content.

Two bright-burning wedges of log
balanced at the top of the grate,
he pokes out the powder-fine ash
from the bottom of its deep bed,

perches the black kettle above,
and sits back, fire and battered chair
and nosing dog more richly his
than households of valuable goods.

It boils in no time and he crooks
the teapot over three cheap mugs,
pouring a thin dark stream of cha,
then puts out bread and cheese and jam.

*   *   *   *

Over tea he takes down postcards
and snapshots pinned disorderly
on the wall above the cupboard:
one from New York, New Zealand,

the neighbour's son who's a pilot
in the air force now. The wide world
orbits these walls of Welsh granite
and time's fuel for that steady fire.

"They didn't do too good a job
to that place, the previous people.
This'll be right when that shoddy
modern stuff's to be done again.

"It was then they improved the well,
too. Yes. Beside the road, below
the gate, in a little basin.
Fresh water for the passers-by."

*   *   *   *

When we go he comes out with us
into the clear but blowing night
to bring in the cows and the calves
that stand and wait at the yard gate.

They lower their angular heads
and watch us musingly pass
between them, breathing starry steam,
before they amble in to him.

I catch a last glimpse of his back
under the light, his shoulders
round and solid as a boulder,
Queenie alert, trotting at heel.

The Ridge

ON our last evening we drive down
the valley to where it narrows.
The sun is low already, the air
chilling over the flat floodplain,

a bare quarter-mile of fat land.
Starting up the far side, the slope's
brutally steep, hardly easing
as we climb in the last daylight.

I go more slowly and he waits
to take my hand, then leads me up
between the broken roots and holes
of a storm-mangled belt of trees,

an outlying arm of the dense
wood that hangs on the valley side.
The top's a bald domed pasture where
my ears start to ache in the wind

pouring across the deceptive,
receding skyline he pursues
until he's persuaded the ground
slopes down from us on every side.

*   *   *   *

A struggling, rushing horde of cloud
out of the west, piled and harried
by the gale, blackens the grey sky.
The last rays shiver on the hills.

167

We can scarcely make out the ground
coming down, hurried by the gloom.
The higher crowns of trees still sway,
but calm's fallen on the valley.

Against the restless colonies
of rooks, homing from below
in ones and twos, calling, wheeling
out for one last flight before night,

then settling to contend and sleep,
an owl shakes out his seldom cry,
hollow and keen, like a pennant
pronouncing his kingdom coming.

III. DISORDER

ON the hips of the evening patrol
the holsters flash like slow white wings below.
Run down the dial on the radio;
the pirates have all been silenced.
No ragga, no rap, no house, no soul.
But Radio 4's reassuring
people things are normal
with the tenor of those upper-middle accents.

He's gone for a while with the gun,
locking the door behind him.
I'm too high up for a jump,
no-one pays any mind to shouting
these days, nor screams, nor sudden reports.
Count my cigarettes
and take one, count my almost-worthless change.
Being indoors is a blessing of sorts.

Horrible lingering beer and garlic farts
he laughs about making, for a start…
Marriages may be designed in heaven
but the blueprints get sent down to hell
and hell does a job of the usual quality.
Before this whole mess began
he rushed us through the registry,
said it might give me a margin of safety.

So now I'm his captive, and that's official.
By then the worst seemed possible,
like the Chinese curse: May you live in eventful
times. The mob or the people
(take your pick) were too vengeful

for their own good. Imagine the mood
of the Security Council.
They say it'll soon be business as usual.

The TV ads are the same,
that's part of the calming game.
Except, among some images
of things you can't get now for love nor money,
they're running all these funny slots,
like a Recycling Centre, mini-cabs,
a Pregnancy Advice Bureau,
with tinkly amateurish jingles.

It's dead quiet in the courtyard.
Deal another hand of patience.
The red queen's behind the black four,
the black jack's on top of red three.
This is the door and this is the window,
this is the key and this is the door.
I've only to get them in the order
where first's after last and the ace will be free.

*   *   *   *

So much for English reserve.
Why on earth would they tear down Eros?
The hand with the bow's
lying by the road.
For a while it was indeed
a bloody Circus,
tented with tear-gas.
Doing the red-nosed clown dance under the blows.

Like crushed coloured sugar
the pavements are covered
with glass from the neon displays.

There's a blood-stained trainer
unattached in the gutter.
It's quiet but not peaceful these days
and being footloose isn't an occupation
to make you popular with policemen.

We pass by looking purposeful and meek.
You often see them with a hand unconsciously
stroking the gutta-percha
of their pistol-holsters now
like somebody fingering the lump
they've convinced themselves might be cancer.
Step around the broad unlucky streak
that's been smeared with a mop, that still looks damp.

No luck at Leicester Square.
There's a burnt-out car
been pushed down the shattered entrance stairs.
No good going to Charing Cross
cause the whole Northern Line's a dead loss.
("It's good to know some things don't change.")
The smoke-blackened front of the National
looks more like Stonehenge.

The presence is thicker towards the Embankment
where the down-and-outs are still gathered.
There's two charred and mangled
double-deckers turned over in the Strand.
We go up through Covent Garden.
The guy they shot with a shotgun
and a grand and a half cash money
in his pocket got it here, on Bow Street.

The legends already abound
of the ones who got rich quick and went to ground
and the ones who got dead quicker

and went underground. "Yeah,
suckers," you hear them snicker.
"So suffer," you hear them mutter.
"It's getting late to be walking," says Rex.
"It's half an hour till curfew."

*   *   *   *

The water's on again for a while.
It'll soon be off.
I fill up bottles and buckets and jugs
with the retsina-coloured stuff.
Are they really putting drugs in it?
It's half an hour till curfew,
he has to be back soon.
I taste it. It tastes vile.

The phone's still dead as a doornail.
I pick it up and dial his number
and say his name to the deaf and dumb receiver,
check my looks in the mirror
that's lying on the table – bad, too pale.
I look as though I'm crying snow.
His kind of kindness was to leave a
couple of fat lines of coke.

"That should see you fine,
that should pass the time."
Or was that his idea of a joke?
I roll up a twenty-pound note.
I remember when what you snorted
you snorted through something that might have
          bought it.
Then I'm sitting there clenching my teeth.
Even what he gets himself is cut to hell with speed.

Nice gift, you bastard, thanks!
Go to the bathroom cupboard to get some trancs.
The bottle's there but the bottle's empty.
I could have sworn there were fifteen or twenty
in there. Does he go off selling those
as well, or is he afraid I'll overdose?
No chance, bastard. No matter how long you kept me
I've got something in me to outlast it.

What's that look in the bathroom glass?
What's that expression?
Those tiny eyes and the face all pointy
and pallid with tension?
It's the gaze of a white laboratory
rat trying to pass
through a particularly tricky
behaviourist's maze.

I go and lie down and my thoughts go racing
through the tranquil greenery
we left behind in Wales,
only now instead of measured pacing
through the scenery
it goes flying by like the painted flats
in a theatre gone loco, with details
heavily impastoed, unnatural.

* * * *

I can feel that short lively weight
swing against my leg in the sports bag.
They'd shoot me on sight if they saw it,
but the places I'm going
and the people I'm seeing
and the way things are going

it's good to be carrying
some strong persuasion along with the scag.

But out after dark with a sawn-off… ?
There may be quicker ways to top yourself
but I haven't got time to think of them.
Half an hour till curfew.
I just hope some copper
doesn't give me the option
between here and home.
Baby, your baby's done roaming.

She thinks I turn that key because I'm cruel,
I know. It isn't true.
But give her an inch and she'd run a mile
after that fool, Paul,
and this is no weather to be out in.
We're in for a stormy autumn
and things won't get better before they get worse.
She needs a man with nous to protect her.

You see those neat little hawks,
kestrels, now like you never did before,
those slim brown gentlemen
taking their morning and evening walks
or hanging out on a corner of the sky.
They're getting fat off the vermin, the rats.
They'd have my canary before she could fly
halfway from her cage to the nest.

If she ever loved me once she doesn't now.
You think that's easy to live with?
I've seen the short fat creases in her brow
and the hard way she swallows
all the time, frowning
and trying to keep her dinner down

when I talk to her, whenever I'm round the house.
And I take it for her own good. And if that isn't love…

Just two guys going quietly
on the shadowy side of the street
with no more than ten minutes to go.
Morons – made me start,
coming round the corner suddenly.
Hurry home, boys, hurry home.
Didn't your mummies warn you
not to be out after dark?

*   *   *   *

What the hell are we doing, Paul?
We're looking for a man you've never seen
and you don't know where he lives exactly,
to find a woman he's keeping indoors
(which seems pretty unlikely)
who the next-door neighbours themselves,
if he is, probably don't know is there at all,
or if she ever has been?

OK, why not? I'm game.
Up Hatton Garden things look pretty much the same.
No matter what happens
nothing's going to hurt the trade in jewels and gold.
You'd need a bomb or oxyacetylene tools
to get through that steel shuttering.
So what if it is a little bit stolen
and you're buying the ring today that yesterday you
            sold?

Just when I'm thinking
coppers seem thin on the ground tonight

comes a jam sandwich
howling and blinking,
hammers to a halt by the garage.
We shrink back instinctively
from the swipes of that freezing blue light
and hurry on – don't hurry – innocently.

We've got no night-pass.
It must be nearly quarter past.
All these steel-grilled windows full of clocks
and not one of them telling the time.
It's somewhere in these blocks,
you reckon? You see that bloke jump
coming round the building? What crime bumped
against his conscience?

So why'd you pull me back when he's gone?
You mean to tell me he's the one?
There are ten thousand guys with a ponytail.
She didn't go into much detail.
Slip through the shadows and duck
through the archway he went in. It's too much luck.
Always fancied myself as a private dick,
if you know what I mean.

No entry-phones on these tenements.
Race across the courtyard and in at the stairway door.
Did she mention a black moustache?
Maybe he's grown it since?
Yes, and maybe he cut off his hair…
Alright, alright, I'll hush.
Counting the steps that are echoing
down on us in the well, to guess which landing.

*　　*　　*　　*

Goes leaping upstairs like a madman,
half a flight at each bound.
By the fourth I'm wishing I'd given up smoking,
my heart starts to pound
but my head feels light and floating
as though I was stoned
on the anticipation – or,
to give it its proper name, fear.

"Are you sure it was the fifth?"
"I can't be positive."
There are four flats to each storey,
so what do we do? Suddenly
inspiration leaves him forlorn and passive
like the dot disappearing
on a TV switched off.
Well, let's put an ear to each door.

    Her arms on the table,
    her head on the backs of her hands.
    She starts and jerks up straight
    when I come in, awkwardly stands
    and backs away a step. "Sorry I'm late."
    "Do you think I mind?" "Are you alright, babe?"
    "I did those lines you left, for once.
    So apart from speeding off my bonce… "

    Her hands catch and clutch
    and reluctantly release,
    torment and twist each other for comfort
    like the woman in a black and white thriller.
    Her face is a bad colour.
    "Please let me go, Bill – please.
    It's too much. It's going to kill me, staying here.
    Is that what you want?" Her voice getting shriller.

"Paul! Paul!" I whisper hoarsely.
"Here – listen here!" "That's her!"
I have to tell him. He's not without mercy.
I have to try. He must see what it does to me.
His face clouds over with hurt and confusion –
that need for protection I'd almost forgotten
that first drew me to him,
but it's too late. There's a sharp rap on the door.

"Now what?" "Knock." "Just that?" "What else?"
And what if no-one answers?
And what if he closes the door in my face?
"But stand back a bit, Rex,
around the corner.
Two will make him suspicious."
The door goes in two inches on its chain.
"Yes?" "My name's Paul. I've come for Beatrice."

  "Sorry, mate. Wrong number."
  "Come on, Bill. Apart from her
  I bet there's plenty more at home
  Old Bill 'd like to see."
  Peeking round the corner,
  I watch him, in a low unshaken voice,
  talk to the grease-printed door-jamb.
  "Don't threaten me, pal. It isn't wise."

Now for me to look mean and effective,
or at least show there's a witness.
"Hello, Beatrice," he calls.
Who's he muttering to in the hall?
It can't be a deal. It can't be – "Paul!"
"Shut your mouth. Now listen, pal – "
A bunch of red-polished nails appear on his scalp,
dig through the slicked-back tress

178

and his face disappears,
dragged backwards by the hair.
"Now, Rex, now, come on!"
And we bang our bodies into it
and burst through the chain.
She's sitting on the floor,
her mouth knocked sideways a bit, her lip split.
For a moment we all just stand there breathing.

"You wanted to protect me, Bill.
I understand that."
"Come on, the game's up."
"Shut up." She gets up.
"But here's the man I want to be with."
"Come on, let's keep things simple."
"I told you. I don't want to hear your voice again,
        pal."
"Please, Bill, be sensible."

He says nothing. His face is white.
He goes into the room to his right.
They look at each other, not speaking,
a hand stretched out towards her cheek,
and then they're both holding tight – tighter.
Come on, Paul, be sensible. Later,
man, later. Please. He's got the message.
We've just stepped out in the passage

when the door bangs open behind us.
Our host is smiling widely
with a sleek and ugly
length of machinery held out casually
towards us. "You've got two choices,
boys," he says, "and one of them's to go home."
We're rooted solid, but she steps towards him
and grabs the barrel and *boom!*

We're under a shower of blood and bone,
the thing sounds louder than thunder,
and she flies back into his arms.
The whole of her front looks sodden and broken.
He's just standing there shaking
with the smile screwed onto his face
like it's never going to come off.
Something drops on the concrete with a clunk.

There's a last bit of life in the eyes she turns on his
and then it's gone. It's dripping off his nose.
And there's really nothing to do but be gone,
to get before we're got.
Poor Bill's sunk down on the floor, staring at the gun.

I pull him away, and there's no resistance.
He knows. He wipes the spots off her brows
and off her chin and lies her on her side.
He starts to come away slowly
till I drag him, and we run.

IV. EVENING SINGER

I

"IT'S hard to say in the end what it was.
The Disorder has so many stories
untold, and Paul was someone who knew them.
Those times left us all with scars and losses
that the songs recall. But they're medicine.
He drew on a fund of pain to heal them.
And he never lost sight of an odd thing
people forget, that destruction caught light
from hope at first. He was there from the start,
remember, burning down Wandsworth Town Hall..."

You heard Rex Maynard speaking, the close friend,
aide and confidant of the late Paul Dell.
This is Radio Freedom. As your calls
pour in, we give the day to his music.

II

"HE ran, he lived on the lam for a while.
They gunned him down before Reconstruction,
I heard. He just got more and more reckless.
First it was aggravated burglary,
armed robbery, then out-and-out murder.
He even got to be a star of sorts –
blood shining in the dark. He must have known
the old ways would be drawing to an end.
It was in the last few days. For myself,
I wouldn't feel safe now if they hadn't

run him down, out of luck, out of bullets.
No-one who didn't endure through that time
would believe it. But we mustn't forget,
nor our children, the price and worth of peace."

III

ALDERS shimmer by the river, tossing
the light and wind from one to another.
The shadow of the armour of the Dane
and Norman, like da Vinci's *sfumato*
that rounds his figures, imperceptibly
lends an edge to the plumpest and brightest
of Berkshire summers. We lounge on the lawn,
Rex and I, and under a feathery,
lark-riddled sky, watch nothing but the tint
of the sun through the blood of our eyelids.
A transistor on the marble table
is humming not much louder than a bee,
playing the Sunday Top 40 run-down,
waiting to hear how the single's doing.

IV

"WHAT do you think?" We play it back again.
"Cut the rhythm track down to the cowbell
maybe, for one bar after the chorus.
And more delay on the guitar solo."
"I feel it could do with something, the bridge,
something plucky, bazouki or banjo,
perhaps mandolin, to kick it along."
André's bass line's gorgeous there, steep and bare,
looping back on itself... "Too many hooks?"
I grin across the desk at Rex. "No, man,

that's perfect. Doesn't clutter the lyrics."
"OK, Dan, let's take it back to the top
and get those harmonies on the intro."
"Born Number One if ever I heard one."

V

Woman-hater. Never caught around one.
Whited sepulchre, full of ochre bones.
Or should I write, Dear Moses, who's shown us
the border of a fat and pleasant land
through a glass darkly, across the river,
and written his words on the wilderness.
Our loving and sexless, reclusive sage,
the man to thank now that thoughtfulness is
the fashion. Don't think I haven't seen you,
an arena in the palm of your hand.
And all your works are as signs and wonders.

Rex frowns and shows me. A note like the last,
scrawled on a shotgun ad torn from *The Field*,
postmarked EC1. It reads "UNPAID BILL".

VI

UP off the road and over the downland,
the chalk and sand of the racehorses' run
pitted with their hoofs. The patchwork puddles
of the sudden, vertical summer rain
reflect a sky still confused but clearing.
I've got it to myself, I think too soon.
A woman's sitting on her folded coat
beside the hedge. I try to pass her by,
nod politely and murmur "Afternoon,"

but a moment later she's by my side,
slinging her sports bag over her shoulder.
"Hi, Mr. Dell. Mind if I walk with you?"
Jesus, another fan. So far, at least,
she's not rabid, not grabbing or probing.

VII

SMART, attractive, well-mannered; not gushing
and not uptight. This one's been blessed with the
gift of silence, smiling and saying nowt.
She tosses back her long, brown, coiling hair.
Her eyes are a girl's, her face is older.
"I'm sorry to be intruding on you.
I realise you must get this all the time.
I could have pretended not to know you –
well, really I don't, any more than you
know me; but I feel I know you so well.
I mean, I listen to you all the time."
"You're right. I've had to move once already
when the place got too well known. Normally…
But in your case I'll make an exception."

VIII

"WOULD you mind if I ask you a question?"
"I suppose if you must." "I read somewhere
that you lost someone who was close to you – "
"Not about that." "No, I understand.
I did too, and in a similar way."
"I'm sorry." Something about this woman.
I suppose that story's not uncommon.
How our feet have fallen unthinkingly
in step, for instance, just like they used to…

"Are you? No, but what I wanted to say
was, looking back, does it all seem worthwhile?"
"What do you mean, my life?" "Your life, that too,
but all the sacrifice and suffering.
You sing as though the whole thing meant some-
    thing."

IX

"IF I felt I could tell you frankly, Miss – "
"Blackstone. It's Mrs. But I'm a widow."
"Blackstone? You're not – " "Go on." "I knew some-
    one…"
"I doubt if you ever knew my husband."
"No, of course not." "Go on." Her expression's
smooth and deep, unassuming. "If I felt – "
"Not a soul, I promise." "I think I stand
for people's desire to forget their pain,
to believe they actually won their way
to the promised land, whether or not – "
"Excuse me just a moment, Mr Dell."
Her laces are fine, but she stops and stoops
while I walk on. The zip of her bag, then,
clear in the silence, a clean double click.

X

FLUORESCENT tape flutters in the dusk,
draped from gorsebush to gorsebush. The flowers
glow waxily in the deepening blue
and low beams from the cars shine down the lane,
catching the small puddles like polished steel.
Two or three confer around the body,
nod their heads in quiet, angry patience,

and one bobby leans on the swung-open door,
talking to another behind the wheel,
who looks drawn, nervous and out of his depth;
laughs, glances quickly in my direction.
"I wish you'd shown us these notes before,
Mr Maynard." "So do I, inspector."
"Still, let's say – I think we expect results."

XI

Of course there were none.
With a murder so motiveless,
What would one expect?
    You blew the ashes off this heart of mine

Under Jamaican sun
He's suddenly motionless
For a long-drawn moment.
    Breathe a little flame into the embers

Cut to San Juan,
Upheld lighters all over the place;
Same song, different concert.
    So breathe on love and let the starlight shine

Streams and flickers on,
Just his singing head full-face,
Calm and fulfilled and alert.
    World's on fire but nobody remembers

World's on fire but nobody remembers
So breathe on love and let the starlight shine
Breathe a little flame into the embers
You blew the ashes off this heart of mine
    She breathes, and she breathes for the life of me
    And always in the darkness I can hear her breathe

INTIMATIONS

I'M beckoning a tiger.

If it comes
springing in surfs of leaves
it'll kill.

Or tell him I went that way.

*   *   *   *

I WOKE up and cried in the morning,
white as it was promised,
when there was a cold sheet
and a bird singing,
"There's been time for bitterness
but it passed in the night."

*   *   *   *

PEOPLE do not stop loving each other
but become other,
not noticing the phoenix down
gathering in the bedroom corner
in the minutes they spend apart,
washing.

*   *   *   *

BEWARE, my child, the jungle creatures.
They are knobbly and blotchy and their ears stick out.
Don't go near the smallest of them,
For he's a mouthful of pins to prick your finger with.

But see how shiny blood stands on your fingertip!
See how bright are fevered eye and brow!
See how you quietly let your clutch of life slip…
My child, my child – what good's my warning now?

*　　*　　*　　*

TOWERS hang and swoop
from the car to the weeping horizon.
In the factory, fixed on our progress
heart to heart, life's cracking
and spitting down corridors of power
whose fissure glides towards us, bright
and deep as a snake,
or deadly patient detective
maddening our cells.

It is quiet although the wound
of sunset lies huge and open.

*　　*　　*　　*

THE flower, a white rose, the honey husks
of whose heart are dry as bird bones,
turning apart, and the bottle,
half drunk, of red wine, with its label

190

away from me, the sheer portion of liquid
black inside the glass, are islands,
the pediments of golden columns,
and the sea that moves about them
is doubt.

*   *   *   *

LIKE the bird at dawn
loosing a chill wire into the mist,
a handful of notes,
the pear tree's letting pears drop
as hard as tears.

*   *   *   *

TURNING wrong in Sloane Square
I came to a place where the bones
of millions of people had been
flogged to a sick cream
and made into white hotels.

*   *   *   *

THE dog star crawled into the smallest
hole in the world,
found a hole in it,
crawled in further,
sulked nose to tail and yawned.

Desert turned to glass.
Dark space between flowers
burn-patterned skin.

*   *   *   *

I LIKE the world now
the car takes bends
fatally into the black
road's skin open
to a half-acre of diamonds.

*   *   *   *

WITH little ado
I found winter's fretful
        fellow on the step.

All the bones left him
        were one starling's
that the wind turned through.

*   *   *   *

ENOUGH
we touch
then sidlingly
now close, now closer
then sidlingly.

Acute snow gathers the arched,
spitted back of spring's resistance.

       *   *   *   *

IT'S warm in Chancery Lane
and the builders' blokes
leaning under the scaffolding
smile,
folding their broad blond arms in the sunlight.

Bit of raw dust on the old
wood, glass and gilt.
Building trade's alright.

       *   *   *   *

THE dome fell in and the air above
was full of birds and light
and we stopped singing.

       *   *   *   *

WHEN morning called
there was white mist in the garden
and autumn pears as hard as pine
fell in the grass.

       *   *   *   *

ALL done   now

then   come dreamtime

*   *   *   *

TWO TIGERS BY THE SEA

AT least we were safe there
  And kept warm in winter
But there's no going home now.

The sea forms in long black lips
  – Winter's dog on our heels –
While we pad this grey beach

Bright as descended stars
  Watching the shore birds
Flock from the night

And fly south. This is a cold
  Island, and small as a birdcage.
Impossible to move silently

Over the sharp ice in gardens.
  Tigers are hardly indigenous
And the scent of sapphires that comes

On warm winds is untenable.
  I have seen something when I raise
The wide world of one foot

That I cannot say.
    I have seen it falling among the leaves
Of the holy forest.

                    *   *   *   *

    MY nails grow round and long.
    I was not meant for tiger or falcon
    But suppose I am a camel
    Who walks on flat round nails.

MAN'S LAUGHTER

THE LOUT'S PRANK

OUR fathers
who conquered the world,
hidebound, bent and mean,
their kingdom queened,
their will bedunged,
inert aestheticist heathens,
give us this day our daily bread
and fourfold give us their trespasses –
a sweet thought given those
who trespass and get sussed.
Our leaders now test our patience
by defiling us as people,
for we are the conscience,
the poor and the glory
and our endeavour's
well-meant.

KNOCKING TWICE

SEEK and ye shall find, knock

                    Knock.

Who's there?

                    Death.

Death who?

                    Deathide for yourthelf.

FROM THE TEA CHING TO

TWO things fill up the universe:
the known and the unknown.
Of the unknown is made the known,
but how much of the unknown may be known?
This is unknowable
and three things fill up the universe:
known, knowable, and unknowable unknown.

The known and the knowable are not constant;
they partake of one another.
The unknowable alone is constant and eternal.
The unknowable alone brought forth the universe,
all things known or knowable, and their knower,
who is the known unknowable in the knowable
        unknown.

PICA PICA RAIDS THE BIRD BOOK

WITH speckled bread recognition
and grey-brown incubation
boldly snails contrasting closely
about frogs iridescent green

May fed April plumage animals by long lays
21 times black light days eggs
4 only white and usually nestlings
at and by 7 female carrion

both small wedge-shaped birds usually tail other
        parents of sexes alike
young rootlets with leave covered nesting after mud

and about both eggs of sexes lining seeds
build 27 with days and domed fruit structure wild

tree of grain twigs feeding larvae
or insects in their bush and

OPENING MILTON

"GOD, when he gave me strength, to show withal
How slight the gift was, hung it in my hair."

Blind Christ-kind,
wife-loser –
Mary and Katherine,
RIP from birth –
whose daughters "would have sold the rest
of his bookes to the Dunghill women",
whose only son John was
no sooner given than taken back.
Yet from the bated, rigid darkness of that bed

"The breath of heaven fresh blowing, pure and sweet,
With day-spring born"

DANGER!

DO not reach under
raised body unless it is
PROPPED.
Dustcart notice costing
an arm or a leg.

SEVEN DEADLIES

legswap
pawgles
lapsgew **L**ust

spawlge
gawples
lewpsag **S**loth

wapgels
slagpew
gaswelp **W**rath

elsgawp
ewlgasp
waspleg **E**nvy

aspglew
glaspew
gewlsap **A**varice

glawpse
swelgap
spewlag **G**luttony

pewlgas
wagspel
lawspeg **P**ride

THE HANGED MAN

```
          ƎB
          OⱢ
          OT
          BE
    T  O      N
          OⱢ
          ƎB
          OT
```

THEN

WAS a good time
Men had the sense of despair
The Worst
Unsuccumbed to, written down
Failed War
Some men had the sense of women

The Twisties

That now they haven't

The Thirsties

Evil was floodlit
The Sickened
Our lot were green and grimly cheerful
World Whole
How could you tell them
Under all these pastel shades

The Presleys

Now they're into?

Hypocrisy's grey
The Sextease
Our lot was colourful
Severedease
Even if empty, unbidden
Eaties
That was the good's time
Nighnites

i.m.E.P.

THAT confound-
ed grumbling sound
beneath this mound
is Ezra Pound
turning round
where he's bound
underground.

SCREW THE POPULAR PRESS

WITH their cannibal language and dicing for flesh
they furk you in the mouth when you speak.

With a rabbit snare and dark glasses
and their views on other people's lives
they furk you in the head when you think.

With what they own
and because they want to go on
getting more
they furk you in the pocket
where they were begotten.

THE LOVES OF RICK LIME

I'LL tell you in a metaphor
The only thing he met her for:
    A bloom draws a bee
    Sure as A-B-C
But he'll take the rose for a whore.

HAVE YOU STOPPED

GETTING biological out there in Staines,
    Sudbury, Hornchurch?
Do you find your regular tumble dry?
    Try FLAJ.

    FLAJ is scientifically formulated
for a low lather at high temperatures,

　　　　to give your whites a pink that glows
and leave your whole awash with a deep down
　　　　　　　　　　　　　　　　softness.

So Mums remember, next blue Monday –
　　　　FLAJ.
It'll put the ow! back in your housework
　　　　and the eek! back into the week.

21

WITH my mouse-grey shoe
I came to you
all the summer-long grasses through.

Concrete, gravel,
up steep and level
this spider-black sole did travel.

Up to your door stepped,
my man's heart leapt
under the window where we'd slept.

For from your room
did a sly face loom
bearded at the base like a broom…

Has your mouth whiskered
since I kissed it?
O, you have basted some oaf's brisket!

Indoors I'd've went
on blood hell-bent
till I recalled that actually you live at number twent-

y-*one*.

EGO

THE ego's a monstrous mechanism
Because you weren't interested
    I couldn't resist you
If you hadn't laughed
    I wouldn't have got serious
It wasn't love twisted me
I'm in the grip of a runaway invention
    more machine than creature
more monster than anything
    and mine, all mine

FREAKS OF NATURE

Man evolved from a dolphin
stranded in a tree
who grew legs to get down.

Dinosaurs evolved from crude oil
desperately
trying to invent the internal combustion engine.

WORM

Aardvark, booby, gecko and gnu,
The creatures boarding their ship-shape zoo,
The story goes, went two by two,
But a single earthworm, wriggling through,
Told Noah, "I'm my other half too."

CHATTERING PIE

mates some above the or
feeding a make seen highly

have among male preservers some that understood
tends and be are in shy
which common heavily of it

courtship exterminated fancy keepers
takes Norfolk
object the or World
any but
but have surplus elsewhere
not the to reductions are gamekeeping magpies

magpie developed now is into all and common
already hoarding as other city
chase in branches before about it
chatter colonise understood

central is in whose the ceremonial robs
seen birds may including
or of as
and as of in
and and
and in is
but has in gamekeepers alone the go part magpies

its and consists of insects food
grain of usually greater about but
or upset pairs what late this winter young
early eggs spring pheasant
many partridge 100
those more nests be other

in magpie gatherings London purpose parks not
the they may jump long in Dublin
and bird each a

the established instinct is to towns
crows moving highly
is in the they

in liable post-war hide
with only increased food
numbers also War
colourful First
shiny before
which in their by the was displays

keepered this are
in areas bird scarce complicated
to little it on so
occasions game

birds unpopular been it
hovering habits
foot magpies so of their

SIMPLES

NOW I cannot go down
You bear me up as a great ship
However long the storm, day breaks on us

We lie with our arms around
And sail down the river to sleep
However long our day, night falls on us

Birds in the dark make sound
Living on promises to keep
However long we wait, dawn calls on us

THE sung song's there, on the air
though the voice fail the note
    to reach from time to time,
is what is sung not what it should be.

The sung song's there or elsewhere;
though broken it passes
    and never goes away.

SHE says, When they turn to you
my thoughts rejoice and travel
like the snakes according to legend
holding their tails in their mouths
and rolling like hoops down the hill,
as I go with her among the grass.

NOVEMBER trees give off their gold
To soil the autumn rain's soaked black.
Beside the old leaf-scar, tight-scrolled,
The bud's note promises it back.

EARLY or late
makes no difference in the grave.
Who goes calling
will find them always in,
need have no fear of waking them.

Cedar, oak and yew
inch their great shade over them.
Bend nearer then
the matted green, and call
where all are equally at home.

Early or late,
in the grave they are always waiting,
always willing
to be spoken to and listen.
Their green door will always let you in.

≈

THE light is small,
I cannot see far.
I see your face,
fine and serene,
the hollows and the sweetly parted lips.

≈

AN old moon looks on me,
shadow-bit deep.
You're no more keen
to die than I am, dear.
He loves me not
I'm counting on this single petal.

≈

213

SIMPLES

MY theme would be
the world's shiftless sadness
gripped to the winnowing sands
but that running sheet blisters my hands.

My theme would be
how we lay into the grey
waking and dozing amazed
but my birds would descant by rote
beside that current thrush's
live liquid note.

My theme must be
your present absence.
It shadows my singing sense.

WHAT word would be first
to commemorate this piece of mind?
Water like a dancing floor
where the cold-eyed fish leap,
fall and are quenched
in slow diminuendo music.
Why do they set their pointed heads
to splinter their limit and get at
the glare of light in air thus?

For flies
like sultanas
at twilight
they pass
clear through and back.

TONGUES that scorned or flattered
Are hung up torn and tattered
As crows hang on a barbed-wire gibbet.

Tongues that sang true praises
The common wind upraises
As skylarks in the air's wide liberty.

* * * *

I sing in praise of lightness. Diverse dust
Spirals like seraphs through sunlight. All must
Fall, but still the beams hold house for hosts
Of guests. Those sparkling motes were shed like
        ghosts
From friends who are not dead. They are the blessed,
Who shine and spin, whose lighted hearts can't rest.

LOVE is brightness still
though hurt come winding,
is peace that once was rage.

No worm nor wardrobe dust will kill
the flesh within the coat, close-binding
flesh: one lifetime and no age.

All barren colonnades, all
grey gardens
I walk with love. Tall
diamond hardens in my flaking bones.

No ruined place shall hold her small
white arm
though giants built to bird-call,
fall, and harm, and sky-sheared stones.

CHRIST comes to Jerusalem today
And all the world gives a shout;
To the temple as yet unfinished
To throw the stallholders out

And roll all Cæsar's silver faces
In the dust with a clatter.
For thirty such impressed images
His friend would be the traitor.

He comes by a narrow way
Through the jubilant thousands.
In how short time will tough Barabbas
Be chosen in their presence?

In how short time, his disciples asked,
Will the temple be downthrown?
Don't be deceived, he said, by prophets.
To know that is God's alone.

When the Holy City came in sight,
Did he weep for him or them,
The people of the bride-bright city,
God-killing Jerusalem?

SO we'll take up the tune, love,
And play through all its changes,
For an old theme's not worn thin
By days; still the heart opens.

Time's patchwork's not a pattern
Seemingly, but a makeshift,
Erratic fit of instants
Of marring and of mending.

Yet moments (early and late),
Nights (and not only the first,
Side by side under the quilt)
We felt had swallowed all time

Sometimes seem still to have done –
Others might never have been.

HOW many burned, Lord,
how many shot and burned, gassed and burned?
How many buried by bulldozer,
unearthed by hand to be counted?

Lord, if these are your children
help them.
They went in at the gate of hell.
Lord, if these are your children
help me.
I feel those fingers clutch me by my ribs.

Does it take any more
to know the worst,
to have done it and lived
or to die?

THE birds in the bushes have thrown it all over for love
The farmer's out potting rooks in the trees
Evening's gone to smoke
And I've been a year long work-shy

The grass is just harmonicas
And the curlews xylophones
Look to the lilies of the field
And I've spent a short life work-shy

Michael's going overseas for summer
Dave's in Leeds and sometimes writes
I went down to the park in my lunch hour
And looked at the birds in the rain working over the
        river

PLUMS, pears and apples,
sing the folk in the chapels,
while the Quakers
smile: Thou light of the Maker's.

The least
shall feast,
chant the monks of the East.
Beware the Beast.

Won't you come home?
asks the great church of Rome.
Come home to me,
says the dear C of E.

No longer sin's captive,
cry the Baptists.
Be perfect as God is,
hymn the Methodists.

Where's an end to your searches?
enquire all the churches.
And who does live and not transgress?
cries a voice in the wilderness.

SIGNIFICANT pattern in the past of this life
even though a pattern of mistakes
for mistakes were our purpose
and our purpose something other.

*   *   *   *

What can I call true
if not that you are my friend
and I write this down?

*   *   *   *

This is where we live
when no more knowledge
can save us.

No only living
experience can teach us
further to live.

This is what we learn from
the holy books
and our own lives.

≈

FROM a Friday to a Friday man was made,
                    Unmade,
                    Remade.
The cross rose where the fruit's pip fell in the shade.

≈

THE fast fixed star's a star;
the fast star passing
and the faster ones, red and green,
are a plane, and a closer plane.

The further star's so far
and fast away
I'm amazed you can see it
although it's vast.

Where are you? Where are you?
We swim through the night
and find no rest
because you are not here.

Swim through the night, signalling,
keeping our distance.
I'm here, I'm here,
bravely swimming in this tiny

thin air.

THE IMPROVISED VERSION

A. A.

BELL ringing at the brim of sunrise
a screen of wings

> shaking, shoaling
uttermost, express, expansive
shooting the blue

> fish, or
adjectival horn
choiring names invisible in the fire

ALIENS

THERE'S a place far away
where the sun shines hard
and the days are as long as our weeks.
It's very, very hot – hot enough to melt metal.

On this planet there were two people, Adam and Eve,
and they had two sons, Cain and Abel.
Adam and Eve were quite old and the sons young.

Abel was bright and strong.
He shone in the sun.
Radiace fell all about him.
Cain was pretty much like us, like me or you.

But Abel was boastful. He boasted about his powers.
He could fly and he could kill.
When he flew he appeared like a shining red flame.
When he flew down low he set fire to the ground.

Cain made himself some wings and tried to learn to
      fly.
On the first day he couldn't fly at all,
nor on the second day,
but on the third day he managed a short distance
and on the fourth day he could fly as far and as fast
      as a bird.

He flew round and round about his brother's head,
laughing and making fun, till his brother got so
      angry
he shot him, destroying his wings.

Cain fell into the sun, and when he came out
the sun had burned all his old limbs
and stripped away everything
so he came out a new and superb monster.

The two brothers parted and wandered over the
      universe,
joining up sometimes to fight a strong enemy.

ALPHABEATLES

A IS for the Amps
that couldn't compete
with the shrieking hordes
that drowned out the beat.

B's for the Beauty
that no-one foresaw
could come from four scruffs
from a northern shore.

C's for the Cavern
where Brian Epstein

found the local stars
were starting to shine.

D is for the Drum-
kit that Ringo hit
like your funny-bone
with his dry Scouse wit.

E is for Ears that
were covered in hair
yet of great music
wrote more than their share.

F is for a Fame
"greater than Jesus":
a statement that gave
the God-squad seizures.

G is for George whose
shy ways struck a chord
with ladies who cried
out for their sweet lord.

H is for Hamburg,
a grim German port,
where marks weren't many
and the gigs weren't short.

I's for Imagine
that some mixed-up kid
would gun down John Lennon.
None of us did.

J's for the Joint
Bob Dylan got going.
Suck on this wind
where the answer's blowing.

K's the Kaleidoscope
eyes of the girls,
the Cynths and Jackies
and Chrissies and Shirls.

L is for the Love
that is all you need.
For a moment it seemed
the world agreed.

M's the Mersey,
that great shining current
they all four had
as a common parent.

N is for the *Night*
that was *A Hard Day's*,
lasting monument
to a passing craze.

And O's for Oh boy!
Have you heard the news?
Paul must be dead
'cause he's not wearing shoes.

P's for Producer,
the great George Martin,
who opened the door
and let some art in.

Q's for Queen Liz
who awarded them gongs
for invading the States
with groovy songs.

R's for *Revolver*,
a radical disc

you could live without,
but why take the risk?

And S for Shirelles,
young, gifted and black.
Liverpool, Africa,
New World and back.

T's for Ties skinny,
toes pointy and tab-
collared shirts you had
to wear to be fab.

U's for the Unity
coming apart
as the decade wore out
and broke its heart.

V's for the Vast
sums of money they made
proving juvenile style
a worldwide trade.

W's the Wirral,
those church-hall gigs,
birds in vans, local fans,
cheap scent and cigs.

X the ingredient
ninety per cent
of rival bands
couldn't seem to invent.

Y is for Yellow,
their submarine's hue,
which means that this poem
is nearly through

but for Z, the Zebra
crossing they strode
out of our lives on
across Abbey Road.

ALTO

WHERE the clarinet had
snaked and floated kite-like
above the cakewalking
march home from the graveyard,
little brother Parker
flew his fighter-agile
alto for a Night in
Tunisia, Scrapple from
the Apple, Parker's Mood.

The shadow of his wings
has crossed the fretted brow
of every blower since
and sent some down in flames
and dared some to come higher.
I hear him as I warm
and wet the mouthpiece, cry
out in the wilderness,
a reed shaken by the wind.

ARMSTRONG

SON of the herald's brazen tongue,
once proclaimer of pomp
and slaughter's signature,
a small boy came

from hunger to play on the horn
    of plenty a summer's
    brilliant blare, to shout out
        pangs of secret

love from the rooftops and whisper
    his bold acclamations;
    to make of the terror-
        striking trumpet

the voice of hosts it never deigned
    to lead – the dispossessed.
    Garnered lead of their tears
        his cornet turned

to jocund, untouchable gold,
    to fire-pearls that Louis
    of Storyville scattered
        on the blue earth;

His namesake a lifespan later
    set foot on virgin dust,
    but Satchmo taught us to
        walk in the sun.

BEBOP & BLUEGRASS

BEBOP was sitting with his hook thrown in
    to the River Mercurius,
    fishing for his father's gold ring.

Bluegrass came down to the opposite bank,
    leading his horses to water.
    Over the current his voice rang:

"Hey bro, how's fishing?" From Bebop no word
    of reply, so up with a stone
    comes Bluegrass to make him attend.

Intent on the bob of his float, Bebop
    took note of nothing, suddenly,
    else in that silver-framed moment.

But under the stone that was meant to toss
    to splash in the brook, look, the ring
    winking like the sun at daybreak.

Meanwhile Bebop's float had swerved and vanished
    and the big back broke the water
    of a birdfish long as your arm,

when gold in the fingers of Bluegrass flashed.
    Bebop said "Ho!", dropping his rod,
    and the birdfish sped off upstream.

Bluegrass, hearing the line whizz, whining off
    the reel, glanced up as the rod, dragged
    down, disappeared underwater;

saw a yardlong birdfish leap with it clamped
    and snap it clean in two between
    chain-cutter jaws. Open-mouthed he

stared – forgetful he fumbled the ring which,
    falling, caught the fish's gold eye,
    who spat out the hook and took it.

Bluegrass instantly snatched him by the tail
    and him and Bebop, rapidly
    wading over, heaved him high till

the ring dropped from his lips into Bebop's
    hand. He got his father's gold band
    and Bluegrass barbecued birdfish.

Then they both got down beneath the blue moon
    to the didgeridoos and spoons
    and the banjos and valve trombones.

BLUES HIT

WHINE of the twined steel
the glass gadget glides on,
dodging along and back
to the fingernail's pluck,
the tapping and thump of a bootsole and heel,

and the thumbtack-studded rubbed-out felt
on the hammers of a split-backed,
ivory-cracked and ebony-(black-paint)-
worn-away upright
bonging and plinking the big rigid strings

while the wheezing and wail
of a breath-rattled sliver of metal
in the toylike tinplate instrument 's
humming and moaning in sidesucked air,
cupped in one hand while the other hand's clapping
    the end,

and the crash, bump, rattle of the three-piece kit,
kickdrum and traps and ride
keep time, a kind of time
with the belligerent bullfiddle's shoving:
Oohee babe, I need your kind of, kind of loving.

THE BRIDGE
Sonny Rollins

HIS head clears the clouds
of an atmosphere of themes
that hums about him.
Tall lips compel a rubbery
or smoky note out, rebounding
on the surroundings' network of tones.
A colossal stroll's deliberately
taken in difficult air in order
to disclose a new opening.

CHARLES & ERIC

> *Just reach me that skellingtune.*

Would you be hormonious? Don't bowdlerise the
blues.

> *Bowdada? Bowdada? I ain't skeered.*

Bravo, mon mesmeriste, triste muezzin!

> *Scalliwag. Wagtail. Wag and tale man,
> teller. I'll tell how, and how.*

Lurch up here beside me till I buzz your bones out.

> *Oh no you don't.*

Do. I do.

> *Old stout one. I ain't skeered.*

Blood buddy.

> *Aha. A havoc I'll wreak on a rag and bone
> scale.*

Blow, young vagabond!

> *And valuable, remember? Ember? Voluble –
> a member? Pandemonium.*

O rum, O bad and rum, O bird, abandoned boy, my
bester.

Jester. I'll veer, scutter.
Utter, nutter – go!
> *No. Wonder. I'll wander awhile. Gambol and
> squander not your melody, longbreathed
> fellow. I am. Bop. And will be.*

Walk With Man, say? Or Human Marvel?
> *Yes, and Edgy Alien Poet.*

But how'd you lead or board a bear – beard him in a
lair?
> *Underground, daddy, if you dare, you way-
> ward aristo, boss, profuse crater.*

Dare me not, thou duodecaphonic dandy, Dolphy.
> *O mangle, mingle it –*

I'll drive, I'll dizzy you, dazzle and, in a brief word,
deliver.
> *Unmentionable, major man, Mingus –*

Pattercake.
> *Pardon?*

Pattercake.
> *What but? Love but. What what? Otherwise –*

Patriarch… Paraclete…
> *What love?*

Wise love.

CULTURE

I HAVE always heard in your voices the arts of peace
and sounds of day, as of a man who has walked alone
on the mountain with the voice of God around him
in the greenness and the stillness and the breath of
    not a cloud;
one who, taking courage from it, expressed to
    brothers and sisters
how good and how pleasant it is, amid the thick of
    want,

in destitution cutting the rind from the heart like a
       ratchet,
to build among one or two of like mind,
families, neighbours and neighbourhoods,
with a trusting hand, upright in your doings,
the house of civilisation and truth of social living,
under the sun and the sky that shines equally,
under the rain that falls equally, gently
and generously, evoking many reflections,
as a person might have towards the end of day
who has done faithfully and through tribulation,
rebuke and soreness of heart, the right thing.

DOUBLE BASS

MINE is the voice more profound and gentle
       when the horns sob,
more stern while the saxophones celebrate.

Among the machines of music I am
       Ulysses' bow,
that blisters fingers and renders hands raw.

Who masters me is quiet about it.
       I am the wise
and encouraging one, the counsellor.

Is my large brown body feminine?
       Then hold me close
and dance, and be my partner for life.

In cries and whims we'll partner them, for here
       it's not begun,
to tell the truth, till the fat lady's sung.

THE ENTERTAINERS

I
Bareback

THE waist-high net-clad thighs
and clenched and seam-drawn rump
that swoop before your eyes,
the tasselled basque and deep
décolletage that keep
me barely in, and shown
shaved oxter, arms upthrown,
call for applause when, jump
and somersault complete,
I land on slender feet.
These, as Eros fancies,
should surmount sleek ponies' dances.
And yet the truth, although you see no horn,
is that I am the Virgin tames the Unicorn.

II
Conjuror

NONE but me has seen the jack
of diamonds' other profile
yet, nor the queen of spades' smile.

This is a box with no back
and no front, this is a hoop
with no middle. My hand goes
in with a twist – *Allez oop!*
and comes out with a white rose.

237

Watch more closely as I close
my fingers, fill your clumsy
heads with uneasy wonder.
A bunch of flames becomes the
ace of roses, two of clubs
flies up as a pair of doves.
Which cloth was your watch under?

I spell the very letters
out of your name. You too turn
to flowers, to the flutters
of nothing, thin air. Discern
me as I am – the seamless
illusion sent of the stern
and patterless host who shall
entertain us last of all,
our master of emptiness.

III
Harlequin

GOD'S blood, how I'm descended
from king of the wild hunt once
to this – pratfalls and fool-traps,
the captivating favours
of a meringue-faced sweetheart,
Columbine. An untrodden
world I bestrode, with the boar,
bear and wolf for companions,
who now have a yard of dust
wherein to assert my wiles.
Who are served worse than former
demons, your humble servants?
Still this leather visor hints,
mine are eyes that none might meet.

IV
Pierrot

NOT Solomon in all his folly
nor King David when he mooned and swanned
about the palace swollen up with lust
for the streaming limbs of Bathsheba
was arrayed nor played like pale-faced me,
pauper knight of the painted tear-drop.

You laugh to see me pricked, tripped, trapped,
        kicked
as cruelly as you quashed your own
upstart, milk-hearted adolescence.
But when you're next caught at her pleasure,
pining and stung, remember me now
that I bow and lip my clarinet
to stop your malice with music.
My lament will be your comfort then.

V
Stiltwalkers

WALKING Babels, no-kneed, flapping,
we came out of Africa gods,
and still our long legs strike more dread
than hilarity when we pass,
being the spirits who, striding
by indifferent, testify
less to divinity's stature,
than its irreducible oddness.

While acrobats and jugglers prompt
you to applaud your inborn,
unperfected faculties, we,

who are as skilled, provoke an old
and deviant longing, and fear,
to be of a more monstrous build.

VI
Tragedian

HOLDING a grey round stone above you
you enter barefoot in the single garment
that huddled beneath Gethsemane's trees.

As you sail out on the unmoved stage
the gown floods to your knees in the scented draught
till you tip and catch light at the world's lip.

We feel your going run and gather
like mercury in the scooped pumice basin,
the drop's quick cold between our shoulderblades.

In the perfection of your disgrace
no flotsam's drifted back to us to clatter
on shingle or leap end-up in the surf.

Only your stone still hovers where you
and your hubris embraced, becoming clear
as salt dissolved in the ocean of justice.

VII
High Wire

A SPANGLED crucifix,
I inch across the tautened cavern
pitched in the pit of your stomach.

Did you see the canvas
waver from the wind you'd forgotten
still blows outside, and bulge slightly?

It's your breath withheld and
narrowed eyebeams fixed that support me:
I'd tumble like down if you sighed.

My feet curl and dimple
around the rope, and the tense drums hush.
I feel forward on your raised hopes.

VIII

Sydney Stanley
"Syd Stan & His Talking Man"

HE'S as unpresentable as only
the upper-crust can be, unmannerly,
vain and philistine with the best of them,
and irrepressible, my wooden id,
who'll swivel his head and flutter and bat
his lids to a stream of innuendo,
who'll chortle and clack his pendulous lip
and roll off my knee to his no-brow wit.

Most reprehensible of low-life lords,
his vowels are like his humour, ripe as an
overhung bird. Clingingly dependent,
I would not support him for a moment
longer, were he not these children's hero.
Now come out of there and explain yourself.

IX
Juggler

THIS seems autonomous symmetry
and not my doing.
I stand and let it spring from me
as the first cause,
rise, return and fly, while I,
transported,
follow the respiration of the spheres.

It's Brahma who swings the clubs, Vishnu
keeping them spinning
and painting the space with their speed,
till by Shiva's
hand, a fine fling done, they're drawn
down and ceased,
like the life where you look for such order.

X
Hermes

ME you won't see among my acolytes
though all that's illumined by inwit or
        nimble or tricky is mine.

But where's the youth who took your cash before
at the booth? Is that him, by Jumbo's flank
        backstage, slender and handsome,

hair in ringlets under his rakish hat,
innocent looking as a forged banknote?
        He's not to be seen by

night's end, who ducks gusts of clapping, nods, jokes
with the flying lady. His feet seem light
    as, perhaps, were his fingers.

If he charmed, or if he deceived, by me
he'll claim his right, but the thief and the fraud
    find the pitfall finally.

Down this road I rule, my star speeds the fair
dealer only, and favours the rover
    who traces truth through its dust.

On them I cast my mingled ray and shade.
For them the traveller's joy winds the wayside,
    a friendly child brings water.

FOR MUSIC

THERE must be a poem
    whose surface is nervous,
      sensible as skin,
whose power is to roll the stars in
    and whose heart is the heart
      to express glory.

GIG

IT was Thursday night at the Crate and Poker,
you know – the grim one behind the station –
Futile Park. We were called the Bram Stoker
Sextet. Frank was doing his PhD
then on the Gothic imagination.
The music wasn't alive, exactly,

but at least it was undead. Beaky Bob
Bishop on bass; that's right, Bob with the bad
hanggliding habit. Did a good job
on both legs a bit later. Venomous
Vincent, London's ugliest drummer – had
a new girlfriend each week. Anonymous

Andrew on piano, the silent type,
threw up all over the keyboard one night
after Frank had got out the water-pipe
in the Transit. And Mark the Millionaire,
who had that hit with Cheesecake Satellite,
he was on guitar and trousers and hair.

Me on trumpet and chicken vindaloos.
Frank on alto, illicit cigarettes
and bizarre thoughts on the roots of the blues
and their relation to Mary Shelley.
Did some Monk tunes, even one of Ornette's;
had a few gargles, gave it some welly.

When we took it on, the place was a crypt.
By the time we left we'd pulled a few punters.
We were doing alright till Andrew slipped
up in his break in "I Can't Get Started".
He was the last of the moaning grunters,
touchy kid, dead serious, introverted.

Finishes his solo, then walks offstage
to brain the guvnor with the piano stool,
screaming something about a living wage.
Vincent has to hold the guvnor's missus
back from smacking the poor boy with a pool
cue. This is the cultural life one misses.

For the grand finale, old Frank blows up,
ranting about opium and *Liebestod*.
The curtain comes down when Old Bill shows up
and nicks the band for disturbing the peace.
So much for jazz. Frank, I believe, found God.
I got a gig in the pit-band for *Grease*.

HORN

EXTENDS itself / up
beat / down

beat buoyant on elastic pinions

Tenor
the land can only just
make itself in time
to be flown over

A swift full hand
drawing
everything moving

THE IMPROVISED VERSION

SHE was working in a deli or bar at the time I forget
Nursing the soft white belly anyway
He wasn't working at all then anywhere as in any-
where and everywhere
That's she and him which makes it a love story
Which makes it a love story
Meanwhile international crises came and went

245

Somewhere there was a meltdown and a sub went
    down
Assassinations caught them with their pants down
With their parts down one another's throats
Somebody found out about not being born bulletproof
And the guy on the roof wasn't putting up an aerial
Did they give a funny you should ask
They just had time to get some dubious turkey breast
Courtesy of the cold meats counter past its sellby
Into a french stick trying to go straight
When the spasms came back and bang they were
    back on their backs
That's the point of a love story
They gave it their best shot
It was mind over matter they didn't matter and they
    didn't mind
Someone gave a speech somewhere the hall was full
    of mumbling voices
Afterwards somebody asked someone what they
    would do if somebody did something
Music counted the only one who spoke the same
    language
Suddenly he got a job
They had him taking casualties back home to their
    wives and children
Or back to their children and husbands if they really
    were unlucky
And explaining could they please be injured some
    other time
Or they were entitled to reapply with the same
    injury if symptoms persisted
Between the hours of 12 and 12 midnight Mondays
    Thursdays and Fridays
It was depressing work to say the least
They were hoping one day to afford a house a carpet
    a few luxuries

After nine months he was eligible for promotion to
the mortuary
He didn't last a fortnight there were plenty more
where he came from
Where he came from people were falling over them-
selves for that kind of work
As far as he could tell people were falling over
themselves anyway
Just for the fun of it just for a hobby
He took it up she couldn't see the attraction
She tried to tell him there was no future in it
He tried to tell her there was a tradition to maintain
People have always done it that's the point of love
They had their little differences when they had the
time
She was still working in the bar or deli I forget at
the time
Spoonfeeding the joker's busy jaw anyway one way
or the other
They told her it was the service industry she was in
like the church
It was bound to be there for ever
Fashions may come and fashions may go they said
But some things don't change and your wages are
one of them
They were hoping to afford a wardrobe a teatowel a
few luxuries
At which point he entered one of his extended
resting periods
Like scattered rain merging into continual showers
He'd been between jobs since he was filling nappies
He couldn't see how he could have been the point of
a love story
He was willing to take it on trust I mean
If you insist I'll take your word for it

A JAZZ LULLABY

BABY'S sleeping soundly
so rattle those traps but softly
with your brushes, Mr Roach,
and let the sizzle cymbal
sing, but quietly
like a distant blackbird's whistle.

Because Baby's sleeping deeply
and dreaming of the lake
breathe gently, Monsieur Bechet,
breathe gently on the reed
the way you do, the way you know.
No need to let rip, let the clarinet ripple tonight.

My Baby's sleep is peaceful,
brush your bow against the strings
and rock the cradle,
Señor Mingus, if you please,
and be willing as you're able
to rock the cradle by your bass.

Baby's fast asleep,
just touch the keys,
just pet the frets
and keep your hat on, Mr Christian,
and thank you, Duke,
for being so Ellington.

And thank you all for your endeavours.
Now my Baby's sighing soft and steady
rhythm to the solo of her dreams.

JIMMIE RODGERS

TB took him off the railroad
And with a voice that was ferrous
And frail as the light striking bowed
And unending telegraph wires
And as straightforward as their code
He fell on his feet on the way
To singing stardom. High-fliers,
Hillbillies, hoboes heard him say:

"It's death in my chest throws my voice
Out on the air like a night bird
And death on his knees shaking dice
In a box-car with life I heard
As he threw out five and a deuce
Saying that roll won him my soul.
And the whistle wailed a blue third
Like a dog at the moon's dry bowl.

"When the little red rooster droops
His crest, it's jelly roll to blame,
Cause my heart jumps right through their hoops
And if it's another man's name
She wears, you rounders mind your coops
And I'll cock-a-doodle on mine.
The sun can't show his face for shame
When I get up to crow and shine.

"We've got no cause to fuss and fight
In the broadest land that God carved.
You go straight on and I'll turn right:
Fare-thee-well is a trouble halved.

And when you spot me in the light
At the dark end of wicked Beale
I'm two-thirds drunk and still half-starved,
So drop a dime on me, big wheel.

"The porch of my Texan mansion
Is long as a station platform,
Wide enough to hold a dance on,
Swept clean like a college girls' dorm,
And I sit with shades advancing
Looking out from my brakeman's cap
At the end of an evening storm
With my wife and guitar on my lap.

"Don't haul me with six white horses
To lay me down under the yews.
Up on the hill like old Moses
I'll settle and render my dues.
The valleys and watercourses,
Groves and vineyards – there it all lies.
Though I die in harness, my eyes
Saw the Blue Yodeller's Paradise.

"Another record, another
Buck. Set me up a folding cot.
With luck I'll save you the bother
Of doctor and priest. All I've got
To do, like a good wee cougher,
Is close my lids and rock and sing
Myself to sleep." Another shot
Of rye. Fade out the country king.

He left his epitaph written
Around scattered slabs of shellac,
Perishable as his smitten
Flesh, solid as his worth, bright-black

As his humour, his wit and grin.
Two thumbs raised in one photograph,
He vanished like smoke from the stack,
Short-lived, with a last crying laugh.

KIT

I AM a brawling family
        and my name is legion.
I am a crowd of uncles, aunts
and cousins all speaking at once.
        The cymbals look daggers,
        snare tears its hair, beats its
breast, the bass drum bangs the table.

We are in perfect agreement,
        it's just that there's nothing
we like like a good argument.
No-one can say anything but
        someone must answer back.
        But don't dare gainsay us
cause we stick together. Listen –
this furor's chaos's harmony.

LOL COXHILL

EXTRUDED citric arrangements of tones
cantilevered over against the overtones…
Something stirred on the heap of memory.

Esemplastic corrosive displacements of tones
skirting themselves with overtones…
Cockcrow on the mound of memory.

Filibustering epicacophony of tones
sardonically figured with baroque undertones...
Glint of metal on the pile of memory.

An old-fashioned tune's dismantled tones
assemble like ghosts in the overtones...
Spike of grass on the brow of memory.

Splay of clownish inarticulate tones,
poignant buffoon with harlequin undertones...
This was mine on the ash-tip of memory.

Elliptical doubled-edged tones...
Underdog truth comes over
like the sun on the nightly rise of memory.

MONK'S SPHERE

HERE'S a cone.
The piano keys go up it one by one
In a spiral like Mount Purgatory,
The white ones Dante and the black ones Virgil.

Becomes a cube:
It's hard to get a grand piano
In at all, but if anyone can...
These tunes would sing on a Model T upright.

And then a shape with thirty-two faces,
Thirty-two bars of angular elegance.
Is it inside or outside?
Produce your evidence.

Before Monk died
Was there such a word as "torsus"
To name a form like a multi-dimensional pretzel
Or a derailed halo?

This little finger knew Parker
And this little finger stayed at home
And these two thumbs rode with Charlie Christian
And I wish Bud Powell was alive.

Beard of a scholar,
Beard of an Abyssinian prince;
Over invisible smiles and an airman's shades
An astrakhan cap like a furry halo.

THE NTH MEMBER

SILENCE, the fifth member
of every quartet, the fourth
of every trio –

PIANO

STILL your crying,
brass, your thunder
and lightning, drums
and let me speak.

I have reasons
for what you shriek,
wail and clatter,
for what you sing.

My words are each
full sentences
condensed and a
phrase whole pages.

What I proclaim
I have in black
and white. "Even
strength" is my name

and my heart like
yours is strings and
hammers, which with
these keys opens.

'RAMBLING', BY THE
ORNETTE COLEMAN QUARTET

LIKE a cloud that blows unravelling
and heavy loaded, rumbling
many days across the changing blues
of the changing skies of America
with spokes of lightning
travelling west to east, having gathered
in the sunset country,
been fathered on the Pacific,

Unseen, like a sidewinder tracing its oblique track
in the dirt that a dust-devil obliterates
or a tumbleweed bouncing
and like Lemon Jefferson blind drunk
picking his way home over railroad ties
and Blind Lemon stone cold sober
picking out frail and stubborn, stumbling dances
and singing See That My Grave Is Kept Clean,

Like a tune that might form in the mind
of a man who hears that rain rush
and wash Blind Lemon's grave
and the cement of Fort Worth sidewalks
and hears the forked lightning before he sees the
  thunder,
feels the black breath of the storm from the
  cemetery gate,
the train rush and the cloud push on to deliver more
  rain,
in the mind of a steady rolling man given to
  rambling.

SAXOPHONE PLOUGH

DIP the bell in ground
suck the ground notes in
soil and stones and trash

blows out roots — blows out
seeds and stalks — fat leaves
eyelash tender leaves

Dig the bell in hard
deep in the stone foot
of a bare white cross

knuckles a flicker
across the metal
mother of pearl stops

Stark hymns — damnation
plain and quick to save
foot stamps on floorboards

hand claps and palm raised
to rafters — head bowed
midnight — moving star

Undertone snigger
& sweat in the eyes
haunting the crossroads

the pickaxe handle
the piano wire
thirty-eight — twelve-bore

Cry of cracked and now
appearing— tough—strained
voice to paint weathered

off — to elastic
movements — aim to please
… announcements half torn

Twelve bar piano
dews sliding down cars'
bodywork rocking

till morning subdues
coming up — the still
reeling — slowly— grey

Mist in the bottoms
round under the fat
leafy thickets — shut

black tender eyelids
still rocking till the
light — still grooving till

SON HOUSE

A BANGING sheet of zinc,
folding, shearing, taking off,
hurricane origami.

The old cat's rigor,
eyes clear and wide, like the mouth
baring her undulled canines,
the end of sickness outfaced like a night intruder.

Oblique rain beats the transmitted palms and
        porches
and the foolhardier venturers-out.
Finned cars turned on their long American sides or
        roofs;
then the aerial overview and the voice-over,
glinting miles of drowned farmland,
bridges going nowhere in the middle of lakes.

Why is this all-steel National guitar
with engraved tracery like the delicate
filaments and blooms of mud
in the slow-receding floodwaters
floating? And why do four blue fingers
like a TV hand caught reflected
in picture-glass, play Dry Spell Blues?
Four blue fingers and a short fast spell
of brass pipe.

Everything that dies goes under the cherry tree,
loser pigeons, beloved cats,
and coming up to Easter
it flowers.

SWING
for Michael Smith and Prince Far-I

WITH a giant
      shine-toothy grin
the drummer
      dives into his splash,
a frantic swimmer he
      who butterflies away from
the whirlpool of Titanic horns he still goes into
      spinning and marking time.
Swing, brother.

      Dropped from the eyes of tenors
gently rocking, blowing their dots,
      the clarinet's
sweetheart-elegant,
      black, long, tear-
like body cried
      for strange fruit by name.

Swing
      turned into livity
spirits robbed with gravity
      by the neck
until the wind that rocked them
      gently blew rock steady
enough to bring the house down.

TENOR

      ADOLPHE Saxe saw
      the world, that it was good,
      but thought it lacked somewhat

a brass serpent
with the voice of a cow in heat
    if it so pleased,
    the musical
accomplishment of cats
    at midnight, dogs
in the moonlight, howler
monkeys in tops of trees.
This metal vocal chord,
    extravagant
external larynx and mono-
    morphous menagerie
        attached itself
    to a man called Coltrane
    and, making his humble
    lungs its hard-pressed servant,
        it spoke to God.
        It spoke and what
    it said was loud with love.

THELONIOUS

MISTERIOSO was in his little rootie-tootie
round about midnight, driving slow
for the brake's sake, when he took one
of those brilliant corners and ran into the
evidence. *Trinkle-tinkle* – the tune of falling
headlight glass, played twice.

He got out and checked the street – he wasn't
being followed – then went straight, no chaser,
to the nearest phone.

"Ruby, my dear," he said, "tell Oska T. I've
found the blue monk, down on Panonica, just off
Minor. And tell him, well, you needn't bother
with the four in one. He ain't rhythm-a-ning."

He listened to her jackie-ing for a while, then interrupted the epistrophy. "Yeah, yeah, honey, don't worry. We'll see Bemsha swing for this. Now listen, you ugly beauty, meet me as soon as you can. Yes, I mean you." And he gave her the name of a nearby club.

"That's right. You want me to spell it? Ba-lue Bolivar Ba-lues-are. OK? Bye-ya."

He'd just slid into a corner booth and downed a couple of green chimneys, when in walked Bud.

"Hey, ya stuffy turkey," sneered the gunsel, "Guess ya heard about Monk's mood?"

M. looked up. "Listen, punk, just ask me now, if you want a case of boo-boo's birthday."

"Okay, okay – no need to raise four."

[*Answer: 32*]

TROMBONE

I CAN'T keep the chuckle out of my tone;
into my most mournful soliloquy,
among the downturned notes and sliding sighs,
the echo of laughter's prone to enter.

Let others have tongues of fire. Mine's human
and given to the telling of stories,
where always, as I say, however lu-
gubrious, a bubble of wit will break.

How could one be iconic with this long
implement to hand? Still the painters of
the Middle Ages' Paradise suggest
angels are not averse to playing it.

VARIOUS ARTISTS

THEIR garb was rather foppish
Their harmonies barber-shop-ish
The song they sang was pop-ish
And after a while I wished they'd stop

The clothes they wore were punky
They sang a song about a junkie
Their rhythms were wild and clunky
And I didn't really mind if they didn't go on

Their expressions were intent and serious
They played many notes and various
But their credentials were spurious
And shortly made me weary

Their suits were dark and formal
They played under the auspices of the Duke of
        Cornwall
Such stiffness isn't normal
It was hard to warm to them

A band of pavement gypsies
With an insidious kick like rum and Pepsi
And a style of choreography that bordered on
        epilepsy
Made a sound that gripped and grips me

UILLEAN PIPE MUSIC

IS the wind that plays through
the bent grass, the blown reed,
through the hollow trailing legs

of a wading bird
and fire tracing the known shape
of a hilly mountain,
a stream of whittling water.

The grass battered to fire
by the wastrel wind,
the water like blown glass
and the true dark note of the black soil
that drowns all it buries,
onward, ominous hum
in the entrails of the universe,
tottering song
and the nasal noise the stars actually make
sounding like wide cold silence.

Bent towards the fire
singing and playing onward
towards the embers,
everything dying
and getting up
and dying again
along the thin wind playing.

PRAISES

PART I

1. OF EZRA POUND

WHO wrought to overturn the world's
disorder, overturned himself,
wounded and was wounded;
fought with bitterness the death
injected in the tongue,
whose tongue became poisonous;

Whose acrid, jittery early works
are not inaccurate darts,
whose Jesus was the knotter of a scourge;
who was a Provençal Confucian from Idaho,
a Jew-baiting Jeremiah
and Jonah watching tendrils from his booth of wire;

Who outlived "an old man's frenzy"
and ended like his Paradiso,
stone-like – that is, glinting and unyielding,
clear-cut, elevated, wordless;
who saw the crystal sea
and Hell in the minds of men.

2. OF THE BLACKBIRD'S NIGHT-MUSIC

A GREY-RINGED pink-rimmed eye
says you've been a lullaby
too often, starting towards the equinox
in the third hour
your song like the rain that sweetens midnight.

Premature muezzin,
summoning from an aerial
or gutter minaret,

in darker blue than cobalt glaze,
a mate, to seize the day and hatch out summer;

unparalleled Parker among birds,
the urban avians' matchless inventor,
invert and anagram those
scintillating almost-melodies,
proffer your glinting jets,

the profligate makings of human music,
which we who grow in sorrow,
if not haltingly, then slowly raise:
a tuneful oak, deciduous, symphonic,
where you and she may nest.

3. OF THE DAFFODILS

THAT start from the cool bark-like glaze
of your broad-shouldered vase,
brilliant, silent, giving
as the sun, so densely gathered
that they picture.

A modest spray of mimosa,
soon-withered, sets them off,
the fringed leaves folded flat
like palms, the gold dots dustier
and heavier.

Translucent yellow hilarity
without malice, fanfare
without pomp, and sexual
openness entire and guileless –
immaculate:

how, though one by slender one
from the sodden humus
you declare your solar
loyalty, the singly stated
is perfect chorus.

A man the angels sang for praised you:
not even Solomon
in splendour outdid you.
A man the angels worshipped made you
a wise word.

4. OF A PORTRAIT BY PICASSO

OF a normal woman gazing calmly
and amusedly at him who formed her
pairs of hands and eyes and nose. Of the first,
her right's a cactoid clump that overhangs
the chair – several blunt prisms sprouted
one from another – while her left is crouched
and scaled and bossed in ancient monochrome.
Across the bare stone plaza of her head
large elliptical features move and meet
as gravely graceful actors in a piece
masquing the biography of her face.
He seized the upper hand from space and made
imagination emperor; draws our
eyes like needles through the injured era.

5. OF RETICENCE

SCORN of the ignorant, praise of the wise –
        value these,
though one's to forgive and one to treasure.

Idiots are vehement, reticent
     the clever,
like the river, sure, not controversial.

An edified mind moves one embracing
     many ways,
like the river, the stiller the deeper.

6. OF SPRING AGAIN

WHEN green-white flames spurt from the tips
of saplings glimpsed against the lid
of lead-grey sky by parallel
sunlight raking the avenue

and like the dinted glassy boss
of water where a spring wells up
the prunus shows a cool new surge
of leaf with two or three blossoms

floated up on it like bubbles
before the whole froth surfaces
and all the trees in their own way
test the air with genitally

sticky or bulbous or frilly
outgrowths and irretractile risks.

7. OF MOZART

DOTTED in unequal sequence down their stalks,
     disclosing themselves by the fistful
while, coy and corpulent, the raspberry hides,

the armed and taunting bramble
dangles out of reach,
these that, once their faint-bloomed gloss has burst, will
stain mouths purple, perfectly poised
between tart and sweet – blackcurrants, globe by
globe, show how complete's
their inky pregnant likeness
to Wolfgang's crotchets.

8. OF JAPANESE CHERRIES

WHICH by night, when you're climbing the steep
Georgian hill
with one shadow cast by the streetlight leading
morosely
and the other behind you evading your glance,
are black and white that the brain makes pink and
brown.

Most artificial of things in London's nature,
in the gaudiest interior they'd raise a chuckle,
stout smooth branches gleaming like polished
furniture
upholstered with fab ruffs of chiffon blossom.

Such eagerness to please would be merely comic
if their superabundant, fruitless generosity
had not the charm to touch the question poignantly,
whether your own after all less effusive

emotion were worthy of Easter. A light wind rises.
They flutter like a madness of moths around the
lamps.

9. OF MAPS

GOING imaginary thousands of miles
where rivers are as quick to navigate
upstream as down, and mountains and deserts
no bar, in the earthless places peopled
out of yarns with wise and brown-eyed, smiling
hosts in strange headgear, lapped in atmospheres
of poetic fog and brilliance, scented
by phrasings, relieved with hatchings of song,
between Stovall's Plantation and Clarksdale
my nails raise dust in the home of the blues,
hover at Lhasa, the roof of the world
a creased leather skullcap beneath my palm
while, paused by specks in a paper Pacific,
two fingertips drift in serenity.

10. OF WINE

FOR being,
though sometimes like verse
so poor you can't imagine
why you let it on your tongue at all,

at others
an opening book
of sunshine, rhyming soil and
season, the song of labour and time,

till, testing
the light through a glass
raised again to the few, who-
ever are this bottle's company,

approving
the beam's reluctance
to divine it too fully,
its inclination to linger, you

feel, *Lucky*
us, friends, again we're
given to hold the essence
of our grave and hospitable earth.

11. OF MORE WINE

PROVIDED by the Lord for revellers in Galilee,
where none sat askance and sipped, with pious
indulgent smile
or palm across the brim.
They soaked it up in the reeling steps of Noah the
brewer,
our Saviour among them, an enjoyer.

If Socrates could sink the volumes Plato pours for him
and still talk wisely,
could not the Nazarene imbibe the like and do still
what he
did best, namely love God?
The Son of man was not some maudlin boozer,
who called his death "this cup".

There are no icons of tipsy Jesus
and we take our sherry austerely at the altar rail.
Men in white gowns give us pills and medicine.
They tell me that you're coming to another wedding
soon.

12. OF THE FALL

WE make our mistake
concerning learning's
fruit and find by it
the law of freedom,
our right to do wrong.

Should sin then abound
that grace may prevail?
God forbid, said Paul.
It's not our mired way
makes the firm ground firm.

Elohim no more
walk among our trees
in the evening dew.
Our fault comes home to
roost like a vulture

in whose shadow this
beauty arises:
Jesus the joiner
hangs in a bare place,
dies and rejoins us.

13. OF PHONOGRAPHY

TAKE the heavy base of the jumped-up juice
squeezed from a long-gone-underground jungle,
simmer, mix and cool it, mould and brand it
with the fine labyrinthine groove that goes
through darkness to silence, counter-clockwise.

Find an old man banging his meal-ticket
music-box with a dying fall, and kids
shouting to shake their elders' approval
down like peaches, who would be studs and kings.

Make a million of a few moments,
winding notched spirals through our memory;
build monuments of breath from a short-lived
addict emptying his lungs and spirit
into tintinnabulating alloy.

14. OF THE BOOK

WHICH though small is the largest of works,
like the soul, in neither time nor space;
whose beginning and end co-exist,
occult from nature, contiguous
with life, and ours to perceive alone;
never read by the same person twice;

Which is not the thing that bears its name,
the flammable, fragile, speckled sheaf
of leaves, but what arises from them,
sublimated, in presence of mind;
which has neither form, colour, motion,
smell, sound, flavour, duration nor place;

Which modifies the pulse and habit
of the hands that hold and open it.

15. OF THE HORSE CHESTNUT

LEAVES emerging eight
to the bud and more. The leaders
    already spread wide
droop forward along the axis
    of the branch. Above
their smaller reflections open
    back towards the trunk.
Under these staggered pairs, balanced
    and commensurate,
grow lateral ones, yet smaller –
    which foursome, rising
to a level, fills the plane in
    the four directions,
having clustered in its middle,
    stiffly vertical
still, and crinkled and sticky, its
    minute self again
and even once again. These will
    overshade the stage
that cradles them, to be themselves
    outgrown. The light green
involuted tines now spiking
    from the structure's heart
will wave and deepen uppermost:
    The last shall be first.

And all this was built in the bud,
    a single complex,
as the flower will be when it twists
    up from the new growth,
splashed naive, fresh pink and yellow
    on crowded faces.
Retracing the themes to the tree,

see how its spiralled,
too, closely on itself, in one
    integral outburst,
its branches spun by what numbers?
    The shoots' one and one
and twice two, or the fingered leaves
    fives and sevens – or
their fertile dynamic combined?
    "A dense pyramid-
shaped crown" as the tree-guide calls it,
    the iterated
algorithms harmonised so
    that the sum is one,
the several different symmetries
    of parts deriving
from, yet none directly quoting
    its noble total.
Our counting's only a writing
    words the tree itself
pronounces, the tree's poetry.

16. OF THE SMALL BIRDS

WHO (not which for such as these)
of the handful of species
frequenting the narrow yard,
have most inspired, with their hard
bright chatter, renewed courage,
shouting their sense of outrage
out from the rooftops when some
bullish pigeon, his handsome,
glassy and flexible neck
extended, with a brute peck
drives them from the crusts,
and next a blackbird with thrusts

of his gold beak, as useful
a sword as it is tuneful
as a flute, keeps them from lunch.
They flutter and puff and hunch
themselves, still proud as pharaohs,
indomitable sparrows.

17. OF THE MORELLO

I

WE planted when we came,
   barely waist high,
     a gift
     that, leaving
  in April, we watch
for the last time completely
swathed in flowers, under a sky
   like summer, and that now
     overspreads us.

   The brown honey-bees
  go fumbling into blossom
after blossom, whose work we shan't see:
the cherries neither so bitter nor black
  as we expected, but clear-fleshed,
     red and yellow, acid.
     The blackbirds got them before us.

   So entirely white, so beautiful
and plentiful is its flowering this spring
it's painful almost to look at, unbearably
   fragile and temporary. Imploring
     every wind that rises to blow

gently on it, letting go, we leave
our wish as a charm upon it, that every
hand that follows on ours may lend itself to tend it.

II

(July. Still here.
Smearing Vaseline
on bark that's rent and cleft,
over holes that ants frequent,
having poked out first with a stick
portly herds of St Anthony's pigs
that delve and cluster where the trunk is split.

The thing we most possess is valueless,
shaped to the sunshine ten careful years
up from the shadowed yard. A curse
on property bought and sold
and praises and blessings
on all that grows and,
growing, teaches
growth, grows at
our be-
hest and
in the end
we belong to.

18. OF ST GEORGE'S WEATHER

HAIL scolding, gusts buffeting the window;
Through the white and dark clouds, baby simple
Sky looks down; then a flurry of damp snow
Dissolving quicker than torn-off blossom.

Our brooding turbulence distilled this charge-
Laden atmosphere, not vice versa:
Suddenly from the North, April inverts
The fallacy that we call pathetic.

A blue-white flash behind your head: heaven's
Photographed a moment of exultance.
Barging aside normality, the boss
Thunder speaks in a second: *Hold it there.*

19. OF THEM WHO HOLD

THE bullet must fly if the hammer falls
but that you pull the trigger is not inevitable,
refusing to give to war the honorific title
    tragedy, whose pain and death are neither,
as the light and the dark paint are neither light nor
                  darkness;
and which awakes our suffering with a sense of
                  purpose
    as a shade evokes illumination.

    Corruptible ends of mortal powers,
hounded by shortness and greedy for extenuation,
are poor parables of design's aesthetic government.
    Those who, on seeing the compositions
that slaughter offers the lens, insist these scenes
                need never
be, and being, have no mitigation, are all our blood-
    stained states can afford in mitigation.

20. OF STEEP

WHERE a stone faces France
in the long tilted meadow that butterflies dodder
above,
whose wild herbs underfoot
scent the sheltered air at rest between the tall woods'
troubled tops.

In the persistent shade
of that hanger the fallow doe and her faun are
checked, stock-still,
with poised hooves and low neck
outstretched to catch the taint of us she suspects,
who stand subdued.

Vanished in the thicket,
we endow them as the deer that Edward Thomas
sensed, who walked
daily among these trees,
when, near death, he invoked the encircling night
they traversed

beyond the slight orbit
of his lamp and the solitary hilltop study above,
calling them last to mind
far from here. Now a stone faces France, in the haze,
where he fell.

21. OF THE WELL-MADE POT

THAN which nothing more precisely
  adumbrates the hand
  in all its shapely
 digital melody,

for here are the pressure of heel
  and guidance of palm,
  pinch of opposed palps
 with the dint of knuckle

that the whirled retentive clay holds,
  turned to stone by flame,
  in fluent sequence,
 till like a hand itself

it winds the light around itself,
  flexing foot, neck and
  shoulder in thin air,
 makes space dance to its tune.

22. OF WHALES

I

BY whose making the Lord above all
adverted prostrate Job of his might,
whose eyes are like the eyes of morning,
who make their path shine; the royal fish
with whose mysterious cranial oil
Europe's crowned heads were annointed and
by whose light her books have been written;

but who, unlike any kings, found peace
in power, until creation's crown
himself required their bodies' riches;
who will yet befriend the bandit, man.

II

Would nature's St Peter's of pleasure
be the great cetacean's clitoris?
Despite their barnacled and flinty-
looking skin, they tenderly grapple
towards an ocean-shaking coupling
with mild caresses. Down in the dim
gelid brine they know every nuzzling,
sidle and rub conducing friendship.
The violence of subpolar weathers
is sport to them, who breach howling seas,
surf the tide-race through wrecking narrows.

III

Humpbacks a hundred feet down, hanging
motionless, intone the latest tune
in their ancient unearthly sequence,
bouncing their profoundest lovers' moans
Puck-like in a girdle round the globe,
pelagic arias resounding
the hydrosphere. What hymns do the din-
riddled continents compare with these?
Titanic heads are hunting, sounding
down the lightless depths the plumed, crusted
ruins of our liner monument.

23. OF LAKELAND

THE pens and abandoned byres collapse
and the drovers' road is smothered in bracken.
The fells, in the shapes that intense, fragmenting
    frost and abrading ice have left them,
    crumble and persist redundantly.

    Apart from the chainsaws' whine,
the shepherd's curt whistle to the dog
that follows the straggling long-faced sheep,
    the language of livelihoods
    in which they were woven fails.

    Miners and weavers,
most of the slaters, wallers,
the charcoal-burners have left
    to be reflected
    as their only task.

    The fanned heaps
of scree and talus
that buttress the cloud-
    sporting crags
    challenge words.

    Write,
they command
the poet,
    our
    truth.

    Some few
ancestral thwaites
may keep their ways,
    and new
    ones rise.

One tenth per cent
of the crowd, if it balks
at vacuous pursuits,
 may take themselves
 another way

and unfamiliar hands
take up the still-warm tools the old
let fall, and vital skills survive
 the monstrous isotopes
 that Sellafield bequeathes,

whose half-lives are only moments
to the broad dome of igneous mountains
where some, by a voice in their breasts, may come
 into possession of the earth
 to lead there their following lives.

24. OF PLUTO

WHOM the Greeks were loth to name,
striking the ground when they did:

not the bright antagonist,
subtle malefic agent,

but the eerie and needful
god underlying the grave

whose throne set in sightless halls
is ringed with water's echoes.

Murmuring, we undergo
the loss of our upward way.

Threads of gold and iron twist
us together, tormented

by weight. Mortal presences
crowd the chambers of the heart.

From which unillumable
pressure, restored to the world

of the cloud and the crocus,
between blind stones we rise up

healing, with unearthed power.

25. OF A GUITAR

WHOSE much-depicted outline still in
wood honours a gourd-built ancestor,
worldwide, unstandard shape: what hundreds
    of songs have you grown today?

Harmonic abacus whose taut strings
lift in wit or plangently those use-
worn words, like "love", a chorus pitches
    to shine again on their plane.

Sudden, florid, sanguine as a queen
of Barbary in Spain, resounding
pine and rosewood, crowned with thorny hands,
    palms and nails, sing from the gut.

Moorish garden paths of nacre grow
round the back and the sound-hole. Well-bred laps
cradled you and with gentle pluckings
    coloured the evening ballads,

till, armed with metal and reinforced,
long African fingers overseas
wrung from you the voice of their absence,
    which elided Europe's scales.

Taking you up in place of the lute
or harp in these intricate islands,
by history like the air that feeds you
    my hands are weighted again.

26. OF A CHOCOLATE CROISSANT

THOU flaky fruit of bakers' fertile skill,
Which hideth in thy heart a dark delight –
In penury I haste to purchase still
Thy golden form that makes the morning bright,
This first black coffee's perfect paramour.

In despite of the envious eyes' purview,
And other tongues, embittered as my lips,
My sweet, do close on thine, renew
Each day for me thy glorious eclipse –
Thy crescent swell my belly evermore!

27. OF E.T.

WHOSE puppet masters, making the head that tapers
    from broad hydroptic eyes to a shrunken mouth,
        the scaly arms and distended midriff,
            made their image of a magical
                creature, nearer to God than our-
                    selves, with reference to the child
                        starved of the strength to cry.

28. OF ROBERT JOHNSON

IN the musty ruck of blankets
would be a little hunger left
to sour your love-nests sooner
        not later.

Satan sent them one at a time
with a note tucked into their drawers
saying, There's ten thousand more
        where she's from.

Mississippi rolls and tumbles
the way that they did over you
and under. Arms bend like roads
        in the moon.

Remember how you whimpered
to be forgiven when Mama
whipped you and Jesus didn't
        love you enough…

The glass neck slams down on the frets
and they twist their mamas' dresses
higher up their legs. You take
        to the wide road.

You knew the missions of lust
paid in dust, bust springs and stones.
The needle comes down in your
        unmarked grave.

Robert child, the bare lightbulb
throws your small shadow on the floor,
but Mr Law's horned gizmo's thrown it
        over time.

29. OF BOB DYLAN

MOON blowing away like a dandelion;
Radio wavers, bounced off Orion with codes
Of its own. The song says there's roads
In this hole, where a hound sounds like iron.

Bowlegged old men carry in the bone
The suffering children from Chi-town to Rome
To Biloxi – pellagra and rickets and lice.
The toll of their hardships got caught in your
        backwoods voice.

Across the fields you point out
The burnt shell of your father's house.

Silence, rain, the road not going nowhere, going
        away,
Blackbird singing on the Red Wing wall.
Two lanes of 61, St Paul to Thunder Bay,
Mercury glints on grass, lightning's eastbound
        scrawl...

30. OF FIRE

MOST picturing, of all things physical,
the spirit, fire draws – like inimical
brother water, mobile mind's reflection –
draws us near as surely as convection
draws the air that body's built on, that leaps
and aspires. As the meek liquid seeps
and trickles, is torn with roars, stilly poured,
but intending perpetually downward,
teaches the greatness of humility;

so this, ascending undeterredly,
with lozenges of brightness, from even
the lowest crown of flame, loosed to heaven,
takes for text the persistence of ardour,
the light of the world as self-surrender.

31. OF THE SHOES

OF the poet, the dauntless brogues,
    that find their own way home.
    At the word of command,
    an encouraging cluck,
they're off like two fine chestnut mares.
Also, sleek as the pair of ducks
    I watched in egoless
    race dart down the canal
    a foot from the water
then take the bridge in a single
synchronised parabolic hop
    to land with arrowy
    grace in twin plumes of spray,
    my footwear takes the kerb
and puddled gutter in its stride.
These, if the pavements were a grey,
    broken stretch of Channel,
    would be stout Thames barges,
    first one then the other
catching the best of a stiff breeze
as they beat up the strait for home.
    You won't see me exchange
    for Trojan-panicking
    Achilles' chariot
my Czechoslovakian shoes.

32. OF A NAME

A name whose few feminine syllables
R unknown to the lexicon and yet
M brace and stand for home, whose bright arch shines
O ver all the dusty plain of mean and
R gumentative words in black and white,
E voking like a scent some elusive
L emental moment of encounter.

33. OF SLEEP

TAKE this waking, restless mind
I cannot keep, without your
interruptive rule, intact.
You dreamed up revolution.
Oligarchic reason falls
to the unheard multitude,
long-rejected. What can be
imagined reigns, if briefly.

I'm further from naming you
now, the nearer I approach.
That you are called blessed I know
and that you are kin to death.
Show me the missing persons,
restore my abandoned home,
receive and teach me the rest.

PART II

34. OF HORSES

THE great bright-harnessed greys
that drew the Whitbread drays
some mornings past the flats,
driven by men in bowler hats.
Their long heads bowing, nod-
ding in time as they trod
up the hill, their broad shoes
struck with a clangour that subdues
the too-present present.
Beat more bold and pleasant
than piston-clattering
is the feathered hooves battering
the tarmac. Neither cowed
nor vaunting, mild and proud:
may death outpace the day
high-stepping horses pass away.

35. OF EMPTINESS

I CAN'T get rid of that last little bit,
I've done all I can but it just won't quit,
Heaving and pulling, pushing and shoving:
I'm still not a hundred per cent nothing.

36. OF COUPLING

DOES Reynard love the vixen,
duck the drake or dog the bitch?
Does tom love the queen to such a heartfelt pitch
or is it uniquely man and woman's fiction?

since love is God
to love our mate

Since the tender sinews twine
into one flesh for the beast
as for us, what boots the pantomime of priest
and ring and veil, of hats, hankies and fizzy wine?

to love our mate
since love is God
casting out fear

We knew our fuel not fine.
That clear flame released
stinging smoke and bitter ash and clinging smutch
in the grate of affection.

by grace increased
casting out fear

All fleshly fires decline,
all flags that flower from the blind instinctual ditch,
bright with their special toxin.

casting out fear
by grace increased
since love is God
to love our mate

37. OF CORNERS

URBAN patches and angles where the congruence
of incongruous architecture, inhumane
blocks with a fine-textured sky, or a statuesque
cumulus cloud with low, degraded outbuildings,

give us a metropolis to participate,
say on a June Sunday swept clear by the south wind.
Whether fern or buddleia inhabit it, or
ivy and geraniums, neglect or private,
conscientious tending make of a few square yards
of suntrap, escaped from the kingdom of the real
estate, an earnest of an inner city built
by virtue of our power to discover it.

38. OF KATHARINE HEPBURN

ENOUGH stars glow –
Jean Harlow,
the sheen running slow-
ly down, unwilling to let her go,

or, carved from light,
young Marlon –
and your Venus or
Adonis is your own election,

who shines closest,
brightest, first.
Mine's the slender, wry
and animated Kate, a gazelle,

who makes foibles
gracious, wit
an intensity,
early likened to a Peter Pan,

more nearly though
Diana,
"chaste and fair", but no
less "laughter-loving" than her sister.

An era falls
as aura,
a trick of the light
or time, bathing the lucky in hope.

That whole tribe was
luminous
and yet they dazzled
(which is her excellence) humanly.

39. OF A SNAIL

THE upper horns are extended
like expressions of pure longing,
optic fingers. The lower are
touching, touching, tasting the way.

They arch, stretch tenderly to all
that drifts or trickles within reach
and as hastily withdraw in
perpetual motion. Only

the shell that follows comes slowly,
drawn cautiously on in the wake
of tranquil curiosity,
climbing a stride's length overnight.

They live more quickly than we do
in enormously detailed worlds.

40. OF THE BREATH OF LIFE

FART, yawn, belch,
hiccup, sneeze and sigh,
cough, laugh and snore:

the wind blows
through and opens, bangs,
rattles the door.

A fiddler
makes by the fireside,
though thin and poor,

a music
that makes with the noise
a weird rapport.

41. OF A CLOWN

YOUR empty face mirrors ours,
white as death's absolute joke;
not as glass and mercury
invent, but the clear portrait
of a stranger we look through.

There's a heart that blushes red
as the Chinese lantern plant's
berry through skeletal lace
of its pod, made visible
by your outfit's glitz and tat.

You fall to lighten our days'
uneasy rising and fail
perfectly to beat the clock.
Every knock strikes a link off
childhood, when time was weightless.

42. OF BEES

WE are warm and many,
many thousand sisters,
virgin geometers.
Our mother-complexed home
we sweated scales of wax
from our bellies to build.

She giants on jelly
and makes us devotees
who hatch her usurper.
Only the males escape
perpetual labour,
the melancholic drones.

We clamber in colour
to the best of perfumes,
most exquisite textures;
by each spring tree that throws
me a thousand parties,
courted, wooed, delighted.

We fan each other, dance
the names of flowers, comb
the pollen from our legs.
The tessellated cells
we brim with our lifelong
journeying, distilled miles.

43. OF THE MAJORITY

WHO now preoccupy the ground,
whose passed passions enlarged the sun

and earth's foundations handsomely
with their gifts of significance;
who furnished the uprights and bars,
enclosures and curves that you here
interpret in their memory;
who bequeathed even their bodies.

The dead still walk in your bearing
and wake their likeness from my sleep
when I dream the sea of deceased
raising its slow waves, shuddering
wind and lapsing hiss. One by one
the frayed crests flow into their graves.

44. OF IRON

I

HEART of our blood, the blood of our world,
we move in invisible weather
the unstill core makes, heavy with it.
The compass needles shake and steady,
the pole like the point of a dancer
turning her slow pirouette, starlight
flowing on the upraised hands and arms.

II

When the Plough is hungry, Brother Axe
provides, and where the forest's fallen
often the slit poppy's sap rusts there
in the sun, and Sister Needle seeks
a vein, while Uncle Shovel's making
sure that Johnny Motor gets his way;
but Baby Gun is the blue-eyed boy.

III

Iron, you have magnetised our will,
since no metal equals our mettle
so nearly, unyielding chancellor
to whom we give, bent to our bidding,
dominion, to cleave wood, water, stone
earth, flesh. Tell me, in my own empire,
am I not the blade and you the hand?

IV

Take this hammer. Its head is heavy
for the loss of John Henry, the man
whose muscle and skill matched the steam-drill.
Beat the steel of the thieving systems
into pruning hooks, for lopping off
unfruitful branches and barren vines.
Feed them to the fire to forge more tools.

V

The atom's innocent and the blade
of the murder lies smooth and smiling,
blameless as a baby, though suckled
on blood. It was late in our childhood
we found the strength to reach down and twist
the apples of ore off the lodestone
branches, who are not fit yet for force.

45. OF THE NEW MOON

UNSUPERSTITIOUS till now
of new moons through glass,
I watch the calendar, avoid the windows.

Were my months all lucky
before, or is that the nail
on the head of misfortune?

The youngest of thirteen sisters,
stage left, light enters,
a girl in a white shift.

If God is just, as Joyce said,
paring his nails,
she's thin enough for a trimming.

A tremor runs through us,
an intake of breath:
"Alas!" or "Darling, I – "?

46. OF SUMMER CONSTELLATIONS

WE go outside to find them
but half the stars are missing
from our map, veiled by high-rise
and violet electric haze.
    By a bike-lamp's shadowed rays
we read both the chart and sky.
I remember as a child
watching torch-beams dissolving
into nowhere, signalling.
    The Swan, the Lyre, the Eagle:
at the few we trace and name
we stare as people ever
stared, and feel, finding fixed stars,
presences identified

and faced at last: their gleaming
Arabic names – Altair and
Vega – their reputations
for luck or evil waiting
for us to raise a finger,
absorb their emanations.
　　Is this intelligence they
send, or our own – ancestral,
reflected eons that fall
into our starstruck faces,
what people have gazed and felt?

47. OF NATURE PROGRAMMES

CAPTIVE orang-utans reintroduced
to their lush Indonesian treetops
　　by two Swiss girl scientists,

colobus monkeys in their priestly coats
of black and white pass their milk-white child from
　　breast to breast to be coddled,

and six-foot-long Brazilian otters snack
on baby caymans in a pool – little
　　fierce reptiles fighting for life,

while whiskered Norwegian zoologists
slip down in a polar bear's ice-cave lair
　　to count cubs when mum's away:

　　if these are going on when
　　you and I are gone, then bless
　　the TV that kept them in
　　mind between sitcoms and ads.

48. OF ST PAUL

BALDING, bearded, pugnacious but sad,
   with a bead of light rebounding
     from the bulging copper dome
      of his fertile brow, Paul,
      Apostle to the Gentiles,

in the icons' unphotographic
   likeness, looks longingly, bearing
     the brunt of more personhood
      than most bear in the flesh.
      Out of that burnished bulb,

transplanted, burst the hyacinthine
   eloquence of the Epistles,
     but who in this mournful face
      sees the headstrong Samson
      redeemed from his blindness?

The man who held the murderers' coats
   while they stoned Stephen, born again
     to bring down pagan temples
      till the Roman sword fell,
      is too much a Moses

again for many who love the Son
   of Man – his lines stick in their throats;
     who wrote the great love poem,
      "Charity vaunteth not";
      whom we quote as saying

      "but the Spirit gives life".

49. OF ST PETER

THE brawny legs and blue feet under sparkle
Of the surge; at the cock's third stretch and ruffle,
A stiff neck bowed and gone. Dear water-walker,
Dear denier, your love, of all, is realest
To us, because the most rebuffed, the most tried
And sorely pleaded. Between us and the sun
You stand with the shadow you drag, that heals us,
With your outbursts, your leaps and weeping,
    steady.

50. OF THE MATCH-GIRLS

THIS cropped blow-up shows seven.
Three are caught slightly agape,
off-guard; the rest present their
straightforward faces. Only
two bareheaded – one gripping
her headgear in both anxious
fists. Their bonnets are involved,
plump as plush cushions. The one
detail – apart from the eyes
of all rimmed with deep tiredness,
their pallor, youth and thinness –
is the hand of the other
unhatted girl (half-hidden
by a buttress of the wall).
It's resting on the shoulder
of a sister, lightly placed,
that easy, unemphatic
hand that defies proscription,
solidarity's token.

51. OF BUDDLEIA

PATIENCE of that comma-shaped seed
in the least-promising crevice,
driving rootlets into the lime;
vigour of the slender fan of
stalks, spread and shaking, declining
to let go;

        determination,
next, of the arm-thick harsh-skinned stem,
soon-dividing, irregular
and coarse as the mortar it breaks
open;

        most of all, the old sheds
overcome with violet, pending,
tapering rays, plumb of the wall
levered out of true to let them
through,

        lift the heart. Our saddening
domination, acres of brick-
work where no nourishment obtains,
these, in a generation, will
reduce to rubble and flowers.

52. OF CUMULUS

WHAT baroque or rococo,
stasis-resisting, coiling,
proliferous building (light
and shade broken a hundred

and one ways across it and
mixed in as many degrees)
aspired to once, you also
in restless, appearing-so-
effortless grace, example:
the expression, imbalanced
and grand as all creation,
of the thoughts that, heavy with
purity, ceaselessly fill
the unmoved mind of heaven.

53. OF LOVE

WHAT'S praised
or despised?
It weighs their worth.

What's low
and what's high?
Love's more than both.

From loss to be raised,
of pride to be disprized,
it's our own hope.

Governs the sky
or dives in a hole?
Each had its speed from love.

Waters creep-
ing or thunder-
ous don't replenish us more

than that stream's steep-
down caper
on us from above.

Earl of the ocean's crop,
one pearl meek as vapour
it keeps in store.

54. OF THE PILLARS

THESE firm grey women, widows and spinsters
        who maintain the church
show, should you look more closely, their granite's
        a bloom of crystals

shaped stronger and slower than fashion knows,
        petals of sable,
milk and rose, of mica, quartz and feldspar.

        Timelessly hatted
and arm in arm, they leave the porch and keep
        a third between them,
whom they uphold and are joined in above.

PART III

55. OF THE ASSYRIAN BASEMENT

THE corpses of lions slung on poles
and headless dead flung in the river,
merciless killing of prisoners
recorded with pride, incised finely
in low relief. And all, like the leg
of the king himself, the mouth and claws
of the quarry that rears confronted
and the horned bow between, at full stretch.
No

limb is its smooth self here – a trunk,
a cord of twisted strength: aesthetics
of aggression perfected in these
cool grey friezes, by which a Hitler's
or a Stalin's jut-jawed warriors
and blockhead heroes backed by blue sky
seem sheer dissembling, domination
painted up in colours of militant
sainthood.

Halfway down, a long-faced lad
looked long in the moonlike face, "perhaps
of a cult figure", bald eyes placid
and the Buddhistic lip curled, where will
to power is sated by slaughter
to stillness.

Here's the young grey self you
shot, tête-à-tête with the cruel god,
longhaired, pale and muffled, mesmerised
by that calm and comprehensive stare.

56. OF FLORENCE

SNAIL-LIKE city, self-contained,
river gliding at the foot
of deep, long streets that, curved like
rays by gravity, arrive
in squares where spacious arches
triumph, but decorously;
which light calls home; the spiral's
core the Duomo, coloured in
the key of earth-tones – marl-grey,
green, cream and terracotta.

From the hilltop piazza,
San Miniato al Monte,
it shows as Aristotle
made requisite for beauty –
whole, apprehended as one;
though the outbound train reveals
the naff daily hinterland,
cash-and-carry blocks of flats,
little trees wreathed with plastic
from the Arno's winter floods.

Whoever saw of London
the entirety? The clay
bowl's pointed with domes and spires
dissolved in fumes at the base
and fume-like jumble of roofs.
But once on the homeward night-
flight, the wing dipped, the strew of
lights, like fibres of a sea-
form, bespoke integrity,
consonance and clarity.

57. OF ANANSE

RED-BROWN, crossing the bedroom floor
at a high-stepping scuttle, caught
in the corner eye, audible
and startling at midnight. Instinct
interprets you at once as no
insect. There's a purposive line
to your biased sidelong progress,
a hunter's devising and craft.

Grey-brown, saved from the bath, two wisps
of tarry-wool on the silk-gland,
glyph on your back undeciphered.
Submitting with legs indrawn to
the help of a hand, a cast of
invisible threads caresses it.
Go net the light and put on weight
where fly-worlds gather, shaven star.

58. OF A WASP

'S vigorous arabesque
waltz and rest with its armed
and pointed abdomen
palpitant while it's pressed
on the bowl-rim to feed.

Heraldic segmenting
in radiation's key,
black and yellow; fearless
elegance of a taut,
sensuous frame, taunt you.

Watch feelers that played on
your syrup like foils, bent
by a foreleg and groomed,
the vizarded head turn
side to side in a knight's

gesture, gone in peace. From
the harm of an errant
templar whose splinter-lance
means none, whose fricative
fanfare hails the sun, hold

back that ungallant hand.

59. OF A DANCER

WOULD it be without weight, this bone
garment, or the dwelling flesh float?
It goes to its dear ground again.

Pensive for a few long inches,
fingers try the air. The bare heel
proposes a step, the bold knee

seconds it. Then the deliberate
vertebral column, suppler than
reason, with its subtle rhetoric

sways the issue. Now it tends down,
led by unfledged shoulders meekly,
not from heaviness, as by light

homeless grace's affinity
with the level earth, everywhere
itself, dense and unrelenting.

A ghost in parting might care
less for all but elevation,
though be as tender. It is there-

fore arriving spirit that walks
in through this door, this dancing frame.

60. OF GULLS

THESE scavengers of the ebbing river's
littered shoreline, over unhealthy silt,
broken crusts of polystyrene, quilted
contaminated stones, crying loudly,
rise on thin white oars up from foraging

to re-assume their princely, piratic
hauteur – the casual indifference
to violent air, utter control of it,
immunity to waves and rain and snares,
the wild unmusical voice that moves us

seaward, wherever they clamber and quarrel
on a ruptured hill of plastic sacks or whirl
like nebulae in the haze of drizzle
behind the tractor on the tumbled clods.

61. OF THE ROOM AT
THE END OF THE ROAD

NOT much wider than the road itself,
Simple, straight and low,
With ash-tree saplings tapping on the windows,

Wooden walls, where we wait,
Simpatico, to see where we go
Afterwards, after the road.
Was it long and narrow
As the room, not vice versa?
Without expectation, without an exit,
In the clear light, cool as the leaves,
Waiting is pleasant,
Is living in the perfect tense.

62. OF A MOTH

A CLOAKED one carries the sunset
    under the dun outer folds,
    settles in glare of a bulb
with prestidigitator's pass
        to stroke spread horns.
He has broad shoulders, reflex eyes.

Oracular fragment, troubled,
    batters the shade, then resumes
    that autumnal trance with wing-
beauty hidden. Pauper delta
        of damaged leaf
is the prince of night disguised.

63. OF ERIC DOLPHY

THE love of her life was music, of which
she heard but little, apart from the drop
of water, cheep of birds who came to drink,
the high song of mosquitoes above it.

One day, inspired, she left her native place
and went on a long, hazardous journey
by inhospitable roads, crowded trains,
unhygienic ships and expensive cabs
to a place where the press of feet menaced
and the noise and dirt and haste oppressed her.

There, in a smoky and underlit joint,
where her green home seemed a million miles off,
she found what she longed to hear, late one night,
played on, of all things, a bass clarinet.

64. OF THE DISAPPEARING RIVER

THAT marshals its hundred streams
in the Ethiopian highlands
with their pelts of mist,

conducts them to jagged falls,
enlisting their muds in the labour
of digging its gorge,

then heads, helpless, for no sea,
goes out to waterless wilderness,
the earth's biggest hole

and surrenders to the sun.
There is its vaporous suicide's
grave – unmarked, hard air.

From which ascending, absolved of salt and of
sulphur,
it goes back clear and carries no warning.

65. OF SCIENCE FICTION

THE cyborg shot the father of the man whose wife
persuaded him to holiday in Hawaii
instead of Florida, where he'd rescue the son
of the cyborg's inventor-to-be from drowning.

Without the toddler's chance remark, his invention
never occurred to him. The future the cyborg
came from had ceased to be. The machine disap-
        peared
and the man it had killed was unshot, breathed
        again and

stood up. His assassin, made possible once more,
reappeared and, making that bystander history
again, and again, and again, and again, and
again… The future is its own worst enemy.

66. OF A VISITOR

DARK brown, fluttering in the room at night,
but not a moth. Its pole is not the light
but the open window. The wings hinge back
on each other, tremble open. A black
segment of the air broken off, itself
the ghost of a book, it lands on the shelf:
a butterfly. What other flying thing's
less bodily, so utterly wings?

This the ancients likened to the soul
released from the shroud of the corpulent

caterpillar. She seems out of control,
stumbles even in her own element,
lost, fragile. Fear and pity, but wonder
too, go with her, where she may float or blunder.

67. OF INSECT EVOLUTION

AFTER the Gothic dragonfly,
the Roman ant, Renaissance bee
and errant, chivalric cricket,
after the stiff-coated beetle
and Victorian ladybird,
odd that the last word in that line
should be this microchip, the flea.

68. OF AN ENEMY

EVEN squished you're admirable,
with your hypodermic needle
for a mouth, your curlicue legs
and head no more than two black eyes.

Alive you were a haunting – not
substance so much as a crosswise
drift against the grain of the air.
Dead, you're an indelicate smear.

We're not used to being hunted,
even by such tiny hunger.
It's the taunt, the minute trumpet
of your whine, makes me merciless.

We who lie alert in the dark,
devising against your menace,
to you are all suave skin and warm
outgoing flavour, vein pastures.

Tonight your shadow betrayed you.
Another time your revenant
ghost may make me scratch. I can't say
that I'll miss you, little sniper.

69. OF DOG-DAYS

PLANTS overtop themselves,
insects hatch and hurry
and the breezes blow hot.

Beefy houseflies headbutt
the window. Clouds aground
on pessimistic blue

and the sidelong, catlike
calls of the sodium gulls
fill the glass of the world
with a fierce aquavitae.

Restlessly mobhanded,
the leaves are persuaded
in whispers to disband.
They glisten, shake and nod.

70. OF HISTORY

IN the small hours of a century,
the hours of intrigue, compromise,
the spring of the shy, stubborn dogrose,
the clear July of fragile poppies
ashame our mud and frost from the page.

Where hindsight rolls its prospect of rise
and decline, we can't walk anyway.
There we're yet to be born; before us
on the perplexed horizon, we're dead.
The wind buckles the map in our hands

that handled the tiller or fingered
the trigger. History's bearing down
like the thunderbird: some see the brows
or wings, and some the jabberwock beak
with a mixed metaphor's saw-toothed edge.

PART IV

71. OF CONSTANCY

THE long straight shoots of the cherry
grow three feet and four in the year.

Above it darts from enclosure
directly into the sunlight

and where the least drops of shine fall
it hangs out leaves to receive them,

clear green pennants, smooth and tooth-edged.
Roots tug, the trunk twists and braces,

takes its weight of aspiration.
Pushing rain ahead and hauling

a blue sky ringed with astounding
white behind them, the fronts circle.

Moisture, earth and air and their creatures,
transforming, live by constancy.

72. OF THE NOSE

TUNNELLED tower, spirit channel,
the face is arranged around you
like a feudal hamlet round its castle.

Beauty's most difficult aspect,
you who keep the voice's secret
resonance are therefore the heart's trumpet.

You lend the deep eyes direction
and overtop the smiling gorge,
abrupt, broad-shouldered, fissured or pitted

like pumice, like snow or basalt
gleamed, rufous or yellow as dawn;
on whom the tears' Niagaras, trembling,

shake the air around with silence;
from whose steamy caverns, distent,
erupts the surplus volcanic laughter;

inaccessible mountain home,
above all, of the pagan sneeze,
at whose outrush come forfending blessings.

Within the hill of spices, one
by one, the scent molecules are
given audience as the day is long.

73. OF A STONE

FEATURELESS sea-flint
picked off the levels,
once sea-bed, where sheep bleat;
a talisman rubbed
and revolved for a mile
left-handed, revealing a landscape,

then tossed across the grasses'
lengthening shadows,
spinning in idleness further
in fifteen minutes than the tides' labour
would take it in a year.

And yet, as the broken breakwaters,
sanded smooth and green with weed,
that try to control the beach can prove,
it's the breathing tides always win,

pushing their booty up the coast,
taking the coast itself away captive,
throwing up their spume of waders
that turn in the light a moment
and fall as the lightest of bones,
a turning feather, the driest of sand.

Where the goose-flocks grazing
have strewn the ground with preened-out plumes,
the leathery oar-weeds were waving,
coral insects castled
and forests sank since flint was born;

but the dunlins and I, many-memoried,
will be blown about together
before the span of this dumb
simple round is broken.

74. OF THE GIANT HOGWEED

DRY upstanding rivers
    whose arms snake out oddly
        like lightnings reversed, by
autumn hollow, man-tall.
    Each climbs to many light,
        dark seed-specks through frequent
branchings – a watershed
    map, with the tarns that peat-
        brown streams fall from, merging,

suspended in mild air,
    and this sunken wasteground
        as ocean.

          The fluted
beige stems would rattle and
    whistle if any wind
        stirred on the duckweed-scummed
and rush-rimmed pond they guard,
    heads leaning together,
        unremembered, at ease.

75. OF AN EAR OF WHEAT

STIFF and dry like a feather
with a new-moon curve, picked up
in the stubble no gleaners
search, shaved uniformly short.

All around in the big fields
the hard light soil's been harrowed.
The black ground over the ditch
is patched with unburnt yellow.

Pinkish-grey, industrial,
the bare fields, a half-mile long,
windswept, blank as factories.
Lights come on in the outskirts

along the A road. Angled
like river gravel, seeds are
full and sharp in this light discard,
never to be bread. A dog-

rose pink, thin and pitted moon
peers beside the hilltop town
at the cars' conceited whine
down the medieval shoreline.

Pendulous, with winged husks ridged
like the legs of a cricket,
finely pointed, the fifty-
four grain ear forgives and gives.

76. OF THESE PEBBLES

OFF Winchelsea Beach
which, touched together –
a chirk and warble,
like displaced lapwings'
sharp cries on the flats –
seem to spell out home.

Two bits knocked off, time
out of mind, from some
conglomerate bed
(itself stuck pebbles),
each a rock nexus,
strong miscellany.

No amount of speech
knows them, whose shades, shapes
and surfaces – spheres
becoming blunted
pyramids, rhomboids,
rust, black, white and grey,

331

dimpled knobs, pocked, chipped,
osseous and glass-
smooth inclines, nodules –
words could go round and
round all day like waves
and never wholly

say, both being one
in a million or
ten, being one in
an all-equally-
language-exhausting
unnameable sum.

77. OF BEDTIME READING

THE brown hand holds the white
palm, tanned forearm on sheltered wrist.
Her even breathing's resonant
and calming as the herb
she twisted and frayed to breathe today in
Henry James's garden,
puzzled to name the cinder-grey
feathery leaf, losing herself
in the scent's elusion.

Her sighs are from the far side of a field
of downland a gate gave on to
out of ten clear pages
where mild shade drifts, pierced with sunlight,
from the fourth chapter of *The Europeans*.

78. OF DYLAN THOMAS

"WHERE are you going with your bag of bread
Proverbs and basket of biblical eggs,
When the one white stone of the sun has thrown
Its likeness on the mercy of cobbles
Barely, giving the day a new name?"

"With my bread baked of froth blown off pints
And eggs empty as headaches, to market,
Of course, to sell." His round, unwell face bobbed
Like pickled evasive onions, then laughed
Unpromisingly as the wind struggling
Uphill against the light.

                              "And they buy there?"
"Because I've a stay-at-home gift they hope
One morning I'll have brought to let them have,
Who, fools, can't afford it, nor know by how far."

79. OF UNDERGROUND MICE

YOUR small world's hard
Steel and noise
Grey as the filth that gathers
Under steel and noise

As you survive there
Steel and noise
I can here

Scutter from the warbling rails
And rumble
Lunch on litter
Live by what we scatter

The deafening wheels
Are not so definitely real
As underground mice

80. OF CHARACTERS' ENDS
for Eugenia

THE simpler were disposed to be happy,
entering ever-after where they change
neither their fortunes nor milieus again.
Others made their close before the cover
consigned a past to all concerned, their parts
enriching strangely beyond their passing.
Central or obscure, their ways, as here, are
pathless and unguessable thereafter.

But one or two move off, too much themselves
to be resolved in marriage or in death.
Their backs are disappearing in the crowd
that mills outside the novel's bounds. A stance
or gesture picks them out, until the crowd
seems suddenly all stances and gestures.

81. OF STONEHENGE

THE cars drone and glitter over the down
    on two thin ribbons diverging
        by the dense ring of stones.

The bronze-age chieftains' mounds
look down in rows from the ridges,
low as the dimming crimson hump of day.

Their sentinel places were appointed
from below, where the henge that crowns
the gentle pudic slope

has a clear and gravid
September moon in attendance
and the equinoctial sun, fast-falling,

tree's X-ray frail against the giant disc.
The loyal star, with bliss-stained clouds,
plunges into the earth

where peace flows and returns
from pillar and lintel, the navel
of stillness, whose power we overlooked.

82. OF AVEBURY

SEABED
slabs stood upright
aim level
strata at the stars:

ancient
intercession
in the sign
of gravity crossed.

335

Round a
sunny rampart,
turning right,
we walk their language.

Long-faced
sheep haven't changed
their thoughts on
grass since these took place:

squared-slit
irises stare
then resume
cropping the temple.

Flung up,
a sudden flock,
the local
rooks are much the same.

Unhewn
clear-featured rock
the years run
true to; syllables:

who set
these up in shape
of time, we
who forget, recall.

83. OF A BUILDER

SHE'S climbing in the quick of night
Diagonally up the air,
Legs uppermost. Caught in the light,

She's no bigger than a snowflake
Floating, symmetrical and white,
Along a thread as fine as hair
Her glimmering haste doesn't shake.

A pendulum behind its glass
Keeps nudging the dark into day,
A small wakeful sun of dull brass.
A good two feet, from the lampshade
To the dried poppies in a vase,
She's stretched her fragile founding stay –
A larger plan than Cheops made.

84. OF AN ADLER

WOULD I amount to a scattered shower
if rain was success?
My livelihood's fingers and thumbs

and the first pool I worked in,
lonely as a fish
… o'er weeds and stones…

was filled with these heavy-duty
desk-bound German "eagles"'
(as the name translates)

clatter, purposeful
da-da-da-dickory-ting!
all day long.

That tallish square machine
of a building was much like a clock
but when it struck one I went down in the lift.

They're has-beens now
and words seem less solid,
the words of commerce and government.

Peck this poem out in pica;
lend your sturdy wings-wide carriage
to the viewless ditto of poesy.

My clicking nails
run up the hill
to fetch a pail of qwertyuiop.

Have zero quid, but joy's
flock of poems waxing. Believe
the quick brown fox jumps over the lazy dogs.

85. OF A DOVE

WITH maimed feet snared and hurt,
like God's, by alighting
where she wasn't wanted.

She raises the more painful clutch
of pink atrophied toes,
patiently stands on the other,
closes her eyes.

Her slate-grey iridiscent mate,
who's paraded beside her all
season, sees off
others to let her feed.

So hope pays court to peace, and love
follows after goodness,
and faith attends and serves the truth.

338

86. OF CITY KESTRELS

OFTEN enough seen
distantly, in stiff-
tailed, narrowed, straight, dis-
criminant hover,
breaking suddenly
away in a wide
curve, as dismissive
of its own intent,
sharp wings dicing air.
But uninflected
calls calling you quick
to the window, see
them now present your
own backyard with their
event.

      One above
on the rooftop shrieks.
The mate on the half-
dead barn that pigeons
roost in stands and stills
all flight a minute.
Round and black-browed, stone-
heavy head that ends
the body bluntly:
you feel a seeing
eye you can't make out
and see the little
black knife of the beak.

The tail, tight-drawn, spreads
out in the hawk's wedge
and, gone again, she

points out all she owns,
pausing here and there,
climbing the air straight
to dwarf by her height
at last that eighteen-
storey block of flats,
sun caught under dark
wing-blades where she turns
beyond City Road,
mere speck, yet focus
of a bright sky still.

87. OF A CONDUCTOR

A SMALL man with the eyebrows of a large one,
tufted with white, with white in the small beard too;

an Indian whom Providence has given
a job on top of his job of conducting,
of being the last of the cheerful Cockney
busmen, a-swagger and bantering loudly.

Dark and shy, scholastic physiognomy
from which each Hold on tight! – Move right down
          inside! –
and Yes please thankyou fares please! is delivered
with a mantric gravity of levity

as though your ticket rattled off with a quip
were a tiny attainment of good karma
and one more run up and down the 19 route
shall free him from the chain of death and rebirth.

88. OF RANDALL JARRELL

THE beard never was that Santa-
white it promised...

Striking down slantwise above the left brow,
across two thinner parallel furrows,
one wrinkle makes the sign, in a faceful
of crinkling whisker and drooped glinting eye,
the sign known to science as "not equal".

The pupils come forward brightly, are brown
I'd say from this black and white portrait – crow's-
foot rich with effort also to withdraw
from a world too much with us, coming closer –
after his subtraction, still not equal.

What was promised?
The bird's nervous wing – surrender –

89. OF CHINATOWN

OFF the Avenue it's suddenly Hong Kong
and you find you're in a smaller, brighter crowd,
as to height and faces, more at ease, less loud
with tension; with people who appear to throng
for love of thronging. Whether it's you or they belong
or otherwise, no-one scans you with a proud
exclusive eye to say. Sighing to have sloughed
off standards which, a street away, you left wrong-
footed, -faced and all, you can hum an exile's
song, its intervals entangled with the tang

of an alien muzak and pitching of words
in syntactical scales, down the gleaming aisles
of stores perfumed by equipollence of yang
and yin, branded with dragons and celestial birds.

90. OF OCTOBER

THE fog descends, the flats' outlines soften.
Above they leave off and merge with the air,
the night air grey and porous as breezeblock.

The twin columns of stairwell lights stand out
like spines. The bulk's become part of the dim
furniture filling up the mist's big room,

and all our doors and walls no more than drawers
and divided compartments where we lie
about and dream, no longer so apart.

91. OF A SNAPSHOT

SKINNY in white on the Taj Mahal's terrace,
the nailhead dent of a three-quarter moon
on the noon-blue where the pierced, vanishing
clouds leave by the top right-hand corner…

They made one of each, the wonder-workers.
In the mausoleum's millionth repeat
the dwarfed self-conscious standing in mid-step
on the marble 's unique. I wouldn't give it
for all the holes in this stone screen or curves
of inlay, of carving or of domes.

Make, over the years, a numb tide of feet
stop and match its unplanned self against you,
and remind the votive eyes in procession,
pressed to viewfinders, what's worth taking care for.

92. OF CORN CIRCLES

HALFWAY to death the year stands still,
buckled leaves, where lights shine over
or through them, less moved than polyp
or weed in their submarine world.

A night-mist comes of the stillness
and clasps the hour like memory.
Like fine rain falling from nowhere,
residual waves of a broadcast

ooze from the air. With planks and string
and nothing better to do, two
blokes' jolt of stellar conception
got them weaving circular holes

that set off a wave, as thinkers,
feelers and watchers of the skies,
dowsers and ring-dancers gather
what they will from the flattened crop.

Not signs of higher sentience,
just art evading property,
breath of green and gold on the box
to those odd lit windows up there

in blocks solemnified by fog,
made more like the homes of hermits;
art exciting speculation
as if meaning more than itself.

93. OF A HERMIT

PINES bowed, theirs branches bowed
by glistening pelts of snow
thick as royal ermine,
their bark's rugosities
capped and speckled with ice,

a rough-clothed man blunders
between them, brushes limbs
whose loads with a dry crack
fall, pitting the fresh drifts
they come drumming down on.

The deep, unbitten green
needles sway up and back,
their live sheen touched by long,
last red of winter's rays

94. OF A PAINTED FIGURE
Piero della Francesca's 'Baptism of Christ'

THE chilled white youth who turns his back to strip
in the middle ground, for whom the background's
only the bank of the river and round
Tuscan hills and cypresses beyond it;
whose foreground is his own plucked-up courage
and recognisable sins. That he's next
is all the man before, that man baptised
behind him, means. He doesn't see the man
he came to see, the moment all before
were prelude to, and the rest aftermath,

tilting his dipper, whose drops in the air
split the world in two: neither the lesser,
intent on pouring, nor greater figure,
prayerful, waiting, nor dove above the bowl.

95. OF NOVEMBER

THE morello gives off light as it gives off leaves,
revealing its ribs as days diminish.
Returning the sunshine owed, it papers the paving
it shaded with multiple layers of yellow.

A leaf at the end of a long twig quivers
like the beak of the blackbird who whistles
in the cold his half-hearted rehearsal of the spring.

The sparrows who pecked its early petals for food
and filled it with commotion, desert the naked eaves.
In dripping rain they huddle among buddleia.

Bare-armed in shining bark and abandoned
by all but the grace of its armoured nudity,
it withdraws from none of summer's flourishes,
preparing to bear on them the hard, delicate frost.

96. OF FRIENDS' FACES
Phoebe & Stephen

ONE inclines to a Buddha's disc, infant-
plump and aureate; a Cubist rebus
of glints, points and shades makes the angles age-
less in the other's. With one the matter's

words – he's bossed with a coin's sound, subtle
curves –
while her matter's matter's metaphor for
language – glass – that lets light through and sees it
off, so full inside of surface, covered
by depth.

Both fragile, both flow; it follows
both both go well and come (transparent pun)
together. Should they come by accident
occasionally apart, beware: of words
and glass, shards are equally sharp. Stick, let's,
vitrifactor, versifier, together.

97. OF ELVIS PRESLEY

ADORED and
mocked respectively
for what he wasn't and was,

whether the sapling's surge and rustle
of green, inspired and flexible youth

or later dark brown
cello roundness; royal, light
or midnight blue; whether inflated,
fattened, vibrated, in self-parodic pop,
touchingly; or driven at rock John-Henry-

like, directly – hollowness,
not emptiness but habitation
by a ghost persisted; who said to the folk
who mocked and adored him, "I hope I haven't
bored you."

346

98. TO THE HOLY SPIRIT

I

LET fire eat the year, soil eat ash,
rain give the root the seeping residue;
    sun, come spring, revive and heat wash
snow from the ground, pierce the frost, re-renew
    the reading of the scriptured cell
whose green oratory holds but cannot sway
    quick fire whose creeping smoke we smell
or slow invisible fire of decay.
So in the round dance of a dozen months
an innocence whirls past us out of reach
    that we had hand in our hand once,
    till brightest of the things whose speech
    we knew, persuaded otherwise.
Now we raise our eyes to the fallen world.

II

Beyond its outer turning lies a rim,
    within its inmost point a hub
    it circles on, and sight is dim
from the spinning, hands too numbed by the rub
of it by them to feel for each other
    or fashion from each other prayer.
    So the whirled kindling will smother
and starve in the surfeit of its foodstuff, air.

    Still us, draw us to the centre's
    centre, edge where divisions cease.
    Show to us the man who enters
there as one at home at last and at peace.
We who are about to die desire to live
with him whose strength to call on him
                  is yours to give.

99. OF DAYS

[The face of the deep]

SILENTLY made a beginning,
from which singularity time,
exploding its Sunday, made space
out of nowhere. Matter, the earth,
though existent, pregnant nothing
was yet to be delivered of.
Nothing contained it, it contained
nothing. Was it desire to speak
made all for its sake – all being
one before, requiring no word?
Then to the page, the stage and place
he had shaped to receive it, spoke
the first of chances – not knowing
first that the light was good? It was.

[And it was so]

THE work of the first of these days was all matter,
    all time and all space and all light.
The next was stormy Monday, when nothing was
                                             made
    but order. That seamless ocean
the breath of making moved over, brooding, being
    itself divided from nothing
but God, was split, by the second day's work, in half.

Space, being present but formless,
became a structure part was turned away above
   and part beneath, and dark and light
were joined, as first-born children of God and not-
                         God,
   by the many twins that followed –
left and right, before and after, plus and minus –
   which were fruitful and multiplied.

[After his kind]

IN the jostling diversity and difference
of divided things and forces, God worked
on through the night. The waters he had spent
a whole day taming streamed and roared above
and below. Massive, agitated, vast,
the abyss would have been as astonished
as the angels, had it not been self-
absorbed, to find him in the third morning's
wild light working a tiny universe
into the great one, the rough crust of earth
sporting tendrils, foaming out in fronds whose
delicacy, regressing as they grew,
increased the world's infinite scope. That was
Tuesday, the trees' day, day of greenery.

[For signs]

WEDNESDAY was for ordering the heavens,
   dividing the days and the seasons,
      giving dark its portion of light
      and day a bed for the night,

making the moon's mansions
and the stars' legions,
encamped around
on frosty fields, sound
as they moved or tended
stationary fires, songs ended
in sun's polyphonic chorale
rising, harmonising overall.
Leaves in waves began, the length of the globe,
to clothe the springs, and autumns to disrobe.

[Be fruitful]

COLD-BLOODED from the sea's yet colder blood,
God called the scaled and finned, the jelly-skinned,
and finally the feathered, to possess the air
that vapours flowed above, the waters swept by air.

Armoured, jointed, spined and clawed, venomous,
toothed, luminescent, transparent – the sea
revelled in its first carnival, freely moving,
laughed with its pointed mouths, its many legs
        dancing.

Dancing better yet, with wide arms outspread,
the birds, entranced with the freedom conferred,
like dervishes turned, their bright eyes a little stunned.

On Thursday the green surge of ocean leapt
for joy, yelling, at the land and, shattered
on rocks already weeded, ran back together.

[In the image]

FROM day to day more varied,
Friday's array widened farther
    than ever, and elephants,
ants and voles, worms, wolves and anteaters
    made their way over the earth,
until one thing more alone remained
    to be made; into which last
thing, as into the first, all the rest
    would be fitted. Whereas once
he had spoken into existence
    and then to existing things,
in the end of beginnings, the rest
    being done and entire, he
paused and spoke to himself: "Let us make…"

[It was very good]

SO came the day all was done;
    water revolved from the clouds
    through rivers to the ocean,
    the earth revolved in the light
    that flew straight and unchanging;
    the herb unfolded the herb's
    peculiar seed, the bird
    unfolded its wings, lions
    their limbs and the ewe her lambs.
    Man and woman alone knew
    enough to stand and wonder:
    Things become selves looked across
    at self from which things became.
    But Saturday didn't last long.

CHARACTERS

STAR

BEFORE you pass
as brightness must
let me give cause
to prize the dust,

for your being
of it, to one
who'll read, to one
you were the sun.

* * * *

Venus alone
in our window
watches the bed
where our hearts slow

and unravel,
glides to the right,
nearing the head
her cares make white.

* * * *

May your night-path
not be fouled nor
haunted by that
at your shoulder

you dare not face.
My arm's under
your head, my head
at your shoulder.

I
YOU & I

FELT

SHE makes a mat
of fibres, layers-
thick, pressed, depict
a face she cares

to know. To show
a friend, her built-
up filmy webs
waver and tilt

out of true when
wetted, flattened,
to likeness more
true in the end,

allowing lines
life's variance.
She wants "Central
Ueropeans",

as she puts it,
to portray, some
Ur-people whose
faces ripple

and merge, emerge,
wink and perish
from these fond French,
Germans, Irish.

She jokes but seeks
to do good works
in this technique
learned from the Turks.

CHARACTERS

Her Icelandic
face at fifty
keeps growing its
changing beauty.

PIPES

HE sets up pipes
and elbow, knee,
stiff fingerpads
begin to play,

to work the air
and forge it, twist
with quick digits
and precise wrist

the air from it,
which jigs and reels
like a spun top
that speeding stills.

Energetic
and introvert,
inattention
and noise can hurt

man and music,
but no tittle
nor jot can harm
nor belittle.

Nursed in corners,
this old rigour,
born of bog and
rock, is bigger

than outlouding
now, finally.
As, shinily-
packed, the present

thing is dull at
core, this scintillates.
Time and stout
wet its gullet.

       *   *   *   *

The well-read chant
of a Saxon
who learned the tune
stones stood up to,

psalms and laments
of megalith-
builders' descent,
grasped the myth

that on ice-cliff
and rock-face, roped
to a v/diff
he groped and craned

to confront, some
mountain/goddess
compounded of
peace and wildness,

remote ridge
and close cranny,
of freedom and
severity.

CAN

BUCKLED on crates
in a doorway,
he holds a can
up to his grey

disordered face.
Constant chewing
movement but no
words ensuing,

no gabble nor
mutter. Like Yeats,
his countryman,
he contemplates

world's busyness;
instead of pierced
hare's collarbone,
a can of beer.

BELLE

EYES' careful arch,
lips' reddened bow,
satin, silver,
worn but to show

what moves within
her, unadorned,
that has been wrung,
wronged, bitten, scorned,

still unbroken.
In her war the
mild and menial
with the father,

who is absent,
cold and bold, who
would forbid her
hunt the gold You

further. She knows
the apple he
holds breaks the spell
and happily

ever after
that she lives her
days on apples
red and silver.

BLUE

POLICE hauled her
out of the bar
for having blue
hair, and slammed her

into a car;
they terrified
then released her.
Another one

dreaming the just
and terrible
day of the dust's
awakening,

drinking her wine
in the meanwhile.
She dances, she
shuffles her feet

to the congas'
supple logic,
drawing designs
in the air with

her arms apart
and her eyes closed,
testing the ground
with her bare toes,

testing the ground
to see what stirs.

JEZ

RAT Scabies dubbed
her Jezebel,
though really she's
an Essex girl.

Sex and drugs and
leather jackets,
drumkits, stitches,
motorcycles:

such revolts are
self-defensive,
both shield and cleave
a woman's love.

CHARACTERS

The drunken blood
has far to go,
the sober heart
must stay at home.

Sea's a contract
full of catches,
lives have holes and
holes need patches.

When we stitch we
need a needle,
when we fish a
hook's essential.

Wryness then finds
a recompense
for refting mind
of innocence.

The little girl
has lost her way;
the woman leads
her back to play.

DO

ISRAELI Charles –
well, out of their
army, Hebrew-
speaking, to boot –

calls Mingus "my
man", who wasn't
black enough quite
nor white enough

either. Either
these are stories
or they're stories.
Sang "Sue's Changes"

in the widow's
ear, met the band.
We know allies
by their sorties

into marvels.
Blowing his own
flute to fatback
funk, he got down.

LINES

ODD to have friends
half-worlds away,
from New Orleans
to Japan, say;

Argentina,
San Francisco,
you'll find your heart
strings stretched out to.

Cards and snaps on
a cork-tile board
by your cupboard:
by one broad point –

an eyebrow's curve
or the fullness
of a red beard,
inquisitive

tilt of the head –
you'll fasten them
in memory,
whose faces change

in the beds of
strangers, other
weathers, other
news to wake to.

Walking neurons,
we keep in touch.
Leavetaking, left-
ness of hearts all

over winds more
and more thread by
day and by night
on this mind-ball.

ACT

PALER than yours
and still able
to see, I'd think
no pale blue

iris could be.
Ex-actors may,
past the stage when
the curtain-call

prompts them, sated
with paint, pretence
and perhapsness,
have the presence

of a mirror
held up to life
without comment,
contemplative,

unrôled faces.

    *   *   *   *

Mimes the driver –
without checking
the survivor –

who checks the paint
of his wing first,
where the bike hit,
using a course

of the bank's stone
wall for a prop.
Which is what Bert
Brecht exampled –

witness acts out
a crash – for grass-
roots of a down-
to-earth play with-

out illusions.

BUMP

IN a crashing
waltz time, two cars
clutch each other –
crunching embrace,

shower of glass –
then limp apart.
One in the wrong
grows as it drifts

from the shock an
anemone,
waving idly,
of hands and hair.

She gets out, high
on shot nerves. "I
saw the light. I
just passed my test."

BIKE

A HEAD of long
hair's no helmet…
Your ruling star
like a comet,

bright tress flaring,
was seen awhile
rounding the sun,
then took the trail

back beyond sight,
beyond Pluto,
back where you go
dark and into

the big zero.
I think you thought

we're recurrent,
but maybe not.

Anyway your
short-lived portent
has made its mark,
though what it meant

none knew before
you passed, were passed
by a car too
nearly. Gone west.

The bike's front wheel
a bit buckled,
that was all, but
your struck brain swelled,

you felt nothing.
And we who'd seen
felt nothing, too,
where love had been.

Death's glancing knock's
still unintel-
ligible to
us. Is a bell

necessary?
Ask not for whom
time was at hand:
grave is her room.

CLAY

SLIGHT as morning
rain, the sixteen-
year-old-looking,
lisping pixie,
resilient
also as wire,

throws her slimness
on wild fortune,
the mercy of
smacked-out squats and
drear B&Bs,
from man to man.

(Thunder and rain
in the Ching means
big love coming.
Ready yourself
to be ambushed
by it, undone.)

The poppy-juice
habit won't heal
the crack. Would your
split twin-brother's
mind be one if
you're made nothing?

Pack your troubles:
ailing mother,
half-used lovers,
junk. That grip won't
let the good you
could do them be.

371

Make them freedom
of clay and space.
At the mild pace
of a lakeside,
sky-covered place,
figure them out.

P.J.

ME and the cat
watching the box,
scratching an ear,
washing her socks,

curled in my lap.
Gave me solace,
relaxing as
Thomas Tallis

unwound on tape
his four-part mass,
by the clothes-horse,
watching the gas-

fire, one blind eye
white as marble.
Who else knew my
folk-classical

arrangement for
"The Galway Shawl",
my intros, stretched
and whimsical

so well? So long,
oddball foundling.
Cat-flattening
lorries pounding

Pentonville Road
outside. Indoors
there are still these
layers of scores,

cassettes and fliers,
but no helpmeet,
skewbald housemate
under my feet.

Let them heckle.
A bad decade's
busking, hustling
fades, in the shape

of a thin cat
withered away
before the state.

VIBE

WARRINGTON raised,
he'll come on strong
like a good cheese,
can do no wrong
where the vibe is,
bounds are broken.

His idea of
heaven's a hell
of a good time
for all, none missed
off the ever-
lasting guest-list.

In the throb, strobe-
flicker and din,
with the voodoo/
hillbilly grin,
leaping into
view, gone again.

Not the hangdog
type, though absent
from a sadness
his look may get.
The cat who knows
where the cream went

winks. Drinks the whey
of loss as well.
Laps you on the
circuit of love.

SILENT JOHN

I'VE fished the cold
wracked waters off
Finisterre and
lived where the air
in the mess can
thicken with sides

and grudges as
quickly as thrash
of the cod's iron
sides in the net,
but quarrels are
short as jack-knives.

The cafe strip-
lights hyphenate
his spectacles
and in each brown
bossed eye a seed
pearl scintillates.

To paint, to make
music, you need
time, space, money,
connections... Art
and rock'n'roll,
the movies – all
so bad, so bad.

His seven-year
silence over,
the gestures speak
like the loaded
flat heads of hogs'
bristle brushes;
a Gallic brogue
broad as the tang
of Nuits St Georges.

These kids think they're
street, they think it's
all for nothing
and free for all.

CHARACTERS

I've trawled for squats
round Finsbury Park
twelve years – but these…
They think they're New
Age Indians.
They don't give a
shit.

    The doors are
closing, the dogs
begin to bark.
With the thinning
whorl of hair, his
bullish forehead,
high, delighted
laugh, plunge forward
against the waves.

BOUND

DEAR Piscean
elder brother
who taught me songs
were in the air,

from time to time
recoverable,
like homing beams
are capable

to lead where fear
and shame leave off –
in the future:
you've had your share

of lost contacts,
broken homes. Back
up from the sea,
I, in your track,

the little one,
come safe through marram
grass and small thorns,
two a quorum.

Why feel you've gone
with the flow too
far the wrong way
when you know you

can't throw away
gifts? Confine them
and their smallness
grows, but loose them,

they'll contain and
lead you where you
want to go. They're
older after

all than you are.

KEEPS

To miss a mum
means not knowing
her as she was,
not the lack of

motherly hugs
but loss of her
self acquiring
lineaments,

becoming that
person to love
who resided
unremembered

in the child-mind's
clutches, the son's
past embraces.
Two and two put

together from
scattered ashes
can't bring you back,
but I pick up

the stray traces,
the smudged ash print,
as it were, of
you as you were,

you as a girl,
as the woman
wanting a girl,
and live with it,

drawing on love
as though you lived.

LONE

AN ascetic
in spareness and
strength of physique,
his aesthetic

goes slow to be
sure of his holds
on the world's mad
geology.

A solitude
is where he's glad
to catch the light,
rock and water,

opens his heart
to the shutter.
The Nepalese
returned a sense

of wonder grown
gradually since
earnest youth was
plagued by teendom's

drossy mockers.
I remember
"Draw me something,"
which something turned

out a dragon,
sky-born earth-force,
Chinese fashion.
I copied scores

of that totem.
Picture him ridge-
striding, splayed sun
spilt from a ledge

of cloud, a child,
like the dragon,
of elements,
rare, here and gone.

GIFT

I NEAR the age
he fathered me,
his third-born son.
That a man so

little given
to ambition
for self, driven
by a boy's own

yearning for home-
time and comforts,
should raise such as
I, egoist,

comes home lately,
sailing the stretch
of a lifetime
midway over.

Did his rising
early. Oxford
taught a workman's
son and schooling,

which had freed him,
was his living
(if a calling
then a faint one)

who had found in
family his
fulfilment. Told
us lately of

his only aim
as a nipper –
to get out of
school as soon as.

My grace was him
for father who
counted a child
the chief of gifts.

BUCK

NINETEEN, twenty –
through the velvet
buds the sharp horn
starts to be shown.

CHARACTERS

What was childish,
soft, has edges,
is ridged and stripped
and, locked, rattles

against others'
on frost-swept leas.
Wearing the weight
of its garland

the head swings up
and brings to bear
its wealth of tines,
the glance aware.

BELOVED

ONE with the hawk's
deportment, she,
imperious,
has the cold sea
sway in her veins,
whose warm-sea baby-blues
fill with quick salt
as she damns faults.
No use to say this crag
is old as time:
a fixed coastline
is not in her atlas.
She'll beat and harry it
and carry it
away at last
to build her own soft beach.

JUDE

MUSICAL child
a mad mother
governed, over-
dressed and bewildered,

born in the sun's
last house, she draws
toward her third
score year. Straightforward

as a steep stone
causeway goes down
through the clear waves,
the way to her heart,

to the restless
and constant sea
where world shines more
than here in the air.

Such a one mid-
summer makes and
the young year bears,
pelagic Pisces'

offspring. Maiden
or widow white
she wore and sat
upright at the grand.

Baroque columns
girdled the glade
where polished notes
like the lyre-bird's rang

off dark wood, gilt
and frilled stucco.
That persistence
girlhood gave her hands,

to learn to grip
and skate the floe
of ivory
keys and ebony

difficulties,
held us spellbound.
Dreamed, when the hard
times were over her

head and no hope
hammered open
her fontanelle,
she was the ice-bear,

ice-cave kept and
invincible;
the surefooted,
sea-wise, nine-foot queen.

TITLE

DUKE Ellington,
no kind of peer,
was but the king
of gentlemen.

His wardrobe shed
all shades but blue
at last, the sky's
modest blazon.

CHARACTERS

He'd step downstage
(mileworn holdall
features, sheen of
suit unwrinkled,

charmingly creased
& solicitous)
to name with smooth
exactitude

another sun-
set-splendoured piece.

CLASS

WHO'S on telly?
Chrysanthemum-
haired, the master
cellist, Monsieur
Tortelier
teaches English
roses Elgar's passion.

Music, he says,
is a lesson
in love, whereas
to be *méchant*,
to be wicked
is to be sans
song. The pupils widen

and fall for him.
A little more,
a little less –

is beautiful.
No need, with such
coaxing, to coach.
With the fingerboard arch

of the nose raised
proud of carved cheeks,
where scrollwork grooves
frame a swift smile,
strung to thrill to
the moment's bow,
he leans forward, all ears.

APES

HER body's big
pot-bellied fruit,
swart and furry,
is hammocked in a dip
of the climbing frame.

She holds her hand-
like feet up, clasps
them absently;
or, slack arm over head,
as we might, she sleeps.

Black as their lids
under leather
ridges, those eyes,
that seem not just to look
at but consider

you, are open,
then close again,
most unimpressed.
What depths of time glinted
across a moment!

She turns away
to be the less
disturbed, and you
are turning too when he,
from a straw-stuffed shelf,

rushes and stops –
that is, was not
one moment, then
was there, and all the more
apparitional

for being so
monument-still
on his turned-out
toes and folded knuckles,
silver back sloping

to the high-domed
summit of skull.
Those who made Kong
weren't wrong in their scaling:
less tall than a man,

his presence is
megasaurian.
A minute he
waits, then charges forward,
unblinking captive,

to watch the world.
Seamed and shiny
as anthracite
and round the nostrils like
  bitumen buckled

in an ornate
calligraphic
"m" (for monarch),
now far from his mist-filled
  forest origins

and far from our
understanding,
he stands to face
us down behind our glass –
  Kronos bewildered

by stripling pale
Olympians,
bored by the leaf-
less brick and scentless steel.
  You'll search your monkey's

soul for bequests
of such quickness
and might in vain
before you touch deft hand
  to bulbous brain-case

in salute and
go, hopefully
humbler, to think
him over like the wise
  witty ape you are.

TILL

C. JOHNSTONE'S Scots –
her plastic says
her name, her voice
    her birth.

Behind her, heads
and nothing else
look down, move side
    to side,

the row of tills'
alignment and
identity
    precise.

Seven is dark,
half-Indian,
half-African
    perhaps,

whose nose-stud winks,
her modish mop
curled and front shock
    gingered;

while eight's black hair
and small white face
are perfectly
    Pictish.

And so on down
the line and round
the conquered globe –
    live parts.

C. Johnstone's six,
whose lilt amidst
digits' blips is
    humane.

II
ONE LIFE

BETH DYING

THE rain again,
　　　　　and me still lying here;
on last year's leaves
　　　　　the rain again, tapping
and muttering.
　　　　　Each drop, my godson says,
must rise and fall
　　　　　and rise again, to gain
that little weight
　　　　　that barely stirs the leaves
by its landing.
　　　　　You'll barely need disturb
the leaves, to lay
　　　　　me down beneath, so light's
this body grown.
　　　　　This couch kind hands alone
will raise me from,
　　　　　insensible, to boards,
is visited
　　　　　by angels and regret.
Kind hands, I pray
　　　　　you pray for me beyond.
Where I am raised
　　　　　no rain nor leaves shall fall.

CLAIRE CRIES

I THOUGHT she'd take my life
or break my mind
with pain of her barging
a way from me.

CHARACTERS

Blood flowed down beneath,
no shriek sufficed
her, whose conquering head
lies on my breast.

Her satisfaction's brief
but all of peace
for a while. My blue veins
run to feed her.

Wet petal lips pushed out,
no words, no smile,
know nothing but my own
clay-dark nipple.

This tiny head as frail
as a snowdrop
trembling in icy wind,
green flame through ice;

this tiny head the creased
seed of mountains
opens, sucks in the world,
lets its cry out.

PAUL'S PICTURES

TRANSPARENT house,
transparent world,
where nothing hides
or hides others.

On ground where to
stand is to float,

CHARACTERS

it belongs to
free-standing folk.

Sun-faced flowers wave
their arms. Man-sun,
cornered, beams at
bloom-topped people

whose twig-hands touch
beside the wide-
eyed walls. Chimney
says a curled word.

The water-winged
things pierce a piece
of paper like
kids in the pool.

Laughing, they shout
out colours, choose
the shapes they have
always wanted.

TERM

A SEAGULL skips
down on the bald
mud of the "lawn"
and struts a yard
then takes off in
horizontal
tireless East wind,
climbs and is blown
twisting from view.

What odds do plate
tectonics or
Corn Laws, oro-
genesis and
titrations make
out there? Vectors
and tenses or
not, we'll be snatched,

scattered by that
same wind. Why not
teach us to fly?
We exercise
our genius in
carving plastic,
engraving desks.
Our code is coarse
and shrill like gulls'.

TRYST

WHO meet in mist-
filled streets, blurred spokes
of yellow lamps
turning above,

are those not let
indoors in bed
their naked lengths
to match, but walk

to prove their love
against the cold
that melts breathed words
in meeting mist.

SMACK

DON'T want your blood
on my rug when
some friends come up
to crack your skull,

nor skeleton
crew spacing out
round the kitchen
with holes for eyes.

No more Old Bill
smashing in to
haul me and her
naked from bed;

cash, clothes, gear, books
gone from our room;
no twisted grins,
bathetic lies.

I don't need you
and your smack to
remind me who
you used to be.

WICKED

BRILLIANT nights
spent missing trains,
nights the earth spent
rolling round us,

the tall centres…
Everyone else
for some reason
had stepped offstage

to watch their own
lives from the wings.
We stormed the lights,
bravely swearing.

From us to God,
who died young, life's
sap crackled like
incense. Rising

voices broke and
wavered thickly.
Up everyone's
noses we got.

So where are we
now? A raucous
ignorable
knot of youth fools

round centre-stage
for all the world
as though the play
was about them

and the wicked
nets of city
lights, the yellow
chains are round them.

SHEBA'S DREAMWORK

SEEING the screen
all day has decked
my eyes with odd
grey specks that drift
amoeba-like
between real life
        and me.

Perfect water,
warm and heaven-
blue, and windows
in lichened stone
which each look out
on a different
        country.

My brain's rubbed smooth
as a gutter
by idle words.
        I, who
build palaces
behind these lids,
am worth more than
        wages.

But Ariel's charms
bind Prospero;
Miranda's brave
new world has no
analogue here.
To serve the dream-
less, blind machines,
        I wake,

to whom, in noon
of sleep, walking
halls and sunlit
alleys, many
mansions open.

HOMING

YOU round the bend, the house appears –
a smoking chimney among trees,
one window which may be the one she's at.

I click in a Haydn cassette,
climbing the gloomy rock-verged road
through fading woods to that revealing turn.

Ingenious, unfinical,
unbreakable, perennial –
dear Papa Haydn like a hedge of may

with powdered wig and earthy boots,
who asks little and gives so much.
His woodwinds chortle as I top the rise,

doing forty, turning fifty.
Soon the shortening days will show
just the one square beacon through the stripped
       trees.

ABSENCE

AFTER the last rook's loud clamour,
the pigeons' last fat muted notes,
only the hum and drone of homing cars
drifts to us over the river.

The lights shoot out, rounding the ridge.
My shadow like something hunted
ducks across the unlit wall behind me,
the pastoral etchings he chose.

She sips a cold, black, bitter cup
of coffee, shudders, hugs her arms.
The girls aren't back from school. The house falls still,
thumb rubbing absence of a ring.

His own lights miss the tranquil gate,
the gnarled willow in gilded frames
by miles. They're prying the mist-filling air
of another shire, a changed choice.

POTTER'S CHILD

THE baby red
as clay asleep
in her arms and
she too can sleep

to all but him.
I dip my hands
in the whirling
nub. A cup stands

and opens, slip
easing the birth.
I flare the lip,
shaped to the mouth.

Prophets who railed
at statuary
saw man's making
in potter's art.

CHARACTERS

A jar gracious
as Adam fills
out and rises
then, wobbling, spills

its centre, in-
jured and flailing.
I sweep the lump
from the wheel and

start another.
Adam awake
to the hunger
he squirms to slake

suckles. I dare
the form higher
then free its foot
with wire gently.

May this gravid
Eve of a vase
survive firing,
glow in its glaze.

REVIVAL

UNEXPECTED as the clown's thrown bucket,
        not of water but confetti,
snow that tumbles from cloudless April sky
        drifts past cherry blossom.

Youth that went come back unseasonably,
        a song from when I was young rose
under the minute flakes for the minute
        they fell, stopped in my throat

while I remembered neither tune nor words,
  and the bones within me shone white
again. I almost raised a witness hand
    like the blacks do in church.

The cloud that had shaken that handful out
    withered the sun; a cold gust blew.
But just for a moment, closer than sleeves
    of bloom on dark branches,

close as white light clothes a gas-lamp mantle,
I was fitted for the everlasting.

THE STRAGGLER

BROTHERLESS, fatherless, motherless,
Fox went at midday over the hill.

The huntsmen rode on the ridge ahead,
He walked behind them in red splendour.

The bears, the boar and the wolves have gone.
Fox is left of the fierce and running.

Fox alone is left, the least of all,
Whom I saw, as I followed on foot,

Up on the hillside sit down and grin
With horses and hounds ahead of him.

Fox is left of the fierce and running.
Fox will bark and gambol where I lie.

Watching him, a russet king, I thought
Of my gander's bloody feathers strewn,

And I called to the hunt riding high
To see who's behind them, last of all.

Fox will bark and gambol where I lie
Beneath a yew that knew wolf and lynx.

LUCY

LOOK how the cat says yes
continually with its purr,
for half an hour
saying nothing but yes.

We've but the one short sound
in a moment gone, while the dumb
old patchwork tom
rests in affirmation.

Do they say the old man's
lonely, perhaps, now his wife's dead;
why not visit?
Is it maybe penance

you do here, or duty;
or do you come of your own kind
thought? My half-blind
eye refracts your beauty.

Though born with a focus
so short that an inch from my nose
I recognise
only moving colours,

yours I like; and your voice,
though it's late for me to relearn

your young concern,
just being young, is choice.

Don't worry if the chat
falls flat. If I only had that
eloquent throat
I'd quote the cat's one note.

CANDLE

How it works, the sullen wax
is drunk up by the wick, breathed
out in a calm plume of flame,
I wondered then and a half-
century later, don't know.

After the table emptied,
in secret, for these were for
special occasions, I'd pinch
the round crater at the top
square, press thin prints of my thumb.

The wakening sex that went
with solitude, my moody
penetration of the rain
on glass, the smoky treetops,
gleaming pavements, aches away

at my dreams once more. A tear,
almost milky with salt, dense
with a day's wear and tear, wells
up out of sleep and puddles
the dim hollow of her eye.

Under those lids lives the glance
that first set light to my chill
heart. For all the times it's been
torn, blown flat by troubled air,
sending the room reeling, still

it returns to burning clear,
still flowers and fascinates,
ascending bright and steady
by a means whose physics I
didn't and never will grasp.

WHEEL

Six o'clock spring-
time morning's light
has not yet split
the night's dense chill
when her small hands
start precisely
their work like prayer.

A spinning lump
between them takes
wings as it were,
takes to the air
in the instant
applying of
sixty years' care.

Each as exact
in its space as
freedom itself,

each from the hand
through the breath to
the eye and back
proceeds by grace.

Translucent age:
her white head flicks
in time above.
No emptiness
more fine than these,
containing each
nothing but love.

STRAND

SHE was in that light the sea
carries with it from all its other shores.
    The wind delighted her hair,
her words flew sideways to the shimmering flocks.

Near her the underfoot, the light and air
    were changed, no longer the land's:
walks with her were always walks on the shore.
    Now her body's brown, ribbed sand

    sunk under fathoms of waves.
They angle and collapse like tombs, and foam's
    inscriptions whisper. And still
at a footstep's sound or a waft of glare

the flood of her runs to me, miles inland,
    the salt taste come from nowhere.

SUN

THE old lady's
wrist on the worn
wooden arm of a garden chair
is pale, finely freckled like an orchid.

The breeze-buckled
young grass glistens
in the freakish warmth of mid-March
whose daffodils impersonate that star.

The far expanse
it burns in seems
a hand's span now her eyes are closed.
Closer than all that's stirred by it, that moves

nearby, the life
that lives on life,
the source itself is solitude
shining on nothing. Only directly

touched, her blood has
so nearly lapsed
to pulses slight as those of grass,
can it grant her longer momentary time.

Metallic bud
of a crocus,
her skull, through thin, sunk lids, is filled
with crimson-tainted light and thought dissolves.

Where the breeze and
the beams' faint strokes
mingle unfelt, reflection fades
from the body, from that that had been "I".

RIVERBUS

I
FALLING DOWN

COMFORT OF RUIN

WHERE the A road crosses the Downs
    Between forest and heath,
Leaving behind the ancient towns,
And dips to the ancient city beneath,

Where the white-limbed birch and the pines
    With rough trunks red as rust
Are pressing closer on the lines
Of hurrying cars, they inspire a trust.

A couple of years of neglect
    And the saplings emerge,
Then branches on the bank, unchecked,
And the central reservation converge.

In a decade or maybe less
    It's bramble and nettle
In squadrons whose relentlessness
Begins to break the carriageway's metal,

And before a century'd passed
    As though it never was,
This way would be wooded and grassed.
God knows why that should comfort, but it does.

RIVERBUS

GREENWICH Reach. From zero
eastward the chestnut kestrel
bombarded by a swerve of pigeons
off the pier's roof goes
over the river. At Deptford,

levellers, diggers; Drake
the circumnavigator's knighted
and C. Marlowe's eye
there later that evening
dagged deep. (A spy?)
On the Isle of Dogs
the bronze and grey shell-
gleam of the empty pyramid,
basalt and mineral glass
tomb for no king
sealed in gold, forcing
away the chopped water
from its base. The yacht,
goosewinged, not following
further, the river leans
on brine, crammed, swallows
the sea-wind past
Superb Flats where guns,
oil and grain were winched
and Confucians, Jews and Protestants
walked ashore. A Chef
& Brewer's very half-
timbered nose had piracy
staked on the silt beneath,
to be sucked like a chicken-bone,
broth seeping over the collar,
the nostril, the dog-long
tongue lapping its human
pollutant. Paul looks
bareheaded down the steps
at black casements across the stream.
Troglodytes troglodytes –
the builder vigilant, stone
floating up past the Tower,
Traitor's Gate no
gate at all – a slimed

wall, ice cream.
Capped muzzles doze
under awnings on Belfast.
Under the Gothic machine,
the Pool museum, parked
steamers, Alexandra's
red floral columns
hold down the bed between bridges,
Blackfriars railway and road.
No fish for sale
at Billingsgate nor boats
for hire by the New Globe's
concrete base. While women
worked in the cradles under marching
arches on Waterloo,
Berlin fell. Neptune
hangs his beard on the line
between Cities. Beyond
the Nile victor's needle
wastes grain by grain
into the sweet Thames.

SAND OF THE THAMES

THE sand of the Thames is a fine,
fur-coloured sand, in beaches a stride
or two wide, below the high-water lines;
deep wads in which the heels sink
fringing the mud, the chalk and flints
and the tar-black misshapen shoe-soles
more generally strewn on the shore.

The current has sorted its contents:
over a few yards, the shards
of crockery, fronds and crests,

a tea-cup handle are most collected.
Nearby are the knee-joints of cows,
porous cones of marrowbone,
a medley of chipped brick, pipe and tile.

Incoherent plastic's scattered on the stones,
strips, clips, tops, bottles, toys,
then for the next few steps, driftwood drying,
planks and ply, with sticks
and oddments of branches. A bed, barely,
a bolster of chalk juts out
and the bank beyond is coated in sea-coal.

And here, under the embankment wall
whose weed, raked by the low sun,
shines a jewel-like and startling green,
the river has hoarded its finest materials.
The sand has no inkling of life
tatters of wrack, cockleshell, papery claw,
but is London milled to its conclusion.

One handful comprehends history.
The grains are greyish, lenticular, anonymous,
softly heaped in a pocket resort
ignored by the people whose feet,
as numerous as these, pass overhead.
Now through that press, at last,
I can feel my way by a thread,

the wide stream stringing its debris,
running low, showing the shoals
that ridge it, or full and glittering,
seeming within a hand's reach,
pulsive, restless steel;
can find the way to a place that heals
which tides accumulate and cancel.

REDCROSS WAY

FROM where the debtors' prison was
with back to the dark street Dickens lodged in
when the Marshalsea held his dad
      straight ahead
down Redcross Way to the rivershore
where once were the wharves and Bankside's
                             wonders,
whores and stages and bloodstained baiting pits,
sun on the left lights blossom in the plotted gardens,
formerly grounds of a great house.

Suffolk Place, that was home
to Henry VIII's little sister
and later Royal Mint
for that Fidei Defensor
has left no sign of itself
but a planted corner of peace:
a tall, lopped cherry beside the flats
      and primary school
with broad white buddleia.

An office block of coffee-coloured glass
replaces the manor at the junction,
the battlements and turrets that half-adorned it
above the cottages and hedgerows sketched
by Anthony van Wyngaerde,
      Flemish freelance
(or an agent of Philip of Spain).

The lane with the Templar name
follows the line of its western wall.
What knights had Brandon, Charles, the Duke of
                             Suffolk,

417

the jousting-butt and brother-in-law of the king
    to ward his palace,
stronghold of what lords went before?

The palimpsest of leaseholds
and old paths following topography
make all routes jink or fork or curve.
This way is different,
    direct
to the former Dead Man's Place
at the Bishop of Winchester's postern gate.

Right, to where the legions traded
and the fair was held by the priory,
    prosperity spread
as a cope's hem over blessed feet –
to Borough Market, forklifts shifting
walls of food in the small hours.
Left, round the back of the Clink
to the Anchor Inn and the water.

Beside where people streamed and are streaming
                                        still
    to the crossing
and on to the place on the northern shore
where power beats like blood in a temple,
out here in the primeval suburb
the lager drinkers congregate
to mutter philosophy in twos and threes.

I wonder did the Nine Day Queen walk here,
Lady Jane Grey, when these were walled demesnes?
Duchess of Suffolk, Queen of France
and briefly, at sixteen, England's,
    beheaded by Mary
the First, alias Bloody.

Some such innocence pervades
this much-divided acre.
Car park, parklet, grove and playground
have cover enough, and headroom
for a sleek brace of pigeon
and songbirds of the country, tits or finches,
      mix their warbling
with the blackbirds as usual, singing free.

One week an immaculate black family
were camping in their car beneath the trees,
mother, father, two small children.
Washing hangs on balconies,
the pupils whirl and shriek, conspire in bunches;
and now and then the branches
shed their slight pink fall of bloom
      as days grow longer.

BOROUGH DIGS

I

THE graveyard's under the railway
    And streams beneath the street.
      Dust on our shoes
Was Roman squaddies' hidebound feet.

Quaker and robber and whore they
    Rub their bones in one bed
      While at the door
Of their stews, we knock overhead.

Those whose slaver is on the pots
    Broken below these stones
      Are tongues that shaped
This sea-going tongue's rolling tones.

Johnson, Jonson, Shakespeare, Burbage
    Wet the shards with their lips,
        And he that coined
"The face that launched a thousand ships".

II

Before the legions came, who knows
    What dwellers in the marsh
        Worshipped what gods
Where buses to Camberwell pass?

The fishpond, the leet and the dyke
    That Middle Ages knew
        Ran into pipes
And imperial hygiene grew.

But the wagtail at his gavotte
    In the infants' school grounds
        Plumbs the buried
Line of the brook, the parish bounds.

III

George and Mitre and Blue-Eyed Maid
    Took not such rabble in
        As, silent, drink
The grit and the gravel, and grin.

For the earth's an inn assuages
    Every thirst and hunger,
        Republic of
Earl, monk, punk and costermonger.

IV

The cormorants come up river.
  Mallard pad the shallows.
    Last night a fox
Trots past our door in the small hours,

Stops, waits for the green man walking,
  Quickly crosses the road.
    Concrete and tar
Crown the past. Once the eel and toad

Owned the Borough: no man-sole trod
  Its brine-bothered islands
    And feet that still
Haunt streets, came through reeds and silence.

FOX AT CANARY WHARF

DELIVERED into the dream of steel
        what was that glimpse?
where the light railway bends sharply
gingerly curves through 90°
on its untidy trackway
        all hi-tech
        it's all still perilously
        up in the air
with a sharpish squealing
and brings us at a certain elevation
        that glimpse of rufous fur
this toy-like train, to our destination
the wind-tunnel of Canary Wharf station

421

Bloody wind
        like some revenge of nature
cold colourless and unending
against the cold and colourless
and would-be unending building
through every would-be public space

Coming in at the north door
of Cabot Place East
out of the bloody wind
into the dream
        the oddly prosaic dream
a man was delivered down diagonally
before my eyes
        in mid air
of course I mean on an escalator
        and who did he remind me of?
a man who comes down an escalator
        while others go up
to all intents and purposes identical
and identically shaped women
        pause by shops
in an architect's rendering

        Confessions of an ant:
what glimpse of a point
of a white tip to it?
        I left and went
until I lost the scent of my fellow workers
        It wasn't far
till the smooth stone gave way
and the benches, railings and trees identical
to all intents and purposes
gave way to water-eroded
stone and long beams of rotten wood

and a beautiful length of green
old rope lurking half-submerged
and I'd got as near as I could
to eye-level with the river
and I sat on a stone and smoked
and no one looked

    I now know why
the Eighties hated me
    yes me
despising all I value highest
exalting all I most despise
    It was entirely personal

A certain Mrs, now a Baroness
    she dreamed a dream
where I'm earning my living
where the bloody wind
    never stops blowing

    (Even on a still day
    chill, the yellow leaves
    still flowing

The river was in two minds
neither going away nor coming back
    it made a big fuss
of a boat that ploughed upstream
    waving it away
with a grand wash splashing up the piling
advancing a yard up the shingle
    but next thing
had forgotten all about it
    went back

to fingering the algae-covered loop of old rope
and murmuring

> A shell, encroached by weeds
> and shrubs and rubbish
> an eerie incompletion?

If you see through the money
the buildings seem meant to be funny,
throwing Bauhaus, Doric, baroque,
romanesque shapes on a block
that's still just a box and shows so.
(Nothing dated so fast as po-mo.)
Should business become unjolly
they may be smiled on as period folly,
standing empty:
a monument to M— T—,
Gloriana
of Toriana.

> Being not the future itself
> but an ersatz science-fiction-
> of-fifty-years-ago, Gerry-
> Anderson-built-for-disaster
> sort of a future

Still there's a taint,
stronger than faint,
of supremacist myth
about the numinous monolith,
No 1 Canada Square

> There –
> with the straightahead gait

424

    the directness of a dog
    but the grace
    in its bounding of a cat
    what was that glimpse
    among the weeds?

Since this is to be our tetrahedral
cathedral
let's pour no scorn
on a too-perfect lawn.
If the fountains are over-excited
that can be righted
and time will remedy too much cleanness.
To find the red dog's penis
nose of Thunderbird 3 arising
from the circular gardens would not be surprising;

    Night in Cabot Square
    a still October night
    the feast of lights
    white water underlit
    and the dark itself
    with the weight of voltage
    luminous
    pervasive gleam on steel and polished
        stone

But to see humanity roughen
and soften
the smooth hard edges and colour
the duller
corners; to see Crossharbour, Westferry, Mudchute be
twisted to a better beauty
more suited their solid
names, though not made squalid…

      Strange abstract symbols
      surmount the façade
      of the mouth of the tunnel
      the Limehouse Link
      like some temple
      to Anubis the jackal-
      headed or another
      underworld god

Who'd have believed when these were dug
the whole great port would lie vacant
so soon, staring at the grey sky,
when barely a generation
back the wealth of the world, jostling,
crowded these docks with funnels smoking,
masts and cranes, a floating forest?
         Is fallen, is fallen

Sea-born metropolis
        up on the 21st floor
looking out from the Mirror
        canteen, seaward
eastward, on giant slabs of workless water
        the Barrier housings
        six great nailheads
        driven into a sheet of metal
the broad bending Thames
        shorelands set with dereliction
the half-finished and the decommissioned

And must we not dream we labour
        to build not in vain
that even now in London
        in every moment Jerusalem
with Babylon battles to be built?

See now westward
sun finishes the city
falling through thin mist
Steam plumes from the tops of tower blocks
and the rays broaden
shot through a rift in dour banks of cloud

Wide vanes slowly resolving
above low hills, alluvial plain
uneven urban miles
of sodium silver-white
their brutal
absurdity subsumed to aspiration
equal and lucid
a bed of quaquaversal amethyst

From the top deck of the Docklands Express
above the tunnel
in front of the mystery temple
a glimpse of freedom
vanished among the weeds

Parallel with the simple light of earth
transfiguring scenes
as strong sun can render dereliction
clear and the ugly cheerful
the light of the world, seen shining
through it, makes it shine
The fox is a fact as unlikely
and needful as that

Rufous fur
the black and white tip of a brush
lithely bounding

LA SERENISSIMA

I

STEPS and voices, the rise and fall of strong voices,
remain the Most Serene Republic's loudest sounds,
with the throb of diesel in a narrow rio.

Fantastic bloom, like the lotus rooted in mud:
the clear line and the arc of Tuscan gravity
have no grip where the level and the upright slip.

To mine the meaning of a dream, trace its surface:
between the dry ground of reason and the near
                                    deep,
the city's risen and holds its tenuous sway.

There the changeless gulls that build small nests,
       and are rocked
in hollows of the sea, dreamed they saw towers, and
       spume
of marble façades, dreamed they heard steps and
       voices.

II

Groan of a rope against iron, against the engine;
Tintoretto mounting models in model rooms.
The hoisted victim groans at the Doge's pleasure,
dangling in the red light from the western window
that dissolves the basilica's rainbow glitter.
His tenebrous interrogators ask again.

The tortuous sinews of Christ's extended arm
and exclamatory hands flung out, full of shadow.
The belly of this goddess, Venice, like a ship's
hold, piled and stuffed with Madonnas and
       merchandise.
A tabby grey as lagoon-mist walks on the wharf
where stripes of ripples lie like flickers of rumour
across the stone-faced elegance of palaces.

The seething angels of annunciation burst
through Mary's wall like denunciation's agents,
while carnival masquers whirl across cat-backed
       bridges
and have disappeared before their laughter's echo.
Casanova rocks to the oar's lurching rhythm
and birds circle, crying, over water as smooth
as Jesus stretched his arm above and bade be still.
The dyer's son mounts his ladder to be near him.

IMPROBABILITY

How hard, as we spin past
the oaks of Devon, only
now beginning to neglect
nurture of their leaves
and let them discolour and wither,
and as, at a curve, the dipping
scape displays a mantle
of the raspberry-coloured earth,
newly-turned, beside a lush
viridian of pastures' second greening,
to keep, like the cloud-
chamber's witness in filaments

of mist to the particles' flight,
track of or hold steadily for a moment
the perception of how unlikely,
in neighbourhood of vast
void this vapour-fretted sky conceals,
the oaks' intricate preparing for autumn,
or the orderly hills of Devon themselves,
raised and lowered by the world's continued
irregular flowing and returning,
and ourselves, and our thought
not even entering its own equation;
how untenable for long
the vanishing trail of noughts
to the odds against one of those
rust-edged round-toothed leaves.

LILSTOCK BEACH

In flat calm, when waves it seems obliged
against its will to run, an inch high
barely and a half-mile long, approach
the stones with the mildest of whispers,
a sea you'd credit with neither ebb
        nor flow fronts Lilstock Beach.

Boulders thoroughly round and the flat
perfect pebbles are quiet witness
to the days of storm, but now near life-
lessness prevails beneath the cliffs of
thick yellow mudstone and dark fractious
        shale, clining sinuously

in alternate layers, catching the late
light on the westward curve of each bay.
Such peace, in level descending rays,

as of a planet where life never
came, the peace on earth before it was;
     stone and water simpleness.

A pavement of fossilised mud lies
fissured into cobbles underfoot
and tramlines of upturned strata run
broken-edged towards the sun, grey light
occupying empty pools. There, in
     a loose block lying crossways,

the big spiral dent, precisely franked
ancestral seal, of an ammonite
fossil, the lid of a manhole raised
to look into time. The sun is down.
and the western sky rich and ragged
     with cloud. The sea's crept forward

a foot or two, quietly, always
eating its words. The aeons, as they
crept past, turned this giant nautilus
to a wheel of stone, as a promise
to beauty: no death. We turn homeward,
     at peace in our novel flesh.

LIGHT IN SOHO

STILL, after the clocks have gone back,
after the slick-faced office blocks
have gone up against it, even
the snag-toothed gin of Victorian
roofs cannot hold it back, which comes
unstealthy, but like a victor
to gates thrown open, bronze and plumes
shining, and spiteless as Hector.

Where the trees are juvenile slaves,
are gracious but inwardly grieved,
withholding counsel from alien
speech, and the birds all too human,
the sly pigeons on their maimed feet,
one from the other world, unbowed,
where Poland meets Great Marlborough Street,
brings gold not to be bought nor sold.

In the metal belly and gut
of concrete where that world is ground
and swilled down in liquidity,
in the wide imperial city,
having for what it engulfs no
eyes, only appetite, no smell
nor touch, we live in delusions
of neon, shadows of the will.

But this broad light, making splendid
the façades, kneels on the road's end
and looks in our faces, candid
friend. Above, steel-bright cirrus brands
the narrow sky. Long silhouettes
at our feet, we recall, as night
soon falls, that we are creatures yet;
it is the earth on which we walk.

II
BALLADS

ISABELLA

AT midnight, in fierce long gusts
the wind, raised suddenly from the sea,
leapt on the village

and seemed the voice of your grieving
over a man gone from the island
and your tideless heart.

Slender beauty, sigh out your gales.
Though your rage beat down this mountain ring
you shan't blow him back.

Brute wind, the dark of the moon.
Down in the dry torrent, the tom-cats
yowl their bloodstained song.

Brown-eyed girl, I beg you, peace,
for love of him on that tireless sea,
gale-weary sailor

who fights black waves to harbour
by the timeless rock of your heart.
Peace: let him anchor.

PAS DE DEUX
Fonteyn & Nureyev

WE'VE come by bad adventure to this bay of peace:
 harbour yourself with me.

*The weight of bonds' remembrance doesn't cease
 as soon as the cuffed hands are free,*

and redeemers have proved captors before,
    so let me range.

Until the sun and moon exchange
    their mansions, there's no door
I would not unlock, nor key I'd not throw away,
    if just an eyebrow raised
or finger crooked, or your head's slightest sway
    showed you so pleased.

Your servitude's a mortgage my poor will must meet
    with express desires then?
Be free of me and our freedom's complete.

    I'm free to be as other men,
untied from you: restricted by the lack
    of actual shape
to my joys, and with no escape
    from searching's circling track.
A world is in the cell that holds us both; a jail
    is the world where you're not.

Once I had none; now hope, though newborn frail,
    is all I've got.
Can I stake my slender means on your well meaning?
    The odds on love are long.

At last the long-wintered heart is greening
    and the birds taking up their song.

But what if ice, returning suddenly,
    should shear these shoots
and freeze the slow sap from the roots?
    Who then would revive me?

The earth would never get round to changing seasons
    if she had metaphors

spun and woven from a stock of reason's
    yarn rich as yours.
But dropping thaw undoes the frost of friendlessness
    in new-found fire; eyes melt
away the fear of proffered tenderness.

Having loved and been betrayed, felt
and met unfeeling, I know that danger
    waits in the trust
of arms, and that when, as we must,
    we will love a stranger,
we put ourselves in the way of the harms that crouch
    in the crooks of twined limbs,
that watch for the moment when two fires touch,
    wariness dims,
then leap to sever and leave us clutching the dark.

I have no spells to fend
nor charms to bend time's arrow from its mark
    except that, send
against us what assaults it may, until my breath
    itself is forfeit, I'll
not breathe the killing word Goodbye.

                        Let death
    alone aspire to part us; while
we live, in league against tyrannous tears,
    the espionage
of envy and the plot of age,
    we'll smile among our fears.

This world has never, whatever its songs may dream,
    been friendly to lovers.

But the Virgin's stars from the sky's extreme
    stream above us.

O'HENCE & O'HITHER

SAID Thither O'Hence to Bide O'Hither,
Let us go walking together,
my dear, my bride-to-be.

Said Bide O'Hither to Thither O'Hence,
I like to wander with my nonchalance;
you always want to get there.

The rocks are flying up to the sun,
the clever birds pretending to be stones,
the mountain is in full song,

but they walk across it separately,
do brisk O'Hence and Miss O'Hither,
although they love each other dearly,

for one longs to get there,
where everything's full of elsewhere –
the colours, the shapes, the air –

while bonny O'Hither, watching the bee on the sprig,
says, Surely,
if there's the only where you get

might you not just as well be here?

ROSE

THE green of the park having turned
Through a June and July that burned and burned
From May's ingenuous shyness
To the eighth month's stiff and shining dryness,

438

Flat on our backs, observing castled cloud,
    We say our mutual thoughts aloud,
    Bustle and dust of the city
Remoter than vaporous bergs and floes
    In a moment that holds but me
        And Rose.

    While people pass beneath our feet
Unseen, unseen the other lovers meet
    Above our heads, beneath the trees,
And the managing director at ease,
Almost, with Miss McCarthy from accounts.
    A zephyr makes the roses flounce
    On their thorns, and tilts the slanted
Polished leaves of the plane above. They close
    And spread light hands on beds planted
        By rows.

    The welcoming turf holds us fast
As hand holds hand on the clipped grass, and past
    Our noses the cumuli tumble.
Earth and sky between them raise and humble,
Let us loose and enclose us all at once.
    To let the bones' and breath's response
    To their elements join us there
Was all we required of that hour's repose,
    Until we were looked for elsewhere
        And rose.

    So long as limbs retain the strength
Of the ground where, coupled, we lay full length,
    And the blue sky flows in my chest,
Mind in its searching out a place of rest
Will recur to that stretch of urban lawn
    Where our green partnership was born.
    In the business of December,

On a Wednesday of unpunctual prose,
   That sun still glows like an ember,
      A rose.

CAT LOVE

Is the last thing from calf-love,
Is not even half-love.
The gentlemen's behaviour
Is of most pungent savour.
Not the courteous or meek
But he of most scar-swollen cheek
Will get to seize her by the scruff
And pin her to the ground
With her tail going round and round.
She, for her part, watches them tear
Each other's heads with an air
Of piqued amusement, from a spot
Of safety. That gets her hot.
She rolls herself base uppermost
And rubs her neck against the post,
The toast of musk his tail-end raised,
And walks on air like a lady praised.
With gashed, infected brows
The losers slink behind the house
And when they meet, in stiff slow-motion
Circle, speaking with deep emotion
Of reciprocal hate and parallel lust
Then give each other another thrust,
Glad if they can rip an ear,
Glad to hear the song of fear,
Fangs sunk in thick necks
With curses that would vex

The Devil himself from sleep.
And when to a nook she must creep,
Fat as a furry full moon,
And multiply all too soon,
Birthing a further four or five,
And give them suck and help them thrive,
Given half a chance the brutes
Will kill the kits, their own prick-fruits.
Thank heavens we are not Felidae:
Thank heavens human love's so tidy!

LOVE IN AGE

As age lays waste to beauty
The time-honoured chorus says
And wrinkles are a duty
Paid to days by every face,
Shall our delights diminish,
What was wrapped in air and fire
Sink to a clayey finish
From which no bronze shoots aspire?

As none prefer from the bowl
The shrivelled fruit to the fresh
Or opt for ash over coal,
So of naked flesh the nesh
And new, of roses the bud
And those that are recently blown
Are counted best, are of good,
Even, all that some will own.

On the dog-rose, the last shred
Of pink still hangs. Breeze-broken
Poppies relinquish their red

Standards. But freed now, shaken
By the shameless destroyer,
The hard pod is filled with seed.
So love's lasting spark blows clear
Of cinders with all time's speed.

TELEOLOGY

"I'M not so sure,"
        She said.
    "There may be more.
Perhaps when we are dead
    The final gnosis
Shall relativise our claims."

"Of course," he said,
        "It might,
    But of this bed
And of this burning night
    Apotheosis
Can but rekindle the flames."

"I'm not," she sighed,
        "So sure."
    "Oh love," he cried,
"Come away from the door.
    Come, quickly, close it,
For the draught it makes here maims."

"I'm still," she wept,
        "In doubt."
    And would have stepped
Over threshold and out
    But in the process
Tripped, and, stayed in his prompt arms,

Promptly forgot her alarms,
Transcendence's fading charms
Or metaphysical aims.
So soon they resume the games.

ON THE NATIONAL STEPS

At every stroke the bells of Martin's ring
The blue-grey plaza of the evening air
Is crossed and recrossed by the birds that turn
In shrieking, flowing coils. The night at hand
Impels them; to protest or take its part,
They crowd against the failing of the light.

From breathing fictive space and painted air
Our feet move weighted and our heads are light.
As though by one yet greater master hand
Compelled to stand still at the stair's top turn,
And watch as round the column, whirling ring
On ring, the waves of starlings crash and part.

Each of its galaxy a millionth part,
Each star there flickers darkly on the turn;
Whose little-finger-knuckle brain, and ring-
Bound staring eye, steer a body so light
Its weight would barely register in hand,
The bones and plumage reinforced with air.

We've seen him within who came to set light
To the hard earth, wading the stream, the ring
Of eternity glimmering in air
Unseen, it seems, by all but one, whose part
Shall be to make a way and die, to turn
And pour the water from his raised right hand.

We've seen the players too who wait their turn,
Each like a Bible studying his hand,
That casual group that time will never part
From brush-strokes freely ordered as an air
Of Bach's, harmonic summing of the light
That dances round a common pastime's ring.

We leave them with a touch of hand on hand.
Together we belonged, but when we part
We're exiled from the timelessness of light
In a world where "Well – I'll give you a ring"
Is all our connection. You, with an air
Of loss, watch the crowds into which we'll turn.

Then turn again and through the darkened air
Let ring the words, strong as your voice is light,
"You're part of me. I'd sooner lose this hand."

THE MOTHER & THE MONUMENT

SHE rises up in her night-dress
   And seizing her distress
      In both her hands
Goes where the great commander's statue stands.

She flings her tears beneath the hoof.
   The rider sits aloof,
      His bronze ear blocked,
But by his stern green brow her grief's unlocked.

"I've laid my children on the bow
   Of your saddle; they go
      Gladly to trench
And charge, to snipe and strafe, to din and stench.

"Now they lie far to south and north
  And of all who went forth
   None has come home
And not for one do these hands deck a tomb.

"Yet you ride on, your right arm raised,
  While I below, half-crazed,
   Lament my few
Of the many the world has lost through you."

Like the moan of the shrouded earth
  A foghorn from the firth
   Booms its refrain
Where the dreadnought swings on its anchor chain.

The night rain pearls the breast she's bared,
  Drops from the horse's flared
   And decades-dead
Nostrils, sweats the furrows of that great head.

Yet here and there the stars peep down
  On the blot of her gown,
   Pale on the black-
Streaked pedestal that smoke and smuts attack.

When they found her cold on the lawn
  Next day, the ray of dawn
   Struck red on mount
And rider. But for this, none could account:

Where the warrior sat, a child
  Now sat, wide-armed, and smiled
   Adorably:
A bronze-cast, dimpled child of two or three.

DEAR JOHN
In memory of Ernie Pyle

DEAR John, I wish you could be more specific
As to just where you are in the Pacific.
I sit and stare at the pages of blue
In the atlas, but which green dot holds you?

Dear Mary, Thank you for the socks and pot
Of jam. The Japs have been making it hot
For us here, but at last the beastly weather
Has cooled. I hope we will soon be together.

Dear John, Anne did well in her last report.
Now all of her blouses are far too short
In the sleeves, she's shot up so this last year.
She looks more and more like you. John, I fear...

Dear Mary, You shouldn't be worried and fret.
You've not heard the end of the old man yet.
Though action's about as far as it could get
From here, I keep my head well down, you bet!

Dear John, Are you sure this landing's not risky?
Did you get the bottle of Daddy's whisky?
Charles says please could you capture a Jap sword!
I miss you, dear. I'm half-frantic, half-bored...

Dear Mary, Well, of course I may get slightly wet!
Is Charlie good? Annie still teacher's pet?
I kiss you all. And darling, don't forget –

Dear Mrs Wilkes, It is with deep regret...

HECTOR'S GHOST

AM I his dogs' meat, dishonoured
and laid on the earth as dung
    who was forward
in the line this morning, and tall and young?

I taste the dust of defeat; he
finds nothing in victory sweet.
    Since he beat me
his anger starves for further flesh to eat.

Till it perishes I linger
still the wrong side of the stream
    where with finger
crooked the boatman beckons to leave this dream.

On the far side, victors, vanquished
forget which they were. Their force
    is relinquished
with all their pain who reach that river's source.

So build for me my monument
and play my funeral games.
    In a moment
then, Hector, Achilles shall be but names

to poets of equal value
as similes for the brave.
    Dear foe, shall you
not also, soon, necessitate a grave?

Like me, and caring as little,
you'll be at mercy of arts:
    of your brittle
heap, no stone; no home but in human hearts.

ICARUS BENEATH THE WAVES

THE wonder is not that I fell so low
    But that I climbed at all
And the pity is not that the clear sky
Dropped me, but that I let my childhood go
    Before I dared to leap;
    Not that I went too high
  But, having no further to fall,
I have no deeper seas in which to sleep.

The floor of broken light that shifts above,
    Darkening then brightening
This steep-struck water daily, black to blue,
Bars that friendly fire with which I fell in love.
    Fine shells thicken the sand
    And bones of gulls that flew
  As sudden as summer lightning
And dust of vessels lost with every hand.

The ruins of my wings that sank more slow
    Are waving at my side
And at my head and feet. Father! I cry
As he watches me fail; he could not know,
    To him or to that sphere
    Where I aspired to die?
  There nothing fades, no creatures slide
On my shade like the shy and odd ones here.

You with your cunning by the middle way
    Arrived on some hilltop
Among olive trees, and burnt your device,
No doubt, that would cause the simple dismay,
    Be plaything for a king.
    Had you not made it twice,

I not been there to take the drop,
What record of your work would the world sing?

My vain desires alone immortalise
        Your unexampled skill.
Through me he learns the first thing, just to dare,
And though he takes your thought, the next who
                                              flies
        Above all takes my heart.
        So to plunge from the glare
    To this dimness that earth's tears fill,
To fail was, after all, the greater part.

ACHERON

A BOAT stands to on a stream beyond sound
whose coiling waters are quiet as smoke –
that thread that the bobbin of earth has wound.

Beaten by boredom, a few lie aground
and beg to board where, beneath a riven oak,
a boat stands to on a stream beyond sound

and the great have cut with their fares outbound,
with a berth there booked they shall not revoke,
that thread that the bobbin of earth has wound.

When you and I beneath a single mound
have come to the place where time has no stroke,
a boat stands to on a stream beyond sound,

and the mud bank is strewn and further browned
with leaves that broke from the bay-crowned who
        spoke
that thread that the bobbin of earth has wound,

may we linger a moment, turning round
to share a word, recall when last we woke.
A boat stands to on a stream beyond sound,
that thread that the bobbin of earth has wound.

ANCHORESS

EASTWARD the rising sun levels
and sets alight, surmounts the baseless line
of ragged peaks. Dust-devils
raised by the dawn lie flat, and lizards catch the shine
of a new day.

She climbs the stair, up through the rock
unliving, but warm with the warmth of life.
Only one dandelion clock
of cloud strives with the light, then abandons the strife
and blows away.

There's the nameless plain, men once gone,
that earth shall be again. She combs the sand
and watches the hours wear on,
the shadows shorten, shading her eyes with her
        hand,
keeping the faith.

Unbroken circle of sky
and the bare inhuman breadth of the land
and unseen cities whose high
hopes shimmer, built by the countless, the dreamless
        hand,
balance on her breath.

SHANTY

BENEATH the sea-wind-stunted oak,
The sea-rain drifting in like smoke,
Beading like glass in her rust-coloured cape,
Bedraggles the hair on her nape,
Where she sits on the low rocky shore.

Her lover's boat slides its grey prow
In past the unseen headland now.
The bell-buoy clangs but rarely on the shoal,
A shivering note like one her soul
Sends to the soul of him she waits for.

The mate bids the captain beware,
The captain bids the pilot dare
The channel. There at the head of the bay
Eyes unseen a year and a day
Watch for the day that his ship shall moor.

"Beware," the bell mutters, "Beware";
And "Beware," the mate. "And where
Are you now, my love, with the heart you took?"
Chimes the soundless note from the rock
He'd heard through gales and the waves' white roar.

SITTING STILL

A TEMPLE had crumbled on an overgrown hill.
        Beside the toppled shrine
Where vine and ivy drank the dregs of mortar out
    From courses laid by the long-dead devout,
        A seeker whose beard was no longer short

451

Nor altogether unmingled with white
  Sat sunk in thought
  One moonless night.
 In his eyes the embers shine,
  And still he sits, still.

He stayed and stared, and sat to meditate his fill,
  Attending on his heart.
An old grey ass, seeing him at noon, shook his ears.
 A young red dog came too and shook his ears.
 A girl sent out for kindling sticks went back
 And told her kin a saint was in that place
  To which the track
  Was a faint trace.
 No look nor sound makes him start,
  And still he sits, still.

Believing one who heard the voice and sought the will
  And loved the works of good
Could not but bring them good, they brought the
         hermit food,
 Cleared somewhat the wreck around his solitude,
 Here and there set stone once more upon stone,
 While the stars went over his whitening head.
  Two decades flown,
  And by his shed
 The shrine stood tall in the wood.
  And still he sits, still.

The apes, the monkeys chatter; parrots, peacocks
         shrill;
  Lamps of magnolia bloom
And shatter, and shake their pale flames down on
         the grass
 Of the springtime that sees the seeker pass.
 His village visitors kindle the pyre

From the fire they daily fed for him once,
  That small watch-fire,
  Then cast in bronze
 The likeness above his tomb.
  And still he sits, still.

THE FOOL

HE came down from the hill,
a tiptoe, unclipped poodle
idling at heel,
a sweet green stalk of grass
between his teeth. The poppies shook
in summer wind.
Weather came behind him:
tall rain-clouds, static, piled up on
the skyline, rolled
at last over the crags.
Ditches burst, cisterns flooded, young
crops beaten flat.

Later, sat by the wall
looking down, watching the night fall,
dew wet the sedge,
he rose when the fat stars
of autumn started to glimmer,
drops on his face,
hitching up his collar
against the veering gust that drives
the small dead leaves.
He went past the chapel
to a bed among the long stones,
speechless as them.

Meanwhile looms were busy,
yearlings trotted to the butcher.
Logs split and stacked,
we waited once more for
winter to cut off the passes.
He grew more grey,
like empty twigs of birch
against the light, stark and absent:
also filthier,
daily nearer to blent
with the dirt; thinner, more tattered
and somnolent.

When the ground was frozen
he passed away, whom we'd called "fool"
for no reason.
The doctor and priest both
attended, and were not required,
who'd also guessed
at a name for the care-
carved face we couldn't place, but felt
we'd met before.
"The sea," he said in death's
fever, "the sea is beautiful."
We took his word.

TWO TOWERS

A KING and his yes-men lived in a tower,
The queen and her ladies beside in hers,
    A few short paces separate,
And easy the commerce over the smooth turf.

Until one autumn of dwindled harvest
Bad news coming from the country's corners,
 Turbulence and noise of dissent,
Caused the king to think of stiffer defence.

"Throw down the crenellated top," he charged,
"The fanciful crown of my consort's keep.
 "Take the stone that I need to build
"From all its unnecessary turrets."

So round the hill with one keep taller now
And one less tall, was built a curtain wall,
 A fosse and moat to keep the men
Of barons bent on usurping at bay,

While under the poorly-assembled boards
That capped the shorter tower now, the queen
 And her ladies-in-waiting tripped
Out of reach of the raindrops warping them.

Until one midnight with one hungry mouth
In which no language was discernible,
 Many-headed with one ahead,
The mob like a wreck-strewn tide assembled

And the king's command was, "Arm my engines
"With the bulk of blocks from that neighbour pile;
 "Let the ladies be quartered here.
"At battle's end I shall build another."

But the queen disdained to be taken in
Or to lean on the alms of an equal.
 "In the lee of this briar patch
"Three canvas sheets shall make me a castle;

"The wind-driven rain shall pour me my wine,
"With freezing stars for candles and sconces,
    "What brambles yield for bread and meat.
"Of the sky I cannot be dispossessed."

So when in the one giant's fist the land
Had round them, like the shell of a blown egg
    The frail fortress broke and fell in
And in massed the murder-minded many,

The gibbet was long where they stretched the king
And all his chivalry, fine-fledged magpies,
    And the only ones spared the death
That crew of beggarwomen on the heath.

THE HOUSE

THE wind as it sucks at the stack
Carries a fume as dense as guilt
That cankers blooms and drives the garden back
From the house that Jack built.

They're up to party every night
And things get broken, drinks are spilt,
But it's still as the grave when the red light
Strikes the house that Jack built.

Some days a pallid toddler cries
For Mr Jack and Mrs Jilt
At the square windows like ignorant eyes
Of the house that Jack built.

A blue glow blinks at evening fall
From an upper room. Curtains wilt
On wires, doors are locked to any who call
At the house that Jack built.

Yet strangers overlook the signs
And as they pass in slow-footed lines
Resolve when they build to base their designs
On the house that Jack built.

A MAN OUTSIDE A CAGE

PLEASURE lies in walking round it,
solidly built and intricate,
the bars and hinges gilt and chased,
locks of impenetrable steel.
Odd they seem designed to fasten
from within. None of those I find
on my circuit, despondently
squatting by their world's neglected
bound, have the look of the keepers
of keys. Scratching themselves, they stare
inward, towards the rich copses,
the recreational pools, frames
and fountains where their dominant
brethren, chattering, sport and splash.

They've never turned a hair or turned
their heads to hear me calling them
from outside. I've waved inducements
of food and other rarities,
trying to catch an eye – some sparkling
fragment scavenged along the track,
shard of glass or aluminium,
soldered maze of snapped circuitry…

Nothing doing. I used to sleep
in the dust, curled tight in a kind
of embrace against it, as dusk
began to fall, lights played inside

457

among the leaves. Am I slowing
with age, I'd long been wondering,
since each circumambulation,
beginning at dawn, eats further
into the hours of daylight. Once
I was finished well before noon:
lately the sun's been far declined
by the time I'm back at the stick
that marks my starting. Now at last
I know.

       My left boot heel's broken
at the corner, and those inside
run barefoot. In a muddy rut
just in from the perimeter,
clearly shown in the low red light
today at the end of my walk,
was my print inside. The cage is
growing.

       I turn my back on it,
looking out over level waste
far as the eye can see – the wide
and spectacular emptiness
of my narrowing possession.

III
HISTORIES

ORIGINALS

I

LUIT used his wits
and strove to be alpha male
with favoured access to all females.

But another, Yeroen,
assaulted him one day
with a sidekick.

They tore his balls off
and left him bleeding to death.
The roots of politics,

said his keeper,
whose brother guts were wrenched,
are older than all humanity.

II

I remember Arnhem
as a boy of eight or nine
whose imagination
powered the powerful machines,

Lockheed Lightning,
Tiger tank among the pines
and sandy walks
where the Allies blundered

and lost bloodily.
Typhoon, '88,

their weight and scales
of green iron,

were my knights in armour,
my dragons,
and the afternoon
happy in the sunny woods.

III

There's 2 per cent
between three chimps
in Arnhem Zoo and us,

the genetic difference
between horse and zebra,
which can be made to mate.

Nikkie and Yeroen plot
against Luit the boss.
Nikkie the younger

in the struggle for
power, the social chess
of reproductive success,

the pawn from time
to time of both,
accomplice to murder.

Three hours of surgery
couldn't save him,
who might have lived

in sunny woods.
But a refugee's
not a recognised species

in captivity,
no driving out
of the war-museum

world of the apes who kept him
for this old animal,
however political.

IV

Horse and bison,
rhino, horse and bison,
bison, deer and horse

over, through and within each other
over and over
for twenty-five thousand years.

Why speak of Rome and Greece
and Britain
which have lived but for instants,

and not of these,
the longest culture of all?
They found their church in a rock,

their church of hands and signs,
herds of horse and bison.

V

Shimmer as long leather thongs
move on her knee, on her thigh
or are blown in the breeze;
slight continuous jingling
of the strings of ivory beads
over her shoulder, down on her breast
shifting as she breathes.

The bride stands ready,
the boy stands by.
His lance beside him
is twice his height,
worked from a single tusk.
The eagle feathers twist
and spin in the gust.

The bride-price displayed
on hides at his feet
is in amber, shell and beads,
delicate horses,
the carved-horn batons of healing.
The bands follow into the cave
of horse and bison,
under the slant ceiling.

Potent and fertile, swift and loud,
the drums and flutes begin,
the dancers circle the fire,
seeing the seer,
entranced, with colours come in.

VI

She dips the brush.
It wavers like a snake
on the face of the rock
without touching
then darts across
and back, and slows,
the stroke unloading
ochre on the stone,
on the flank of black-
maned chestnut mare
and foal she adds to the herd.

VII

The great-jawed southern ape,
bipedally bovine, browsing
unmolested in the clearing,
master of the arts of chewing leaves:

how did handy upright man,
his neighbour striding out,
regard this boss-browed munching shape?
As food perhaps – or with a kind of awe

as, jack of all landscapes,
he left them behind,
the last rugged headland
of subconsciousness, slipping away.

Beyond lay melodious waves
of wordsound, weave
of clanship, chipped tools, personhood;
beyond, ferocious futures.

Furtive among the abundant green
keen-eyed erectus sees their silent troop
saunter hairily by and vanish
in dim, australopithecene peace.

VIII

An ape who looked at the sun said,
You are my friend
always. What can I do for you
whose allegiance I rely on?

An ape who looked at the stream said,
Always clear, always coming.
Without you, home would not be.

The sun was blacked out, the spring dried.
If I was you, said the ape,
I'd treasure signs of gratitude,
spring, sun, if I was you.

Smell the smoke of the fat,
you who lead on the hunters.
Fruit in your lap, flowers for your hair,
said the ape, as lovers give each other,
as becomes the wise.

IX

That's natural religion
and where does that get us
in the natural aggression
of apes at war?

Were we pluckers of Paradise's
fruit with our canine teeth
or was that before?
Did an animal ever stand up

to be guardian over others?
Then what with our greed
we lost, a higher place
than the rest indeed,

where labouring saints
on the earth irrigated with sweat
reach to shoulder the sweet
burden and bring it down the ladder.

THE ASTRONAUT ADRIFT

I

THE voices crackle their consolations
Fainter and fainter, and fade on the chance

They claim of a bright side yet. Ad hoc plans
Drift off and I remain in the silence

To which slow tune my walk becomes a dance.
There is no rescue from this radiance:

I, mote, watched by the stars in their millions
Turning through the blackness of heaven's lens.

II

To taste tobacco on the teeth
and tiredness in the heart
and droop to sleep, from sleep
thereafter never to be apart;

or to wander on the shore
and kick the stone that has no sense
of wonder at coming so far,
of loss at being carried hence;

and to watch the infant inept
in manners, in gait and language
chase the gross and scintillant
fly that prises open the blossom;

such are the treasures that world over there
has to offer the stranded hero
from one to zero
counting his air.

In a deep space freefall
he misses them all.

III

They spent so much to get this view
and I'm the only one who did. "You,"
they said, "bear a great burden, and honour,"
but now they both weigh nothing.

They threaded my snaking umbilical
fine as the finest capillary,
but now I'm a free particle.

A parturition defiantly to be wished,
to go away from all flesh,
the earth's one true supernumerary.

I tug it again in disbelief
and the naked junction rears and gleams
above my head, in the sun that I'm alone with,
me and my one true love, this planet.

IV

Roll and tumble, little star…
Through the sweat of my forefathers' arms
I slipped up here,
further from harm than their wildest fear
or shackled dream would have launched me.

All my mothers bowed down
by labour raised me
to cartwheel with heavenly grace
across the face of Africa,
alone in the eye of the God they praised.

Their voices thickened
by the second-rate air they breathed,
they sang aloud or hummed beneath
their breath their hymns of liberty,
the atmosphere of freedom they foresaw me live in.

Our Father has so many children
but none would ever choose
to be flying in my shoes
beyond those curdled storms;
the sparkling simple seas

where they were tossed and lost
I've effortlessly crossed,
a sparrow He wouldn't let fall.
Above that ball of blues
Jackson, their black son, wheels.

V

To few is there given such luxury,
To count closing breaths with accuracy.

The turning void received our embassy
With its brilliant boundless courtesy.

Who rode on flames, as earth's emissary,
Circles in the glare, the sun's devotee.

Comrades, as you pass my antipodes
Tonight, don't pity, but remember me.

VI

Is America all in the dark?
From up here not a spark
Shows a highway or a city
Or a burning ghetto.
From Buffalo to El Paso
The continent's unlit.

The States undergoing their night
Blaze their martyr no white
Cross nor send the red rocket's glare;
No pointing spangles fill
That barren banner, no lights bill
Their One-Night-Only star.

Though sackless, black, and in a coat
Of silver, as I float
Above their roofs I bless my kids
Like Santa and unload
Prayers, that my pinprick passing goad
As bold, less futile deeds.

BLUE LION

THE blue lion is the night.
He is full of eyes
reaching from horizon to horizon.
He watches over the hunters
sleeping on the plain
and sees them taken
by the slavers with their guns.
They are never to be free again
nor to call him the blue lion.

The blue lion is a blue sea
and each white tooth
in his wide mouth is a shark.
They follow for black meat
after the black keel,
fresh, infected meat.
They will be fed daily
once the disease takes hold.
They weave the water outside the hold.

He is made of the suffering
inside the hold.
The blue lion is king of sufferings.
The little children come to him,

471

the mothers, the husbands.
Many who would come to him
can't come to him.
He becomes iron
in the blackness, stench and pain.

He becomes burning iron
in the marketplace.
His entire flank is covered in brands
and to each of these brands
in time he will answer.
It is an indictment not to be erased
in letters of fire
on a tablet of bronze,
in letters of blood on the sun.

The blue lion is torn to pieces.
The bleeding parts are sent
different places
up and down the green river.
Now is always the last
the wife saw of her husband,
the daughter remembers of her mother.
But the parts of the blue lion
will find each other.

The blue lion is a green river,
a brown river rolling,
clear water rolling over the heads,
woolly heads of the elect.
They bow all in white
to the water, they put their heads
in the hands of the baptiser,
they submit to the water
in the jaws of the blue lion.

Sometimes she lives in the country
where the blue lion stalks
and sets the dogs to baying,
and sometimes she lives in town
and has finery and hears a piano
from mulatto to quadroon,
octaroon to Creole.
She does a dance from Paris, sings,
she puts her head in the jaws of a lion.

He picks up a hammer.
He picks up a hoe.
He picks up a guitar.
He puts down a dollar
like any other man.
He picks up a shotgun
when the dogs are baying.
He picks on his woman.
She packs up his bags.

She packs fruit, she picks cotton,
she bust the suds
in the white folks' yard.
She bears witness
never heard by the ear of man.
She grows old, she knows bitterness.
Her daughters grow up to be black women
like her;
they are the blue lion.

The black snake moan
of the whip. Trenches
in the red clay.
A bloody arm
in a blue sleeve,

a muddy grey back
trampled in the advance,
trampled in the retreat.
Crimson splashes on the midnight blue lion.

The Delta Dog's brakeman
brings a copy of the Yellow Dog Blues.
The blue lion's pupils
drop discs of black vinyl.
A black man with a diamond in his tooth
drives a big car, a Packard
which belongs to him.
His axe is in the back seat.
A white ignoramus calls him "Boy!"

The blue lion thinks of Africa.
He gets a job in Chicago,
composes Ko-Ko,
In a Mellotone and Muggles,
breaks the mould.
He crosses the ocean by Cunard,
by the White Star Line.
Congratulations to the coloured band,
an audience with the King.

Meanwhile, rats, restlessness,
rancour, terror, hopelessness
of meanwhile being forever,
generations passing through
the fire to Moloch.
Sterno, murder, crack, misery,
the racist etcetera,
the ripping up of the future.
The blue lion thinks of a king in Africa.

And begins to resist.
And begins to register.
And begins with rhythm
to gain ground,
to be present beyond all exclusion.
Oh God that auction block
I thought began to shake and rattle.
I do believe the stone
shall rock and roll.

The blue lion whelps in Liverpool
nearby the auction block
and in London, Dakar and Capetown
beyond the road block,
even in Tokyo, Berlin, Moscow,
the blue lion makes a home,
returns home everywhere.
Meanwhile the ripping up of the future
goes on.

In my home, in my bedroom
the blue lion befriended me.
A long way he came;
I could listen to the stories all night.
He became strength to me,
an example,
became the one thing bigger
than inspiration,
an incarnation.

Meanwhile the blue lion lies wounded
in the gutter,
set upon by robbers,
set upon by cops.
Meanwhile the guns multiply

in the gullies and in the projects.
Meanwhile a white estate goes by
with the bass shaking the road, Do you know
Social Living is the best?

Has anyone here
seen the blue lion?
Freed a lot of people,
five centuries old,
purrs like a saxophone,
runs like an Olympic gold medallist,
last seen in chains,
believed to be
bound for glory.

IV

BECOMING LIGHT

SUN CUT

SUN cut in pieces, going down
flashing in trembling pieces
in the twigs' net of oblong
openings, scissoring,
in the leaves' tin-snip blades.

Some will not rise
who see the sun cut in pieces,
shivered, flash red and green;
who soon will be dead

see it in the dark asymmetric
net, in the secateur blades
closing, burning, cut in pieces;
who will not rise with it,
sliding down, non sequitur.

DOUBLY SAD

MY heart was doubly sad
Looking into the spring
For loss of what I had
And hope that May should bring
Again what made me glad.

Now sorrow's harsh, but lack
Of hope is a boundless
Wilderness without track
Or cairn, shade- and soundless,
Where to go on or back

Are neither of them good.
Such deserts were at hand
Though under buds I stood
To see spring paint the land
And the flowering wood.

NUNHEAD

BLACK iron torches turned down on the pillars mean
"That which feeds me kills me". Above, in a circle,
a snake holds its tail, grim sign of the eternal.
Soon they'll lock the gates and loose the dogs from
       the lodge,
a cottage-mausoleum, but there's fox-taint still
mingled with the warm humus of English jungle
and a feast of lairs where trees have toppled the
       tombs.

The wealthy for a moment may make us obey,
with their "final and funniest follies", their pleas
for contemplation, in epitaphs uncomfortable
as this tilted obelisk to all five children
of Mr and Mrs Long, capsized off Worthing;
bones by their bones beside their offspring in their
       tower.

In waist-deep grass, past head-high brambles, we
       stumble
on names. The birch and wild roses strike up
       through their
shady precincts, where stems lap over Wife of the
and Fell Asleep, Asleep, Sleeping in Jesus turn
to touch drunken heads with Daughter of the
       Above.

480

A plot of Anzacs, clipped and swept, is kept in line.
Their upright stones, whiter than canvas, state no
        cause,
birth, nor relations' thoughts: nineteen fifteen, sixteen,
seventeen and so on are all that appertains.

In the newest bed of chopped clods the naked
        sponge
the flowers have fallen off spells DAD and the pine
        peg
puts him late in the race, nearly fifty thousandth.

The lettering's careful and dumb about absence
that chipped the clipped words from the hearts that
        composed them.

Where we feed what kills us, the thrush expends his
        song.

B.B.

NOT a prophet, he
stood in the marketplace de-
nouncing property.

He was not hasty
but considered; nor hateful
except of waste – the

discarded plateful,
minds that are leashed by guts they
desire to make full

though they never may
be. Saw history uphold
what he had to say:

that blood would be stilled
and Devil take the last waltz
if greed wasn't stalled.

Himself unstifled,
he survived to find his calls'
echo turning false.

White rooms, hospitals,
scent of fir and sound of birds
made off with his last words.

i.m. J.S.

I

THE rain's teeming down on no grave tonight:
Ashes to ashes, they ground you fine;
Now you're scattered and gone.

It suits a man so fastidious
To be neat for his last appearance,
A simple heap of dust.

And it's fit that you go by the fire's
Gate out, who were an upright live wire,
Badly insulated.

Fit that the skies aren't spilling by starts
And fits, but soaking, unbroken, beats
The rain on your leaving.

II

But silence, John, and nonentity
I wouldn't have thought your cuppa tea,
Unless lust for nothing,

Desire of the void, oblivion,
Flipsided your hunger for living,
Darkness surrounding flame.

Now you're done with burning and mingled
In air. Next time my nose is tingled
I'll know whose grains to blame,

Cause when the wind blows, when the shivery
Leaves of autumn rattle, it'll still be
John Stevens in your face.

III

The creator who made us inspired dust
Signed our hearts with "Paradise – Or Bust".
You took the short, fast side

Up the mountain, and couldn't reach it
But shouted and waved "Seen the summit!"
Then your heart burst with pride.

BYRONICS FOR RONNIE W.

I

I'M taking up this stanza in remembrance
  Of a dear friend just recently departed
And hoping I can make of the encumbrance

483

Of the triple rhyme, as he in his art did,
A lively, tripping reel and not a glum dance.
    There's one verse almost done before it's started,
And on we race, without let-up or up-let,
To take the final fence, the closing couplet.

II

I'm optimistic that I'll get the hang
    Of the mettlesome form and make it canter
Or trot on command, like Byron who rang
    The changes on it, finding it for banter
Much better suited than for *Sturm und Drang*
    Or any kind of windy, wordy cant – a
Crime of which he accused the Lakers' gang:
Of that, and being Judases to freedom,
And, worst of all, so dull he scarce could read 'em.

III

Now Ron, who died untimely late last year,
    Was of this stanza lately much enamoured
And got his bardic mill in such high gear
    That just before his sudden end he hammered
Them out by the dozen. He could be freer
    Thus, it seems, to shape his thoughts as they
                                        clamoured;
As though his brain was troubled by the rumour
Of what it nursed within – a lethal tumour.

IV

What kind of man was this I elegise?
    A poet by calling, by class patrician;
Direct in his speech, of substantial size;
    A climber, a father and a musician,
An Irish piper on whom were no flies.
    From such a thumbnail sketch of his condition

You really know no more than next to nothing
Of who he was, that good man, Ronnie Wathen.

V

There are colourful escapades a-plenty
    That other, older friends could tell, I'm sure.
What he was like at thirty or at twenty
    I can only guess. How in the wide, pure
Air of the mountains or in some cramped tent he
    Looked, let others relate. I'm of a newer
Generation, and one perhaps less truthful.
But here's a fact: he seemed forever youthful.

VI

I said before he'd heard the Muse's call,
    Yet he was rather tardy in responding.
Perhaps he resented being her thrall,
    Which is, after all, a painful, desponding
Position that can drive you up the wall;
    And arty pretensions were not Ron's thing.
But she had her way with him in the end,
Sending verse as fast as it could be penned.

VII

Apart from Lord Byron (his final choice
    Of mentor), the one whose spell wouldn't break,
With whom he plunged head over heels, was Joyce.
    He had long stretches of *Finnegans Wake*
By heart, and wakened for me its weird voice.
    He could play the pipes and – for heaven's sake! –
At the same time recite that dense, Morphean
Language – an achievement close to Orphean.

VIII

In fact most things Irish Ronnie revered;
    Her rocks and her rivers, her soaking rains

And the splendour of skies suddenly cleared.
    As for the music, it ran in his veins
As Guinness does in hers. He'd mountaineered,
    Piped and rambled her crags and pubs and lanes.
Did he long, like the good (or wicked) lord,
To work and wield, or fall on, freedom's sword?

IX

I doubt it somehow. However he'd grieve
    Or rage at the wrongs done the Emerald Isle,
His heart was gentle. To shatter and cleave
    The heads and limbs of folk was not his style,
Even for a higher cause. To bereave
    One widow and two children was a vile
Enough deed, and though he'd battle all
Night in an argument, he wouldn't brawl.

X

So there you have him – or perhaps you don't:
    An upright, downright man all round; just mad
Enough to be sane; maddening too, I won't
    Deny; strong and generous, with a scad
Of talents to boot. On the Wathen front
    All's quiet now, and reaching a decad
Of these stanzas borrowed from Byron he
So much liked, I'll end: God bless, goodbye Ronnie.

BECOMING LIGHT

ONE by one my memories lose their weight.
These few that are heavier – griefs
and fragments of dread
and one, both minute and massive,

486

that's the rose-scented globe of an instant
when a child was in a garden
– these depart more slowly
and only after many attempts.

Whether it is a heaven
they have risen into before me
around whose gate they wait
purged and sanctified and stripped of pain,
where they may be robed in white –
whether there is a heaven
I can also no longer remember.
All the ideas have floated off too
that I may once have had of such things.

They are drawn away beyond my reach
in the great gravity of brightness
sucking the sad weight from my memory;
until naked of all but the moments
I wait for the moment
when these last few sounds become silence,
these last few colours sink back
down in the rose-scented globe,
both massive and tiny,
that turns to night and folds its petals
behind me, finally closing me out,
and the scent, weighing nothing,
returns to the day it came from
and is folded once more in the grasp of a child.

I have finished my arduous forgetting.
I am becoming light.

ZEUS'S CAMERA

MY Antipandora it opens
and everything good flies in

The mountains, the sea, the sunset
my friends and relations

On the far side of their appearance
the counterbox to mine

As soon as this shuts that opens
containing their essence

Which flies out rejoicing, replacing
themselves with something else

One day creeping round behind the scenes
I opened mine on that

Which, being good, with triumphal flap
flew into this. No sooner

Shut the one than the other sprang wide
inside. I don't know what

Happened, but something snapped. My black
box flew like a raven

And sat on the mountain, with lids spread
against the red sun, laughing

While out rolled another sea, another
sun and yet more mountains

While out streamed a million white weddings
spreading out like the Milky Way

POEM FOR OTIS

LOOK at the starlings tonight round Trafalgar Square,
on a night like this near the autumn equinox

exploding in waves against the sombre sky,
in waves of who knows how many tens of thousands.

You were born in a moment like this.
How may souls burst with you into the air?

Angular, precise, a piece of the puzzle,
each hundred-thousandth body locks exactly into its
       place in the world:

but who can follow the course of one of those
       flickering specks
swept and whirled in the waves of its fellows?

How light and hard, soft and dry and bony is a bird
       in the hand,
the bright eye and the stiff gape evoking the lizard
       ancestor.

Perhaps from this piece we could work out the shape
       of the next
above and below it, insect, twig or bird; then perhaps
       the shape of the world.

But you, being human, are different.
You belong everywhere and nowhere

and these shapes are not locked: a baby hand
that has barely brushed the surface of its capability,

a speechless mouth and weightless mind without
       past or future,
whirled shrieking into the air. And this chaotic world

begins to be born again in you and takes on order
piece by piece, and we gather, looking into the world

you are shaping, to see that peace prevails.
The starlings whirl shrieking into the sky,

the stars whirl silently into their places.
They are waiting on the world you make.

SHOOTING SCRIPT

IN the fourth act, suddenly,
as the lights go out,
for the leading players
there are no more lines.

If he speaks, over his torn shoulder
to one beside him, equally
suspended in a slow dissolve,
none but the captain overhears.

About the central fact
only the head of the hammer
and the nailheads allow of eloquence.
Bang, they say. Bang bang.

APOCALYPSE

WE almost cherish the terrors
of a coming crash whose rumours
are like those wind-chased, capricious
ripples – catspaws – across the swell.
Powerless either to impel
or impede the steady step of waves,
they crinkle, darken and vanish.

Something will be clear; we differ
as to what. Some hope that falsehood
alone suffers. Was disaster
ever known to be fastidious,
or what tornado's torn up rot
and left just the rooted goodness?
It's rats and flies flourish after.

Barely a grain of husbandry
to its name, an economy
soon must founder whose foundations
itself consumes. While we work on
under spoiled heaven, misgiving
nags the heart (that overtaxed word
but true); is daily registered.

To cleave the welter and make stark
would perhaps be relief enough.
An easy wish, to stanch the flux
of glittering, flustered wishes,
the perpetual emotion
of foetal hopes and fears whose germs are
ambiguous information.

Chlorine, shrapnel, Maxims and wire,
naively plotted at the zenith,
prove but barbarous overture
to our novel ascent to hell;
survival to tell it the sting
in each tale. But the world's been hung
by a hair above a furnace

since city and empire were forged,
which burning tongues spoke of. Patience,
preach the pauper seers, pointing out
where catspaws walk on the water.
Beyond the hours of Mars there comes
triumphant peace. Live low and hard;
wait for the high and light to fall.

To death, dearth, plague and the tyrant
our era presents nice firm going
and who could believe they'd go harder
as they come up to the last fence?
The earth flies from under their feet
in a bloodclot rain, and whips raised,
colours flying, they race to the post.

ENVOI

THE thing is finished and the maker
stands off to look, to listen,
and likes finding it there,
likes the fact that it's now a fact,
coming back up close to touch
and even – why not? – to sniff it again.

The parts are all orderly,
the passage from one to the next
lively and rhythmically sound;
the difficult parts, where resistance grew,
have been brought to completion,
hold their own, are perhaps the best.

The maker, though, is less than most
obtuse to the ghost it gives off,
the ideal image escaped again
during the labour of building its home;
having after a while, perhaps in the very presence
of this fact among facts, to begin afresh.

For this was a motion, originally, of spirit
that is now a thing, finished,
and the spirit is restless, resident
hopefully here but demanding already
a new home also, to suit a changing form,
a different visitant trailing familiar incense.

So this goes off to join its species,
all of them born of the one matrix,
whether language or canvas or stone
or the air-altering instruments of music,
and the maker sits down again alone,
taking up tools to redeem the loss.

So soon in satisfaction comes a sorrow
such as has been in the world since God
saw the soul of Adam leave Adam,
who made all things that are made
come apart, unlasting,
resolving in the end to reunite them.

AN ICON

THOUGH praise be of
the dialects of love,
it's less than all
the writing at her call;
in sad complaint's
expensive blue she paints
on either hand
a void in which we stand;

draws our sombre
ground of ochre and umber,
angry dashed-on
crimson and daubed damson-
blackness of grief
drinking down in relief
the chromium-
yellow solace of sun.

She composes,
even out of losses
and lacks, the shades
of the mountain's blunt blades
and spiny growth.
There all harsh and uncouth
passions convert
to an honest desert.

There the elect
sit despondent, lie wracked
with hard labour,
in a rock-cleft stable
to bring from light

to light the bawling, slight
and helpless thing,
the child who shall be king,

whom we who sing
from no angelic rung
nor can adorn
with a wrought, flawless crown,
must sing as best
we can, or just witness
where love descends,
eternity's present.

THE GHOST PATH

CIRCULARS

WEIGHT of things unneeded and without weight
vacant lectionary teaching wastage
catalogues of no consequence of things
never to be ordered uninvited
invitations on forcible glossy
card and paper leotards ties forced smiles
virulent pizzas etc sad
accumulation irking appalling
of offers not even considered mass
to shed before we go in at our door
or can leave through eddies of blurb black ice
of ink denying avenues of thought
The tyres make the sound of a slurp reversed
on the wet tar tonight under no stars

THE COAST PATH

I

DEPTHS & ardors,
The country undiscovered as we walk,
As we are gathered by the flowers,
Consumed by the grass.

Across a void
Of neither flame nor cold our words are steps
And our exploring soles as yet unlearned
Whether on this way to freeze or burn
Would sooner sound a sole depicting echo
Than soon arrive.

II

Sea-pine needles
Splay and bend, extend a southern fringe above a
      northern sea.
Cones of the sea-pine, soft and sweet as honeycomb
      in April,
Close, lap scale on scale,
But as our hearts, to guard their seed.

Leaves of sea-pine
Curve, as languid latin lashes lifted
On an iris pale and varied, nordic blue.
Curve, and tend toward the spiral
Of all gradual things.

Cache of his grey synaesthetic tendresse,
Snail-shell spiral,
Spiral of the pine-cone and the nebula
And of the crown whence flows
The deep slow wave of your hair.

III

They cross and cross,
The waves, in a binary world whose terms are never
      and always.
Creation and destruction are lost in each other.
Neither grid nor swirl, tentative nor disorderly, this
      chaos,
This beginning.

IV

Black crosscut shapes,
Riding easy
Over springtime
Tilth, won't rise here,
Fly straight, afraid
To scan the jade-
Green void they cross.

Old mother salt –
Whitened, wrinkled, afflicted with the wind –
The crows are no children of yours
That span the water fast and low
Side by side to the island.

V

On which each word we speak would be unrepeated
As the flowers are among the waves of moist grass.

Gorse and campion, thrift and pine,
Two crows that cross the jade-green water.

A threefold world
Whose terms are always and never and now.

VI

One wingbeat one
Heartbeat one green
Crosscut wave
One step with no echo
No echo.

VII

Our steps are words,
Depths and ardors rain-enfolded.

We take ourselves
To each other

And are seen in the eyes of flowers
For what we are,

Imaginings of grass,
Who have wound in the coiled

Store of each ear
Our footsoles' echo

From earth returned
As understood.

A LETTER FROM DENMARK

DEAR Norman,
         I wonder have you buckled
on the armour? When I think of you dearfolk
it brings my one image of settlement:
the old light-coloured dog beside the stream
meandering among shrubs; flowers and stones
in the red earth of the iron-bearing hillsides;
your changes the gradual ones of growing
as of declining; your children going
into the independence inevitable
from following in your footsteps, to find the same
        peace

in their loves, if right example
can make even that dice run straight.
Not that, caught in the twists of a life too full
of shocks of late, I might know what storms
have torn at the vale whose name is balm
to me, at Brimfull; but please God it's not so.

Of course it's vacation brings on this welcome bout
of contemplation. Denmark is a fine land
of whose language we know barely two words.
Taking a headline at random, Birthe
translates for me "Gud skabt alt – af kærlighed"
or, God shaped all – of carelyhood,
that is to say, from love. As good a place
as any to begin. The family resemblance
to Saxon is followable from the letters.
In speech, hard consonants are deftly held back;
like many things here, unpronounced. To fashion
a landscape like this requires an equal
almost-absence. Gentle – to take too Latin
a root; and subtle seems even more southern.
Beechwoods and meadow, birch and pine by the
        strand
of boulder and beach. Much untouched and
        flourishing;
in an un-Roman way, rural; civilised
but not urbanised, no one lives far here
from air, earth and water, among a people
soft-spoken and surprising as their country.
Rich and low and full of bloom, of the small
ground-loving greenery, finely weaving, needing
the closer look to reveal the meaning
as in the art where Celtic and Norse combine,
calligraphy, carving, illumination,
bronze, and the broidery of gold, enamel
and jewellery.

This homeland of my colouring,
the tow-haired blue-eyes, launched a culture whose
     stamp
is on that heartland I write to, fell and dale,
beck, tarn and combe, whose granite foundation
in strength outstrips all expression of passion,
defying with definiteness, as here
with modest enchantment the scene shies description.

In a sunny garden I enjoy trying;
peace leaves me free for the struggle with words.

"With the farming of a verse" as Auden put it;
but where these are comes the clash of tongues no
     wisdom,
however pacific the bed in which it's nursed,
has made its way without. For surely, for all
organic metaphors, it's better to say
with Jesus and the apostles, the truth
is sharp as a double-edged sword, and must fight
this world which has its own god. The clatter
of conflicting voices is the music
of everyday, in which the winner makes
a stillness in which to be heard, till silence
seems the option of the wise. Shall quiet
find a champion? Have you buckled on
the armour, Norman, as Paul has prescribed?
Should the calm speak, what turning upside down
would earth feel as she listened: the tired
and strange turned fresh and home, the dog with fell
like wool of the lamb walking between chosen
and tended bushes, or careless wildflowers
thrown as gauze of chromium, mauve, titian,
azure over the bowing summer grass.

THE GHOST PATH

What is the word from the garden? Have you heard
the sayings of the untroubled meadow?
Report them, writer, as they bear on our case.
It is clear we are on trial for our lives.
Can you recollect the reading of the charge?
Where is the witness will speak for us, bringing
leaves to cover us, the branch that reconciles?
The judge is stone-faced and the jury snarls.
What is the word from the garden? Writer,
that spot of ink under your eagle's-beak nib
is all the evidence in our defence.
Swoop now and snatch it, out of the eye of the sun.

I look forward to hearing from you soon
and until then remain, with loving thoughts
for yourself and for all the family,
your former pupil and your though-long-absent
mindful and admiring friend,

                                    John Gibbens

THE QUEEN

CUNT has conquered,
The streets are full of fish.
Towers are sunken
According to her wish.

Her rufous servants
Have doffed their hats.
They stand to attention,
Their little heads she pats.

She rides in a carriage
That rolls on two wheels.
Her home's in a forest
Between soft fields.

Her back door's locked
But some friends come in there;
Her front doors fine copper
In a folding pair.

Her hall has red carpets
To greet her guest.
Dew wets the forest
When he comes in to rest.

With lance borne upright
He pricked through the valley.
She slips down to kiss him
In a narrow alley.

The clock runs backwards,
The mails are delayed,
The noon gun's knackered,
The cats are unspayed,

And cartloads of kittens
In her lap find succour,
For she never called an orphan
Or a beggar "motherfucker".

And some call it chaos
And some call it peace
When cunt has conquered
And the streets are full of fish.

DIAMOND HEART BLUES
A Portrait of Duke Jordan

IT cuts clean thru glass
& it sparkles like tears
w/ a brilliance to last
@ least for 1m years

Born in the black heart of coal
That old flame still burns in your soul

When the fountains of the deep
Lie down in the dust to sleep
The time'll come to lose
Your diamond heart blues

The hammer of hate
Just can't break it
The thief in the night
He can't take it
And the hand of the cunning
Man didn't make it

When the gold bells ring
Down from the hill
And the great world's
All lying still
The angels will swing
Down to shake it
Free of the rust and grime
Of a weary long time

Every edge
Every face will still shine

An undying sign
Bright as the best
Of good news
Your diamond heart blues

CONSUMPTION OF THE STONES

THE obdurate made to seem
Yielding; soft made stark, fleeting still,
In abeyance from time,
Were the codicil
To God's will,
And judgement's gleam.

Crisp acanthus, coiling lock,
Flared fold and fluting, by toil
Of skill nursed from the block,
Which blue fumes of oil
Blur and soil,
Degrade to rock.

The saints lose face in the west,
Firm-mouthed martyr and clear-eyed king
As though once more faint-fleshed,
By the sour rain's sting
Declining,
Absolved of rest.

THE PLAN

THE plan's where our letters
Perfectly fit their slots
And the replies come back
Wholly devoid of nots.

508

THE GHOST PATH

The four helpers meet us
In the prince's courtyard,
Showing us how simple
Is all we thought was hard,

According to the plan;
Whose largest surprise is
Our clear goal dissolving
As the Lord devises.

THE BIN

WHAT shall be done
with them we deem insane?
Locked out
of sight of green,
they'll rattle, like stones in a tin,
their various pain.

And in their lift,
as broad as a room,
shall be writ
"Shit"
of course, and more
simply "Show me the way to go home".

Music there shall be
none, nor flowers
but hours
in large supply
in which to cry
Moi-même!

We're all on film.
All tuned to the one

programme,
none receives the same.
Some dumb. Some have, partly,
voices. Not only earthly.

FILM OF THE FIRST WAR'S
SHELL-SHOCKED

THESE are the war artists
their Chaplin walks
their dancing scalps
their uncontrollable trembling.

No grim poem, painting or story
more eloquent than their ballet.
Terror and pity threw the switch
opened the shutter.

In the middle of the dead
skulls and worse
they became baby bodies
torsos fair-skinned and hairless.

Young men from northern Europe, limbs gibbering.
Tongue never told what their shakes speak.
Oh me shivering china
be still be still be still.

UNWRITTEN

Slipshod fobbers-off,
cunning but not fundamentally clever...

The zone of the cursable extends out of sight.
I walk to where my last-thrown word-stone landed,
centre of a new and undetermined circle.

The sycamore
that wore a mail of green glosses
all summer has recomposed itself:
its few brilliant tatters
against a numb green trunk limply flutter.

It is winter after a fashion
which is the season of the discontinuous,
a dish-rag sky congested with transmissions.

The function of the media, in which all concur,
is not to inform but distract
the living from their living
and the dead from their quiet.

The silver birches, undefeated,
have leaves unlost,
leaf-language still to speak,
have twig-tresses trailing yet.

That no deed be unguarded,
no look unglazed or glance unfended
into the heart of the machine.

Shall one leaf fall unwritten?
Shall one leaf fall as one life falls
among six billion unregarded?

The cherry-plum ascends by downward-sweeping
sprays of branches.
The sycamore thrusts upward
smoothly curving limbs.
In December
these machines are all heart.

Shall one leaf
fall down unwritten?

MIM

THE numbers seem to ask for something to be said.
Although we made the numbers, our day's too busy
Not to obey them. The light of stars is fragile
And quiet, and lights of the city loud and strong.
So it is for us, living inside the numbers.

Thinking backwards, we approach the future side-
      ways,
One eye on it anyway. What's a thousand years
Between continents? A few inches, a few feet.
She can't turn to watch us build cities on her back.
She shoulders the wheel that builds mountains and
      the sea.

Earth, the moon and the sun avoid the decimal
But time in the dock of a wrist stands to be judged
By four crooked magistrates on a palm bench
While the thumb's fat sheriff is practising his knots.
We can't plead the fifth, and no quarter is given.

Now we round the corner that's not there, shifting
      gear.
History changes when we change our minds. Perhaps,
Maybe: two words that are cleft in the mist of
      tongues,
One sprung of chance and one of strength. That
      haps; I may.
But the stick pushed on has no step back, nor neutral.

A smell of burning and a squeal of steel go up
To meet reverberations of the midnight bell.

In the cellar, unscheduled, tap roots of laurel
Pierce the mortar of the vault, shaking hands with
      eyes
Of tubers piled under mild blue phosphorescence.

From liturgies of suchlike congregations, rules
Of prosody and perspective sprout, are moulded,
Infected, reborn. They contain new names for God.
A self-sealing envelope opened in the dark
Spurts a soft violet light from its glue. Our jumpers

Crackle when we undress. Something's being given
Off by, or is it concentrating on our skin?
We walk wrapped in latency of conflagration.
Herald and hail misplaced are midwives to a corpse
And a rhythm's on the verge of reinvention.

WALKING FROM WAPPING

HOME, after press night,
the Culture section put to bed
(Irish edition) and the small
small-hours rain often floating
up into the floodlights
falling over Tower Bridge.

2am-ish, next day's *Times*
and *Sun* already read,
the hour the news is born...
On a clear still night
in the black water of St Katherine's Dock
fish mouths seeding circular ripples.

From the fo'c'sle of a Baltic trader
a lamp left shining
or in the saloon of some outlandish white
millionaire's yacht, a green-tinted light
but no-one stirring:
that special deadliness of sleeping affluence.

Up the steps, past Dead Man's Hole –
a sign explains it's where the river's corpses surface –
and into the harsh illumination,
dwarfed by the blank operatic towers,
huge blue and white links of the suspension,
the muddy flood curdling round the piers.

Occasional quarrels of gulls echo
from midstream, where they roost on the moored
        waste barges.
Unfazed by the lone pedestrian
a young fox digs in the Potter's Field,
runs up the riverbank walk,
disappears between two office blocks.

One night it was a snipe or a woodcock
crashed out of the shrubs in boxes
in front of some corporate headquarters,
made me jump down there in the mausoleum
of commerce at the foot of London Bridge,
but of course it was life more abundant in fact.

The twisted narrow alley round the back
end of the cathedral, I never took:
Green Dragon Court, unlit, on a drizzling night –
no thanks. Out in the square
I stood staring down the grating where what
I realised was a rat only after it had gone had gone.

THE GHOST PATH

Someone stacking boxes of oranges
loudly joins in the chorus of a disco song.
The lanes through Borough Market lined
with levees of Savoy cabbages, cauliflowers,
sandbag stacks of potato sacks,
buzzing of forklifts, artics backing and being
      unloaded.

This was in the days before Borough High Street
was anyone's idea of fun –
just the odd gaggle of clubbers
coming down from the Ministry
to get a cab at the junction that's been a junction
for a couple of thousand years.

LENT

FAT doves ascend in last of the February light
where pallid blossom of the cherry-plum
shakes against blue pallor of the sky
to clamber with little grace where twigs are thinnest,
pecking buds and latest petals for a food
that makes the cold earth taste of milk and honey.

THE PRICE OF EGGS

SO, full marks to Nostradamus:
Reporters in earnest arm us
With the bombs of indignation
As a people's desolation
Stumbles out across the mountains
And into the salving fountains
Of televisual attention.
That cryptic seer's apprehension,

Or so I'm told, in quatrain rhyme,
Was that it should be Mars's time
Before and after Y2K;
Though since it's doubtful since his day
That days are bloody any less
I'd say less mystic hint than guess
Were needed to slate, out of four
Fatal horses, the grey of war
As odds-on to make a showing.
From the long-bow to the Boeing
Man grows in strength to do man hurt
And that's the only racing cert
Of the human race: what we can
We will do, and we brook no ban.
Science, like the samurai's sword
That can't be sheathed without blood poured,
Has never yet unveiled a power
Whose cutting edge, within the hour,
From the knapped flint to carbon steel,
Some soft neck wasn't made to feel.
But technologists aren't to blame
When our Higher Thoughts achieve the same,
When every One True Religion
Bakes a pie of peace's pigeon.
What are these badly butchered cuts
Besmeared with bits of brains and guts?
Wherefore these flesh-and-bloody wrecks,
Ill-made anthologies of ex-
Members of homo sapiens?
To the pursuit of happiness,
Freedom, justice, the rule of law –
To all the words that go to war
These blackly barbecued remnants
Are the quickly piled monuments.
In some semantic cavity,
Some verbal singularity

Meanings are caught, stretched, swallowed whole
Like particles in a black hole.
Perhaps, as cosmologists think,
From that nothing wherein they sink
They emerge on a farther side,
Though utterly transmogrified.
A soldier is a kind of nurse
In that parallel universe,
And intimately videoed
Humanitarian bombs explode,
And the line smart weapons defend
Is that means justify the end.

   Could it be the aim of Nato
That the earth become a state o-
bedient to the laws of Plato?
They'd not give a cold potato
For peasants like the Kosovars
Except to prove us avatars,
We Western powers, fit to shape
A level and gleaming globescape.

   Once for women, gold or cattle
Hairy chieftains went to battle;
Once for slaves and imperial gains
The smithies forged the blades and chains;
But now we arm for harmony
And it's striking how far money
Is from ever being mentioned
By the many well-intentioned
Watchers of the martial mania
Who from Brussels to Albania
Live in hardy symbiosis
With the terrifying process.

   For every move our generals make
No other interests are at stake,
None, say, commercial or the like
In any site our bombers strike.

Through the telly's beaming prism
No motive more than altruism
Shines in our collective action.
Odd phenomenon, refraction…
Every colour of the spectrum
Shows and, as it were, the plectrum
Strikes each chord, from red of rage through
Saffron kindness to sorrow's blue,
Yet of one hue there's not a hint:
Although this business makes a mint
And buying Stealth craft you can't stint,
There seems no trace of verdant tint,
The colour of the stuff we print,
The folding stuff, the stuff that's green:
The bankroll's role's behind the scene.
We'll only see the shade of cash
Go up in smoke and fall as ash
As we conquer, buckle and curb
The Balkan pitbull, Johnny Serb,
Then from ruins of defiance
Build a land of grateful clients.
    Am I objecting overmuch?
Can such words as "just" and "war" touch
Hands, and not become double Dutch?
    The mainspring of my mind's a twist
Of ire, a wrath no pacifist
Could let unwind. The stricken queues
Of refugees that cross the news,
Their hardship, tenderness and tears,
And, past the pain that yet appears,
The brutal truths we've still to learn
From valleys where their houses burn,
Both freeze the blood and make it boil
And tighten, tighten anger's coil
To greet each strike with full heart's chime
Rejoicing to revenge the crime,

Until a sour harmonic pings
Back in the echo of those rings –
The thought those lives we shatter 'll
Be, as they say, "collateral".
How much blood of the innocents
Shall we require as recompense?
Shall child for child repay the bill?
Divide an integer by nil,
The answer's still infinity.
While in the murderous minute he
Might think the deed done in it e-
vens scores, man's wrong. No-one's quit. He
But magnifies iniquity.
Although no airtime's charged with pity
For Serbia's civilian dead
We surely know their blood's as red,
Surely feel their killing's just as
Much an instance of injustice
As any wrong it would amend?
   Now let's hear from the people's friend,
Our liberal Prime Minister,
His speech less left than sinister,
Mourning the sainted Jill Dando,
Britain's TV darling – and o-
bituarising, with just the breath
Before, the condonable death
Of broadcasters bombed in Belgrade.
Of course some missiles get mislaid
And of course we're told "our quarrel
Is not with them" – same old moral.
But then to blow up people you've
No quarrel with – does that not move
Us to righteous indignation
When done to us – that violation
Worse than murder, which we christen
Sheer cold-blooded terrorism?

THE GHOST PATH

I wish I felt some conclusion
Awaits these couplets' profusion.
I only know they're bound to end.
But as I round each fearful bend
The prospect's the same: more chaos,
Heartbreak, hatred, bloodshed and loss.
Call back the boss, as soon as poss:
The one that we nailed on a cross.

MIND THE GAP

PROCEED with caution. Discreetly eye those
Who are passing or precede you.
Let no lurching virus
Prevent you observing silence.
Let no contact impede you.

To keep moving, to know where you're going
Are virtues of a corpuscle:
No backing, no slowing
At a branching or narrowing
To clog this vein's dim bustle.

Occupy your thoughts, but seem impassive,
Bracing a foot to be wheel-hurled.
Attend every message,
Undergo the wrongs of passage,
Consider this the real world.

READING THE TUBE

HAD I an eyesight like the honey-bee's
That sees the flowers burning ultraviolet,
That saw not pulp and gum, but litanies

Only, hiving – the million orts of these
Books, papers and mags, moving inviolate
In air, in the buzz of romance and violence;
Saw drone statistics pressing suit on Love, queen
Among phonemes, the Om of swarming offspring;
We workers would not seem to tremble and swing
In gliding cages, pecking such inky treen
As finches cuttlefish-bones, but being seen
In bluebell woods of sense, would be heard to sing.
    At a carriage return, the doors' curved sheets
      Slide back. New black galaxies push for their
        seats.

BESIDES

THE besides of the lines,
angled iron, coded hatches
("40", "M"),
the vectors' secret breadth.

On a hanging tag, meticulously painted,
two bee ex eight stroke one four,
as though every brick in the railway's skin were
      numbered.

We go down by where in winter we came up
to dripping fingerbones of buddleia, knuckle-grip
      on mortar,
or mid-year daze of ragwort's sulphur crowns,
the rosebay's drift, violet curves and white.

Imprisoned common
raised on a thorax of Victorian vaults,
untrodden, overlooked.

We are going down to where the lights are pending
     from knowledge,
places that are not, by the mile.
My nakedness is buried there,
among the steel-wound and the colour-sheathed
     cabling.

Clot of revolving dust between the rails,
the seed-self.
Signal breaks up and gives out.

BEYOND

HALF-MOON among the bones of silver birch,
last of its yellow coin in threadbare hands.

Winter shows to the city its clearest stars, the few
     brightest,
Orion clambering up in the blue, frozen field.
Whatever his prey tonight, it has nowhere to hide.

And a winter has come among the years. Our tasks
     seem husks,
our hearts are bare. We have been paid unkindly,
asking warmth and harmony, to give and be given.

A ridge of woods, from a high window, southward,
promised the presence of beyond, the skyline of
     Eden.
There are the oaks of understanding, ferns of mercy,
the bird-guarded horizon of our yearning, though it
     be Croydon.

COUNTRY WAYS: AN ECLOGUE

Passenger: Excuse me, is this the way to Forestonehatch?

Local: Beg pardon?

Driver: Fore-stone-hatch.

Local: Not round here. Down that way's Furrysnatch…

Passenger (aside): What do you reckon?

Local: Is it Furrysnatch you want?

Driver: Actually it's Beauchamphall we're looking for.

Local: Oh, Bumhole is it?

Passenger: Mm.

Local: Right then. Along here, to the bottom, and you'll come to the abbey –

Passenger: Allen St Carioc?

Local: Arsecrack, that's it, and about a quarter of a mile on, there's a lane on the right, with the big old gateposts just before it, and the sign for the manor –

Passenger: Northby Chase.

Local: You know these parts, then?

Passenger: No, no. It's what it says on the map. Do we turn right at Northby Chase?

Local: That's it. Go down by Knobcheese till you come to the lake –

Driver: What's that?

Passenger: He means this place. So will we see this lake, then, Carthoops Mere?

Local: Ar, Crapsmear, you'll be seeing it all right. Alongside the railway, left under the bridge –

Driver: Look, it's nearly dark. Can't we just go straight on? See, this way, by Further Wyfoot?

Local: You don't want Fartwhift. That road's all flooded after the rain Saturday night. No, you go along there by the reservoir, and you'll come to a place at the end –

Passenger: Teythwaite.

Local: Twat, sir, yes. And by the church, there's your turn marked. Course you could come round by Furrysnatch, but this way's shorter. Arsecrack, Knobcheese, and just up past Twat, that's Bumhole, with a lovely view of Crapsmear.

ENNEAGON
Poems of Don Plummer

Mud pole men need no poem,
dump loud menu on lumpen dome.

Mud pole men deem lemon open,
peel lode up on duple plenum.

SPINDLE 1

SPINDLE mint bonded
snowdrop by carriage
to the eyebrows inapt
flake and furrow

Re-adding the series perils
axle and catseyes
an AB circulation
of a dieselled aisle and interval

From with by through
to Mytholmrood
a spanked edition is
towing the cow upward

which a mag of botch
spreads on the Fastnet
or a crack-hoofed crocus
to enter the spindle of rain.

SPINDLE 2

HALF-MO potash spindle
not to make that judge are
the foreheaped calcites
beneath your very sofa?

I think we can say
inaccumulate
or a spotting of thousands
without service charge

quartered south and east
microfrequent pistils sally
mauve forth
which no bulls rasp.

This people who span
who piled who knee
& need no letters
invent the parenthesis)

SPINDLE 3

LIPIDS scintillate in the alembic
elf-locked
a keratin spiral
levered from the thumbed spine.

Dumber than metal
a mirror napped
on rogue dejections
either smattering of cards.

A mud hammer wakes the bole
unspun in corporation
or on this dole of sessions
upgrades itself by the light of a spindle.

Doors made faster
were it taken forth
or dried to ceasefire
lessen your malign lenses.

SPINDLE 4

HAWKED out oxymel
webbing to gudgeons
noting the flat neck
of crabbed flocks.

Spares and empty folders
purporting to blend in
rings by a conjunct density
marble our turbid meat,

526

hence the feeler and hither
at its oddless wager
nor grieve the sale
uneven in edge of oak

attempting eternity
by dint of repetition.
Forgive the plug
thus saith the spindle.

SPANDREL 1

WE the ordered by nine began
        who art unmade
stung wings at a hiring folded closed.

A seasonal collage of loans
        distempered or carious
Pater's polymer of absorption overall

where censed gilt joint bosses compound
        to the yoke
believed by swanshell in the signature.

SPANDREL 2

WEB chord scales the life of St Maggot's child
        kept isohedral
from beyond by what superposition of wait.

Rock presses through water gasping for light,
        a cock's egg
scraped its nail on the sea dust.

That a spinsters mite should raise the lichen window
      is rechromed negative
as stone grows from the vine like stone.

SPANDREL 3

WED vesicle pittering to extinction
      our gusto yet a while
that flensed obdurateness plash abraded flags.

Tweak that bracket, make the horizon pale
      as blemished thread
or hems assumed refractory and absolute.

Each depth respired at another hole
      clamped against the brow
that spools a wax bandage of its laurel.

SPADE

AT all the black flung
body and mass over west
thrip sod glebe and tilth
broad flux of utter dung
scarf the worn down flare

O twig O stub ditch
how to gurn the drill
will milk flint of paws
nor urge scabs to thick
by rust of a bark

THE GHOST PATH

Fence of turf jars flown
the green to the blue
that mired whey of horns
sung by the brown barb
to the pluck of gates

Gob bleb tump and clart
spur to the swift rose
twine to addle hedge bloom
or udder twins by mid
which smiles brake the blast

SPUD

FLED storage muted and a pale file
as much knuckle as tongue, no further
tegument required or suspected, this lewd bolus
embalms our stellar regard, stuns all appetite.

If it were blue, a chlorinous speckle
exacted of the plume, torn from rule
by the somnolence of that claustral metallurgy,
all might be foreborne. But not such.

The pyramid's chopped and the long skull
split. A calendal hierograph seeps, written within
to augur its own unveiling. What persists?
Only frost, the noval obscurity of salts.

BEGINNERS

THEY come again
To be said again,
The bronze-leaved cherry-plum's
Precursory blooms,

Distinct because first,
As before a cloudburst
The early drops
Make clear full stops.

A week discloses
Ten thousand tiny roses.
Now the fountain of sticks
Makes do with five or six,

Just half a dozen stars tonight
Out of all that light.
A speaking voice
Or the rolling of dice:

Which elected from the flood
The occasional bud,
Of so many these few?
Likewise, who chose me you?

MEMORIALS OF THE BOATMEN
OF ST AGNES

PITCHED against crabbed seas
To where the drear descended,
That they began and were ended
The stone agrees.

On the teething reef
To hang or stumble, as though
They could no otherwise but go,
Bearing relief

From whey-thin islands
To curdled, deceasing brine,
Stung with the sere lifeline, to mine
Ore of silence,

The quick and the dead
Out of the greed of the waves:
Why this, their unforthcoming graves
Have left unsaid.

Granite they spring from
Mills them into the kingdom,
Its lichens their wreaths. They spill, lift
Up as spindrift.

WEDDING SONG

THESE two have come to the altar
To prove again, again,
That something does not falter
In the withered world of men;

That though the leaves are ashes
And though the waves turn dust,
Though rings contain their crosses,
Yet there is trust.

And if dumb fingers grope
Nightly for a ghost content,
That there is fire, that there is hope,
These two this day have meant.

And if time's judging sand
Has an open and shut case,
These two put hand in hand
To plead that love takes place,

And though the dragon's woken,
And though the ground is shaken,
And though the tree is broken,
Love's place is not taken.

So two before the one
Who shaped them of red earth
Stand to show what shall be done:
Two souls' wedding, one life's birth.

Index of First Lines

536